MW00843346

Latina and Latino Children's Mental Health

Recent Titles in
Child Psychology and Mental Health

Children's Imaginative Play: A Visit to Wonderland
   Shlomo Ariel

Attachment Therapy on Trial: The Torture and Death of Candace Newmaker
   Jean Mercer, Larry Sarner, and Linda Ross

The Educated Parent: Recent Trends in Raising Children
   Joseph D. Sclafani

The Crisis in Youth Mental Health: Critical Issues and Effective Programs
Four Volumes
   Hiram E. Fitzgerald, Robert Zucker, and Kristine Freeark, editors

Learning from Behavior: How to Understand and Help "Challenging" Children in School
   James E. Levine

Obesity in Childhood and Adolescence
Two Volumes
   H. Dele Davies and Hiram E. Fitzgerald, editors

LATINA AND LATINO CHILDREN'S MENTAL HEALTH

Volume 1
Development and Context

Natasha J. Cabrera, Francisco A. Villarruel,
and Hiram E. Fitzgerald, Editors

Child Psychology and Mental Health
Hiram E. Fitzgerald and Susanne Ayres Denham, Series Editors

PRAEGER

AN IMPRINT OF ABC-CLIO, LLC
Santa Barbara, California • Denver, Colorado • Oxford, England

Copyright 2011 by ABC-CLIO, LLC

All rights reserved. No part of this publication may be reproduced, stored in a retrieval system, or transmitted, in any form or by any means, electronic, mechanical, photocopying, recording, or otherwise, except for the inclusion of brief quotations in a review, without prior permission in writing from the publisher.

Library of Congress Cataloging-in-Publication Data

Latina and Latino children's mental health / Natasha J. Cabrera, Francisco A. Villarruel, and Hiram E. Fitzgerald, editors.

p. cm. — (Child psychology and mental health)

Includes bibliographical references and index.

ISBN 978–0–313–38296–3 (hbk. : alk. paper) — ISBN 978–0–313–38297–0 (ebook)
1. Hispanic American children—Mental health. 2. Hispanic American children—Psychology. 3. Hispanic American children—Social conditions. I. Cabrera, Natasha J. II. Villarruel, Francisco. III. Fitzgerald, Hiram E.

RC451.5.H57L35   2011

616.89008968073—dc22   2010030702

ISBN: 978–0–313–38296–3
EISBN: 978–0–313–38297–0

15 14 13 12 11   1 2 3 4 5

This book is also available on the World Wide Web as an eBook.
Visit www.abc-clio.com for details.

Praeger
An Imprint of ABC-CLIO, LLC

ABC-CLIO, LLC
130 Cremona Drive, P.O. Box 1911
Santa Barbara, California 93116-1911

This book is printed on acid-free paper ∞

Manufactured in the United States of America

CONTENTS

SERIES FOREWORD

The twentieth century closed with a decade devoted to the study of brain structure, function, and development that in parallel with studies of the human genome has revealed the extraordinary plasticity of biobehavioral organization and development. The twenty-first century opened with a decade focusing on behavior, but the linkages between brain and behavior are as dynamic as the linkages between parents and children, and children and environment.

The *Child Psychology and Mental Health* series is designed to capture much of this dynamic interplay by advocating for strengthening the science of child development and linking that science to issues related to mental health, child care, parenting, and public policy.

The series consists of individual monographs or thematic volumes, each dealing with a subject that advances knowledge related to the interplay between normal developmental process and developmental psychopathology. The books are intended to reflect the diverse methodologies and content areas encompassed by an age period ranging from conception to late adolescence. Topics of contemporary interest include studies of social-emotional development, behavioral undercontrol, aggression, attachment disorders, substance abuse, and the role that culture and other contextual influences shape developmental trajectories. Investigators involved with prospective longitudinal studies, large epidemiologic cross-sectional samples, intensely followed clinical cases or those wishing to report a systematic sequence of connected experiments are invited to submit manuscripts.

Investigators from all fields in social and behavioral sciences, neurobiological sciences, medical and clinical sciences, and education are invited
to submit manuscripts with implications for child and adolescent mental
health.

Hiram E. Fitzgerald
Susanne Ayres Denham
Series Editors

PREFACE

In 2002, Praeger Press launched a new series devoted to advancing understanding the relationship between child psychology and children's mental
health. The first volume focused on imaginative play in early childhood
and subsequent volumes examined a wide range of research, policy, and
practice issues influencing the mental health of children and adolescents.
The collective force of the 10 volumes published thus far has provided
national stature for the *Child Psychology and Mental Health* series.

Although population diversity has been represented in past volumes,
they do not provide systematic inclusion of the broad issues confronting
minority populations. A chapter on juvenile justice disparities among
Latina/o youth, one on tribal boarding schools, another on the historical
impact of slavery on contemporary African American families, or the leg-
acy of internment of Japanese families during the Second World War, does
little justice to the rich set of issues affecting the mental health of children
from America's increasingly diverse racioethnic population. Most
conservative estimates indicate that by 2050, at least one-half of U.S. children will be members of currently defined minorities, and many of them
will speak Spanish as fluently as they speak English.

In providing justification for the volumes on youth crisis, I noted that
professional and public documents increasingly draw attention to the per-
vasive problems affecting individual, family, and community development. It was not difficult to point out that the extraordinary number of
children with poor self-regulatory skills (internalizing and externalizing

disorders, oppositional defiant disorders, attention deficit hyperactivity, poor impulse control) and poor school achievement; and the extent of the impact of single parent homes (primarily without fathers), the long-term effects of child abuse (physical, sexual, emotional), and neglect; the rise in gangs, substance abuse, aggression, poverty, and the dissolution of a sense of community, are factors that have fueled a crisis in children's mental health in the United States. In many instances, these issues are exacerbated in children and families of color, exacerbated because of poverty, institutional racism, and a deep sense of anomie. However, in many other families of color, children do succeed, families are functionally well, and hopes and aspirations are achieved. Although single volumes have addressed this issues, including volumes written by many of the authors attached to the current series, there has been no comprehensive, focused attention directed to articulation of the core issues of child development and mental health within the major minority groups in the United States and internationally as well.

The conception to postnatal age five years are vital for all children's development. It is during these years that children develop the neurobiological and social structures that will facilitate brain development and its expression in social-emotional control, self regulation, literacy and achievement skills, and social fitness. However, while the early years are extraordinarily important in the organization of biopsychosocial regulation, a dynamic and contextual approach to life span development provides ample evidence that there are critical developmental transitions that elementary children, youth, adolescents, and emergent adults must negotiate if they are to construct successful life-course pathways. What also is clear is that public access to state-of-the-art knowledge and recommendations about future scientific and public policy practices is limited by lack of concentrated information about developmental issues facing children and families whose skin color, culture, and racial identities are different from those of children from the dominant population.

This set is one among 10 volumes targeting the educated public; individuals who not only are responsible for public policy decisions, but those individuals who are responsible for raising America's children, voting for policy makers, and making decisions about policy issues that may or may not positively affect all children. Two volumes each will address child development and mental health issues in African American children, Latina/o children, Asian children, American Indian children, and children from around the world. The collective 10 volumes capture the state of the art in knowledge known and knowledge to know, and will examine social and public policies that impede or enhance positive mental health outcomes among an increasingly significant portion of America's children as well as children around the world.

This project would not have been possible without the good will and hard work of a dedicated set of editors, uniquely selected for each two-volume set. Their efforts combined with commitments from an extraordinary group of social, behavioral, and life science scholars enabled completion within our projected two-year project period. I cannot express deeply enough my thanks to authors for enduring countless email deadline announcements, quick responses to track changed manuscripts, and their good spirits throughout the editorial process. Of course, behind the scenes are the individuals who manage the production process. Prior to enrolling in graduate school, Lisa Devereaux provided initial assistance for tracking the flow of editor and author contacts. For most of the duration of the project, Julie Crowgey has served as the project manager, coordinating editors and authors and publisher to move the project toward its completion. She truly has been the glue that has held everything together. Additional thanks to Adina Huda and Gaukhar Nurseitova for their always perfect and prompt technical assistance with graphics. Finally, I must acknowledge Deborah Carvalko, Praeger editor, who conceived of the idea for the Praeger series and recruited my involvement. It has been a pleasure working with Deborah to produce all of the volumes in the Praeger series drawing attention to the interface between child psychology and mental health.

Hiram E. Fitzgerald

Chapter 1

DEMOGRAPHIC OVERVIEW
OF LATINO CHILDREN

Rubén O. Martinez

The first decade of the twenty-first century has been a time of major changes among Latinos. Not only has the Latino population experienced substantial growth, it has experienced geographic dispersion, increased hostility by American society, and severe negative economic impact by the Great Recession that gripped the nation. In 2003, the U.S. Census Bureau announced that Latinos had become the largest ethnic minority group in the nation, becoming at the same time the second largest ethnic group in the country, following White Americans, an older population group. This was a historic shift in the population, and more will occur during this century.

Both the growth of the Latino population and the aging of the White American population had become evident to demographers in the 1980s. With Census 2000 came widespread public recognition that indeed these demographic changes were taking place. That recognition, along with events such as 9/11, engendered widespread homeland security fears and practices that have dramatically impacted the lives of Latino youth, especially those of undocumented Latino workers. Raids by the U.S. Immigrant and Customs Enforcement agency, for example, have traumatized Latino families that have experienced the forced breakup of the family unit, with children sometimes left unsupervised following the arrest and detention of their parents. Others have experienced extended periods of "detention" in the nation's jails, prisons, and detention centers.

At the same time, despite the occurrence of these dramatic events, there are some indicators that the well-being of Latino children has improved in some domains of life. For example, to analyze trends in the well-being of children, the Child Development Foundation (CDF) uses a Child Well-Being Index (CWI) based on 28 indicators across seven domains of well-being: safety/behavioral concerns, family economic well-being, health, community connectedness, educational attainment, social relationships, and emotional/spiritual well-being (Hernandez and Macartney, 2008). For the period 1985 to 2004, the CDF found that the gaps between Latino and White children had narrowed in terms of safety/behavioral concerns, with reductions in teen births and crime victimization, and family economic well-being. According to the CDF, the gap in the health domain was eliminated mainly because the indicator deteriorated for White children in the areas of activity limitations, obesity, and low birth weight births. The gap in social relationships is also reported to have narrowed due mainly to improvements in the proportion of Latino children living with a single parent and in residential mobility. On the other hand, gaps expanded in community connectedness and persisted in educational achievement. Although preschool enrollment rates increased for both Latinos and Whites, the gap remained large. No improvements were reported in the educational achievement gap. Finally, there was one domain in which Latino children ranked higher than White children from 1985 to 2004, and that is on emotional and spiritual well-being, with little change occurring overall in this domain (Ibid.).

This chapter provides a demographic overview of Latino children and youth. It begins with a brief overview of the Latino population in general and then turns to the children with the focus being on their geographic distribution, family contexts, socio-economic characteristics, education, health, and values, identity, and perceptions of their future. As is commonly known, the experiences of families frame and circumscribe the experiences of children and youth. Where we are able, we make comparisons to other race/ethnic groups in order to provide reference points and a broader context for readers.

We define children as persons under the age of 18, or 17 years of age and younger. In general, we will use the terms "young children" for those between the ages of 0 and 12, and the "term youth" for those between the ages of 13 and 17. We will sometimes present statistics that deviate from these definitions due to our inability to break down the data accordingly or because it makes sense to include young adults as well (as with dropouts). Although in most states 18 is the age at which individuals are treated as adults legally, it is also the case that in our larger society the period of "youth" has extended into the early 20's, with college students often treated as "young people" rather than as adults, with many college students accepting these constructions of pre-adult and adult roles (Arnett, 1994). That experience, however, may not necessarily extend to Latinos, who are more likely than their White counterparts to be in the workplace at that age than in colleges and universities, and may be in adult roles earlier in life (Arnett, 2003).[1] Finally, official reports provided by the U.S. Census Bureau and other agencies do not always use standard or uniform age categories, so the overall result may appear like a collage, but it is one that gives us the best possible statistical portrait of Latino children given the limitations inherent in the endeavor.

LATINO POPULATION SIZE AND PROJECTIONS[2]

In 2000, the Latino population numbered approximately 35.2 million persons and comprised 12.5 percent of the U.S. population (Guzman, 2001; Niner & Rios, 2009). An additional 3.8 million persons were part of the Commonwealth of Puerto Rico, but they are not usually included in statistical portraits on the mainland (Ibid.). The Latino population on the mainland increased in size by nearly 58 percent between 1990 and 2000 (up from 22.4 million). It was estimated to be at 46.9 million in 2008, reflecting an increase of nearly 33 percent since 2000. In contrast, the overall U.S. population increased by 7.4 percent between 2000 and 2008. Projections based on 2000 figures set the Latino population at 49.7 million in 2010 and 132.8 million in 2050. The overall U.S. population is projected to be 310.2 million in 2010 and 439 million in 2050. Thus, the Latino population is expected to go from being 16 percent of the population in 2008 to approximately 30 percent in 2050, reflecting an overall increase of 167 percent. In contrast, the overall U.S. population, including Latinos, is projected to increase by 41.5 percent. When Latinos are taken out of the equation, the non-Latino population is projected to increase by only 17.5 percent between 2010 and 2050. Surprising to some readers, the non-Hispanic White population is projected to increase by .01 percent between 2010 and 2050, when it is projected to comprise 46.3 percent of the overall population. As this demographic shift continues, it will occur more rapidly among young children and ripple through adolescents and young adults.

Latinos are a heterogeneous population comprised of three relatively longstanding population segments, recent newcomers and Other Latinos. Today, except for Mexicans and Puerto Ricans, the majority of Latino adults are foreign born (Grieco, 2009). Historically, Mexican Americans have been the largest group. In 2000, they comprised 58.5 percent of the Latino population, followed by Other Latinos 28.4 percent, Puerto Ricans 9.6 percent, and Cuban Americans 3.5 percent. Other Latinos includes

Spaniards, South Americans, Central Americans, Dominicans, and other population groups. It also includes persons who identified as Latinos but did not specify origin. Estimates for 2007 set the figures for Mexican Americans at 65 percent, followed by Other Latinos 17.4 percent, Puerto Ricans 8.6 percent, and Cuban Americans 3.7 percent (U.S. Census Bureau, 2009a). The differences in the numbers between Mexican Americans and Other Latinos from 2000 and 2007 seem to be due to the greater specificity given to origin in the 2007 figures, thus boosting the percentage among Mexican Americans. Latino children under the age of 18 generally reflect this distribution by subgroup. Because the majority of Latino adults are foreign born, the majority of Latino children today have at least one foreign-born parent (Fry & Passel, 2009).

Latinos are the youngest and most fertile major population group in the nation (Tienda & Mitchell, 2006). In 2008, the median age for Latinos was 27.7, while that for non-Latino Whites was 41.1, and for Not Latinos it was 38.9. As such, it comes as no surprise that Latinas had the highest fertility rate of all the population groups in 2007. Indeed, while women in the other groups had fertility rates in the high 50s, mid 60s, and low 70s, Latinas had a rate of 102.1, meaning that there were this many live births per 1,000 Latinas ages 15 to 44 (Hamilton, Martin, & Ventura, 2009). Preliminary estimates of births in 2007 show an increase of 1 percent overall from the previous year and reflect the highest number of births registered in a single year in the history of the country (Ibid.). Finally, Latinas have the highest teen birth rates (26%) among their Black (22%), White (11%), and Asian (6%) counterparts (Pew Hispanic Center, 2009; Also see Ryan, Franzetta, & Manlove, 2005).

Figure 1.1 provides average percentages of the different subgroups comprising the overall population of Latino children under the age of 18 for the years 2007 to 2009. Those of Mexican origin are the largest group (71%), followed by Other Latinos (18%), Puerto Ricans (9%), and Cuban Americans (2%).

In 2008, Latino children 19 years of age and younger comprised approximately 37.2 percent of the (non-institutionalized) Latino population, while the same age group comprised 25.7 percent of the non-Latino population. The non-Hispanic White children population (19 years of age and younger) is projected to number 46.7 million (23.2%) in 2010, compared to 18.9 million Latinos (38.1%). However, because the non-Latino White population is projected to remain relatively flat over the next 40 years, while Latinos are expected to experience rapid growth, by 2050, the two groups of children are expected to be similar in size (Latinos at 43.7 million, and non-Latino Whites at 43.0 million) by 2050. At that time, Latino children are projected to comprise approximately 33 percent of the Latino population, while

Figure 1.1
Average Percent of Latina/o Children Ages 0–17 by Group Origin, 2007–2009

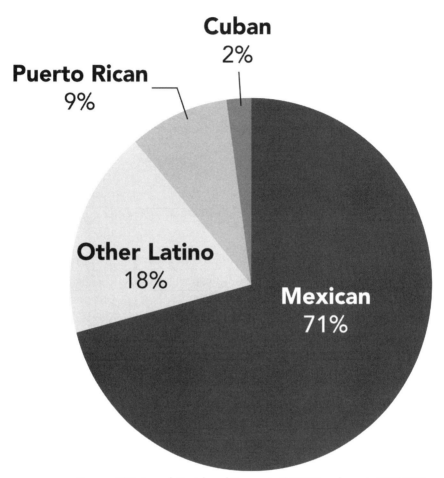

Source: CPS, Annual, Social, and Economic (ASEC) Supplement, 2007-2009.

non-Latino White children will comprise 21.1 percent of the non-Latino White population. After 2050, Latino children will most likely begin outnumbering non-Latino White children, and will be the largest group of children in the nation (see Figure 1.2). Recently, the U.S. Census Bureau announced that in 2008, Latino children under the age of five comprised 25 percent of the nation's children in that age category (U.S. Census Bureau, 2009b). Continued growth will mostly be the result of natural increase, although immigration will continue to contribute to it. Already, most of the growth is due to natural increase (Johnson & Lichter, 2008).

Figure 1.2
Projected Growth of Child Population by Race/Ethnicity, 2010–2050

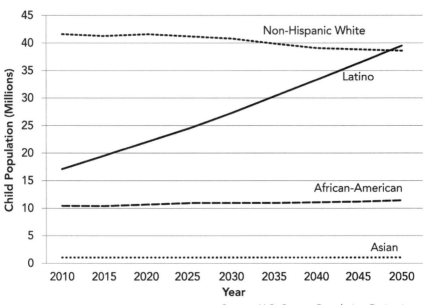

Source: U.S. Census Population Projections.

Using numbers for children under the age of 18, Figure 1.2 shows the trend lines for the growth projections of Latino, non-Latino White, Asian, and Black children. While the slopes are relatively flat for non-Latino White, Asian, and Black children, that for Latino children is steady in its upward trend. This shift in the composition of young populations will require changes in the capacity of institutions to meet their needs, particularly their educational needs.

In sum, the Latino population is a heterogeneous population comprised of Mexican Americans (or Chicanos), Other Latinos (mainly immigrants from Central America and South America), Puerto Ricans, and Cuban Americans. Latinos are a relatively young and rapidly growing population. It is projected that by mid-century Latino children will outnumber White children, marking another historic shift in the nation's population.

GEOGRAPHIC DISTRIBUTION

The Latino population has become increasingly dispersed geographically over the past three decades (Liaw & Frey, 2007). While the three major groups were historically concentrated in the Southwest (Mexican

Americans), the Northeast (Puerto Ricans), and the state of Florida (Cuban Americans), newcomers have moved into western, southern, and midwestern states in greater numbers than they had in the past. Consequently, the South, Midwest, and more recently the West have seen significant increases in their Latino populations since 1990 and 2000. According to Philip Martin (2009) and other scholars (Durand, Massey, & Parrado, 1999), among other factors, this dispersion is a consequence of the amnesty granted undocumented workers by the Immigration Reform and Control Act of 1986. In short, lawful permanent residence brought an estimated 2.7 million of persons out of the shadows where they could travel freely and pursue opportunities openly, and bring their family members with them (Durand, Massey, & Parrado, 1999; Rytina, 2002).

Additionally, the shift of meatpacking and other industries requiring low-skilled labor from urban to rural areas in the South and the Midwest created economic opportunities that attracted the "New Americans" to these regions, especially those with low education levels (Philip, 2009). Once settlements took hold in some communities, over time they attracted immigrant entrepreneurs and became international corridors that facilitated the movement of immigrants (McDaniel & Drever, 2009), including Latinos. The dispersion was driven not only by the attraction of low-skilled employment opportunities but also by the rising costs of living and the congestion of urban life (Frey, 2005). The geographical dispersion of the Latino population includes the dispersion of Latino children, although some scholars still view them as concentrated in a small number of states (Hernandez, Denton, & Macartney, 2007).

Table 1.1 provides the number and percentage of Latino children under the age of 18 by state for the years 2000 and 2008. The distribution of Latino children across the 50 states and the District of Columbia reflects the distribution of Latinos generally. In 2000, of the seven states with the highest concentrations, California had the highest concentration of Latino children, followed by Texas, New York, Florida, Illinois, Arizona, and New Jersey. In 2008, the same seven states remained with the highest concentrations, but the rank order had shifted slightly among them. Of course, California and Texas remained with the highest concentrations, followed by Florida, New York, Arizona, Illinois, and New Jersey. Additionally, while the states of California and Texas together held the majority of Latino children (and Latino population, approximately 52%) in 2000, that was no longer the case in 2008, when they held 48.2 percent of the Latino children (and slightly less of the overall Latino population, 47%).

Table 1.1

Number and Percent Change of Latino Children by State, District of Colombia, and the Nation, 2000 and 2008

State Name	Number of Latino Children, 2000	Number of Latino Children, 2008	Number of All Children, 2008	Percent Latino Children, 2008	Percent Change, 2000–2008
Alabama	25,032	55,544	1,121,877	5.0	121.9
Alaska	10,310	15,830	179,876	8.8	53.5
Arizona	498,660	733,290	1,707,221	43.0	47.1
Arkansas	32,252	65,478	702,481	9.3	103.0
California	4,071,975	4,654,983	9,364,530	49.7	14.3
Colorado	261,603	354,228	1,207,135	29.3	35.4
Connecticut	116,489	140,526	812,213	17.3	20.6
Delaware	13,682	23,385	206,229	11.3	70.9
District of Columbia	11,463	12,499	112,016	11.2	9.0
Florida	708,627	1,013,196	4,004,271	25.3	43.0
Georgia	137,473	298,594	2,548,841	11.7	117.2
Hawaii	35,187	42,158	285,243	14.8	19.8
Idaho	43,334	64,584	412,640	15.7	49.0
Illinois	555,716	691,902	3,179,260	21.8	24.5
Indiana	76,762	128,467	1,584,681	8.1	67.4
Iowa	32,940	52,130	712,613	7.3	58.3
Kansas	74,482	99,706	700,485	14.2	33.9
Kentucky	19,025	39,897	1,008,064	4.0	109.7
Louisiana	30,807	45,400	1,107,973	4.1	47.4
Maine	3,616	6,182	274,867	2.2	71.0
Maryland	72,647	127,270	1,340,583	9.5	75.2
Massachusetts	158,985	187,254	1,427,033	13.1	17.8
Michigan	124,304	152,950	2,390,198	6.4	23.0
Minnesota	56,159	88,366	1,254,644	7.0	57.3
Mississippi	12,138	24,143	766,720	3.1	98.9
Missouri	42,975	73,289	1,421,469	5.2	70.5
Montana	7,396	11,140	220,358	5.1	50.6
Nebraska	37,470	58,444	446,995	13.1	56.0
Nevada	148,311	251,847	667,801	37.7	69.8
New Hampshire	7,862	12,679	293,358	4.3	61.3
New Jersey	340,957	424,217	2,047,582	20.7	24.4
New Mexico	259,279	274,405	502,450	54.6	5.8
New York	897,492	937,772	4,408,016	21.3	4.5
North Carolina	121,146	271,104	2,243,677	12.1	123.8
North Dakota	3,216	5,097	143,048	3.6	58.5
Ohio	80,897	113,751	2,730,377	4.2	40.6
Oklahoma	70,547	111,634	906,035	12.3	58.2
Oregon	108,645	165,025	867,575	19.0	51.9

Table 1.1 *(Continued)*

State Name	Number of Latino Children, 2000	Number of Latino Children, 2008	Number of All Children, 2008	Percent Latino Children, 2008	Percent Change, 2000–2008
Pennsylvania	149,587	223,874	2,762,004	8.1	49.7
Rhode Island	35,282	43,821	228,540	19.2	24.2
South Carolina	28,186	70,483	1,066,227	6.6	150.1
South Dakota	4,552	9,509	198,309	4.8	108.9
Tennessee	39,216	93,119	1,478,594	6.3	137.5
Texas	2,404,552	3,116,203	6,725,771	46.3	29.6
Utah	79,050	134,018	849,635	15.8	69.5
Vermont	1,848	2,659	128,930	2.1	43.9
Virginia	103,607	179,711	1,823,201	9.9	73.5
Washington	178,860	256,992	1,541,175	16.7	43.7
West Virginia	3,898	6,999	386,158	1.8	79.6
Wisconsin	75,848	111,729	1,314,412	8.5	47.3
Wyoming	11,714	15,054	128,457	11.7	28.5
United States	**12,426,061**	**16,092,537**	**73,941,848**	**21.8**	**29.5**

Source: U.S. Census Population Estimates.

The states in the South had the highest growth rates among Latino children between 2000 and 2008. In rank order, the top five growth states in the nation were South Carolina, Tennessee, North Carolina, Alabama, and Georgia. All of these states more than doubled their Latino children populations. Although Mississippi did not double its Latino children population, it came very close, and most likely will by the time the 2010 census is completed. The geographical dispersion of Latino children has brought them into communities that do not have much experience with Latinos. At the same time, spatial movement seems to result in residential segregation (South, Crowder, & Chavez, 2005). This context has important implications for the service delivery systems, which are not likely to have the cultural competencies required for the effective delivery of services, especially in the areas of education and health care, and where there is widespread antipathy toward Latinos. As a result, there is little likelihood that the capacity for cultural competencies will be developed in the near future, unless local leadership recognizes the importance of doing so (Crowley, Lichter, & Qian, 2006).

In summary, then, the Latino population has become more geographically dispersed across the regions of the United States over the past three decades. Although they are concentrated in a handful of states (California,

Texas, New York, Florida, and Illinois), they have moved in significant numbers into southern, midwestern, western, and northeastern states, where communities are struggling with the cultural shifts that are taking place. At the same time, however, Latino residential segregation, which remains a problem, may contribute to poor education and the reproduction of poverty (Frankenberg, Lee, & Orfield, 2003).

FAMILY CONTEXTS

With the legalization of and continued in-migration of Latino immigrants over the past three decades, there has been a shift from the majority of Latinos being third-generation or higher to being first or second generation (Tienda, 2009). Table 1.2 presents the average number and percentage of native-born and foreign-born children under the age of 18 by race/ethnicity for the years 2007 to 2009. Latino children comprise 21.3 percent of the nation's children, 20.1 percent of the native-born children, and about one-half of the foreign-born children. The majority of Latino children (approximately two-thirds) are citizens of the United States by virtue of having been born here, and a slight majority of them are children of immigrants (Pew Hispanic Center, 2009; Fry & Passel, 2009).

Table 1.3 provides the average percentage of children under the age of 18 by household structure and composition by race/ethnicity for the years 2007 to 2009. The majority (70.4%) of all children live in married parents households. This is the case for all groups except non-Latino Blacks. The majority of Black children (61.1%) live in single parent households.

Table 1.2
Number and Percent of Children Ages 0–17 by Racial/Ethnicity (3-year averages), 2007–2009

Race and Ethnicity	Total		Native-Born		Foreign-Born	
	Number	Percent	Number	Percent	Number	Percent
Non-Latino White	41,980,435	56.5	41,510,864	58.1	469,571	16.4
Non-Latino Black	10,829,007	14.6	10,585,993	14.8	243,014	8.5
Latino	15,797,523	21.3	14,363,901	20.1	1,433,622	50.2
Asian or Pacific Islander	3,141,216	4.2	2,445,123	3.4	696,093	24.4
All other races	2,555,651	3.4	2,542,412	3.6	13,240	.5
Total	74,303,833	100.0	71,448,293	100.0	2,855,540	100.0

Source: CPS, Annual, Social, and Economic (ASEC) Supplement, 2007–2009.

Table 1.3
Living Arrangements of Children Ages 0–17 by Racial/Ethnicity, 2007–2009

Household Structure and Composition	Non-Hispanic White	Non-Hispanic Black	Latino/ Hispanic	Asian or Pacific Islander	All Other Races	Total
Living Arrangement (%)						
Married parents	78.8	38.9	67.5	85.2	60.8	70.4
Single Parents	21.2	61.1	32.5	14.8	39.2	29.6
Presence of Other Relatives						
Extended household*	9.4	22.7	22.5	21.6	19.2	15.0
Non-extended household	90.6	77.3	77.5	78.4	80.8	85.0
Family Size Number of Related Children (%)						
1 child	24.3	23.5	18.4	24.1	25.9	23.0
2 children	41.5	33.4	35.6	43.7	35.9	39.0
3 children	22.3	23.3	27.5	18.5	22.1	23.3
4 or more children	11.9	19.8	18.5	13.6	16.1	14.6
Family Size (mean)	4.3	4.3	4.7	4.7	4.3	4.4

*Married and single households with other relative members of householder other than the spouse and children.
Source: CPS, Annual, Social, and Economic (ASEC) Supplement, 2007–2009.

Approximately one-fifth of children in all groups except non-Latino Whites live with other relatives in the household. In terms of the number of related children in the household, two is the modal category for all groups, with non-Latino Whites tending toward smaller families and Latinos and Asian/Pacific Islanders tending toward larger families, with these two groups having an average family size of 4.7 persons.

Figure 1.3 presents the average percentage of children under the age of 18 who speak a language other than English at home by birth origin for the years 2005 to 2007. As might be expected, a majority of foreign-born children across the groups speak another language at home. The highest in this category are Latinos (96.6%), and the lowest are non-Latino Blacks (55.1%). Among the native-born, a majority of both Latino children (63.7%) and Asian/Pacific Islander children (58.1%) speak a language other than English at home. These figures point to a high likelihood of bilingualism among Latinos in the future.

Figure 1.4 presents the average percent of children under the age of 18 who do not speak English well or not at all by birth origin for the years 2005 to 2007. In general, the majority of children are fluent in English at

Figure 1.3
Average Percent of Children Ages 0–17 Who Speak a Language at Home Other Than English, by Race/Ethnicity and Birth Origin, 2005–2007

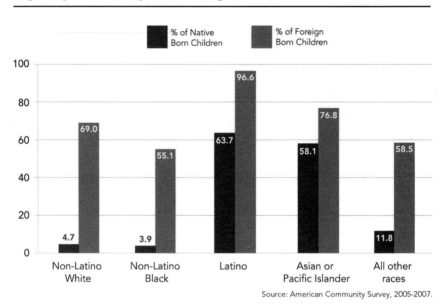

Source: American Community Survey, 2005-2007.

Figure 1.4
Average Percent of Children Ages 0–17 Who Speak a Language at Home Other Than English and Do Not Speak English Well or At All, 2005–2007

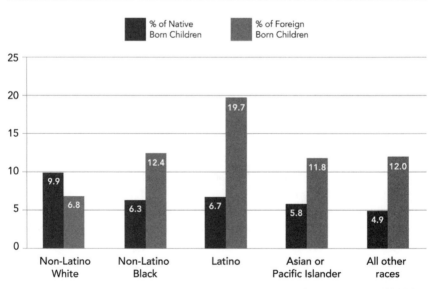

Source: American Community Survey, 2005-2007.

levels higher than "not speaking English well." In addition, as one might expect, foreign-born children are more likely to "not speak English well" or "not at all." The percentage is highest among Latinos (19.7%), followed by non-Latino Blacks (12.4%), Other Races (12.0%), Asian/Pacific Islanders (11.8%), and non-Latino Whites (6.8%). Among all groups except non-Latino Whites, foreign-born children are more likely *not* to speak English well. Interestingly, among non-Latino Whites, a higher percentage of native-born children (9.9%) than foreign-born children (6.8%) do not speak English well. It is not clear which particular White immigrant groups have this experience.

Figure 1.5 presents the average percentage of children under the age of 18 by race/ethnicity and parental education for the years 2007 to 2009. Among the groups, Latino children have the lowest percentage of parents with a college degree (14.6%), followed by non-Latino Blacks (19.6%), Other Races (33.4%) and non-Latino Whites (45.3%). Asian/Pacific Islander children have the highest percentage of parents with college degrees (60.7%). Latinos (29.2%) and non-Latino Blacks (32.5%) were

Figure 1.5
Average Percent of Latina/o Children Ages 0–17 by Group Origin and Parental Education*, 2007–2009

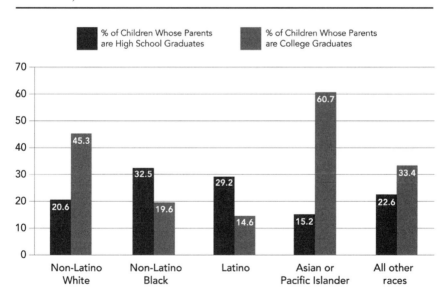

Source: CPS, Annual, Social, and Economic (ASEC) Supplement, 2007-2009

*Parental education is measured according to the highest degree obtained or level of school competed. In the case of two-parent families, the education of the parent who attained the higher level is considered.

Figure 1.6
Average Percent of Latina/o Children Ages 0–17 by Group Origin and Parental Education*, 2007–2009

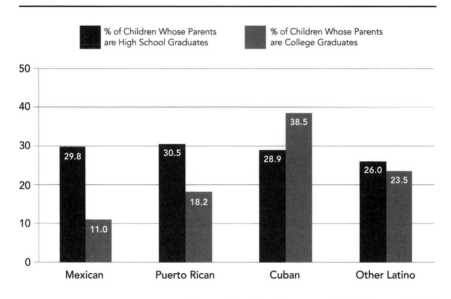

Source: CPS, Annual, Social, and Economic (ASEC) Supplement, 2007-2009

*Parental education is measured according to the highest degree obtained or level of school competed. In the case of two-parent families, the education of the parent who attained the higher level is considered.

more likely to have parents who were high school graduates than all the other groups.

Figure 1.6 presents the average percentage of Latino children under the age of 18 by group origin and parents' education for the years 2007 to 2009. Nearly four in ten Cuban American children have parents with a college degree (38.5%), compared to one in ten among those of Mexican origin (11.0%). Other Latinos are almost evenly split between parents with a high school diploma (26.0%) and those with a college degree (23.5%). Educationally, those of Mexican origin are faring less well than members of all of the other groups.

The well-being of the family has significant consequences for the well-being of children. For example, households with married couples provide environments that promote and support important aspects of child development, such as self concept, behavior, mental health, etc., and avoid the negative impacts of family breakdown (Mooney, Oliver, & Smith, 2009). Similarly, the education of the parents has significant implications for the socio-economic standing of the family. Moreover, it may be that familism, which is a critical feature of the Latino family (Tienda & Mitchell, 2006; Arnett, 2003), serves as a major factor in the resiliency of Latino families that blunts some of the negative effects of low socio-economic status that is tied to the low educational attainment of the parents.

In sum, the majority of Latino children are either first or second-generation, with the majority of them being children of immigrants. Traditionally, Latinos tend to have bigger families than their White counterparts, and are more likely to live in married parents households. They are likely to speak Spanish at home, and to speak English outside the home. Thus, most are bilingual to some degree or another. Their parents tend to have low educational attainment levels. Among the subgroups, Cuban American children are the most likely to have college educated parents, and Mexican American children are the least likely.

SOCIO-ECONOMIC CHARACTERISTICS

With the recession that officially began in 2007 came a decline in real median income (down from $52,163 to $50,303) between 2007 and 2008, and an increase in the poverty rate (up from 12.5% to 13.2%) (DeNavas Walt, Proctor, & Smith, 2009).[3] Latinos not only were among households with the lowest median income levels across the major population groups, but they experienced the greatest decline in median household income between 2007 and 2008. This is not surprising given that the flow of Latino immigrants has consisted primarily of workers with low levels of education (Tienda, 2009). As a result, they tend to be located in the low-skilled segment of the labor force and subject to the vagaries of the economy. In 2007, the median household income for Latinos was $40,165, which declined by 5.6 percent to $37,913 in 2008. The household income of non-Latino White households declined 2.6 percent from $57,030 to $55,530; for Blacks, it declined by 2.8 percent from $35,210 to $34,218; and for Asians, it declined 4.4 percent from $68,643 to $65,637. In 2007, Latinos had the lowest per capita income at $16,203, which declined by 3.3 percent to $15,674 in 2008. For non-Latino Whites it declined from $32,244 to $31,313 (2.9%); for Blacks it declined from $19,136 to $18,406 (3.8%); and for Asians it declined from $31,050 to $30,292 (2.4%).

The poverty threshold for a family of four with two children under the age of 18 years in 2008 was $21,834. The number of persons in poverty in 2007 increased from 37.3 million to 39.8 million in 2008, the second consecutive annual increase in the number of people in poverty, which yielded the highest poverty rate since 1997. The poverty rate for children under 18 years of age also went up from 18 percent to 19 percent. While the poverty rate for Blacks remained statistically unchanged from 2007 to 2008 at 24.7 percent, it increased from 21.5 percent to 23.2 percent for Latinos. For non-Latino Whites it went up from 8.2 percent to 8.6 percent and for Asians it went from 10.2 percent to 11.8 percent. In terms of income-to-poverty ratio, the rate for Latinos under .5 of the poverty threshold was 9.1 percent; under 1.0 it was 23.2 percent and under 1.25 it was 31.4 percent. For non-Latino Whites the rates were 3.7 percent, 8.6 percent and 12.1 percent, respectively. For Blacks the rates were 11.4 percent, 24.7 percent, and 31.6 percent, respectively. For Asians, they were 5.5 percent, 11.8 percent, and 14.5 percent, respectively. Latinos and Blacks had the highest rates across the different ratio levels, and consequently had the highest rates among those experiencing severe poverty (earning .5 or less of the income level at the poverty threshold). Additionally, studies show that foreign-born Latinos are more likely than native-born Latinos to live in poverty (Tienda & Mitchell, 2006). Finally, children in households where both parents are present are less likely to live in poverty than those in single-parent households.

With regard to health insurance coverage, while the increase of the percentage of persons without health insurance from 2007 to 2008 was not statistically significant, the number of uninsured increased from 45.7 to 46.3 million (DeNavas-Walt et al., 2009). With regard to the insured, there was a decrease of 1 million among those covered by private health insurance, and an increase of 4.4 million among those covered by government health insurance. Latinos had uninsured rates of 32.1 percent in 2007 and 30.7 percent in 2008. While there was a slight decline in the rate, it is relative to the increase of the overall Latino population, with the absolute number of uninsured remaining about the same. Among non-Latino Whites, the rate increased from 10.4 percent to 10.8 percent; among Blacks it declined slightly from 19.5 percent to 19.1 percent; and among Asians it increased from 16.8 percent to 17.6 percent. These health insurance rates among Latinos in general circumscribe the health care context for Latino children.

Unlike income and poverty, the percentage and number of children under the age of 18 without health insurance were lower in 2008 (9.9% and 7.3 million) than in 2007 (11.0% and 8.1 million). These were the lowest figures since 1987. Among these youth, Latinos had the highest uninsured rate (17.2%), followed by Asian (10.9%), Blacks (10.7%), and non-Latino Whites (6.7%). As expected, children in poverty were more likely to be uninsured (15.7%) than all children (9.9%). Additionally, children under 12 years of age were less likely to be uninsured (9.0%) than children between the ages of 12 and 17 (11.6%).

Generally, uninsured rates are higher among foreign-born persons than among the native born (Castañeda & Ojeda, 2008). Language and culture, poor health literacy, and concerns about immigration status are among some of the major factors that serve as barriers to health insurance even when it is available through public programs (Abreu & Hynes, 2009).

Socio-economically, then, Latino children are more likely than children from other major population groups to live in households with the lowest per capita incomes. In terms of overall household income, they live in households that have slightly higher incomes than African American households, but substantially lower than White and Asian households. Latino poverty rates are similar to those of African Americans and substantially higher than those for Whites and Asians. One in ten Latino children live in severe poverty. Making matters worse, Latino children are the most likely among the major population groups to lack health insurance (Federal Interagency Forum on Child and Family Statistics, 2009).

EDUCATION

Education is the most important formal socialization component in contemporary society, especially given the emphasis on credentials for occupational access and attainment (see, for instance, the National Career Readiness Certificate developed by ACT). Indeed, education is one of the most important indicators of socio-economic status. Over the next several decades, strong growth is expected in Latino enrollment at all educational levels. Historically, Latinos have not done very well in the nation's schools, which tend to harbor low expectations and non-supportive environments that contribute to high dropout rates. Moreover, Latino students are the most segregated student population in the nation (Frankenberg, Lee, & Orfield, 2005). Using 2007 data, a recent study by the Center for Labor Market Studies at Northeastern University (2009) estimated that nearly 27.5 percent of Latinos between the ages of 16 and 24 were high school dropouts. While there is much controversy over the calculation of the dropout rate, there is no question that among the largest population groups the rate is highest among Latinos, and that it is at least twice that of Whites (12.2%) and higher than that for Blacks (21.0%). Additionally, while there have been improvements in the educational attainment levels among Latinos, relatively speaking, they have lost ground to both White and Black Americans, especially at the postsecondary level, despite increases in enrollments (Tienda, 2009).

Table 1.4 presents the average percentage of children under the age of 18 attending school by grade (and indirectly, school) level, race/ethnicity, and birth origin for the years 2005 to 2007. In other words, the table shows the distribution of students by school level for each group. To a great extent, these figures reflect the relative age distributions of the different groups. Among native-born Asian students, 10.8 percent are attending nursery or preschool, while 8.9 percent of Latino students are enrolled in nursery or preschool levels. Although these percentage differences are small relative to the other groups, the actual numbers of Latino youth are substantial given the size of the population. At the kindergarten level, Latinos have the highest percent of students enrolled (8.9%), and non-Latino Whites have the lowest (7.0%), which reflects the relatively younger student population among Latinos.

In terms of group distributions of students across school levels, the group with the highest percent of students at the elementary school level (grades 1 through 4) are Latinos (31.8%), while non-Latino Whites have the lowest (27.9%). Non-Latino Blacks have the highest percent at the

Table 1.4
Percent of Children Ages 0–17 Attending School by Grade Level, Race/Ethnicity, and Foreign-Born Status

			Grade Level Attending		
Race/Ethnicity	Nursery School/ Preschool	Kinder- garten	Grade 1 to Grade 4	Grade 5 to Grade 8	Grade 9 to Grade 12
Natives					
Non-Latino White	9.0	7.0	27.9	29.7	26.4
Non-Latino Black	9.0	7.1	28.3	30.2	25.4
Latino	8.9	8.9	31.8	28.9	21.6
Asian	10.8	8.3	29.8	28.1	23.0
Other Races	10.2	8.3	30.3	28.7	22.6
Foreign-Born					
Non-Latino White	5.0	4.6	24.1	32.3	34.0
Non-Latino Black	3.3	4.2	22.8	33.3	36.4
Latino	2.6	4.2	26.2	34.4	32.7
Asian	5.7	5.1	25.4	29.9	33.9
Other Races	3.8	4.4	26.4	30.9	34.6

Source: American Community Survey, 2005–2007.

middle school level (grades 5 through 8) (30.2%), and Asians the lowest (28.1%). At the high school level (grades 9 through 12), non-Latino Whites have the highest percent (26.4) and Latinos the lowest (21.6%). These figures represent two patterns among students: 1) the demographic shift that is occurring among students across the groups, and 2) the persisting dropout problem among Latinos at the high school level.

Among the foreign-born children, non-Latino Whites have the highest percentage (5.0%) at the preschool level, and Latinos have the lowest (2.6%). In kindergarten, non-Latino Whites have the highest percentage (4.6%), and Latinos (4.2%) and non-Latino Blacks (4.2%) have the lowest. At the elementary level, Other Races have the highest percentage (26.4%), and non-Latino Blacks (22.8%) the lowest. At the middle school level, Latinos (34.4%) have the highest percent, and Asians (29.9%) the lowest. Finally, at the high school level, non-Latino Blacks have the highest percent (36.4%), and Latinos have the lowest (32.7%). Indeed, studies on immigrant youth and education show that teenagers from Mexico are most likely to experience "educational nonenrollment" (Hirschman, 2001; Pew Hispanic Center, 2009).

Generally, there has been an increase over time in the number of preschool enrollments that reflect increases in the population, but the demographic shift is becoming evident across all the school levels. What the distribution of students across school levels does not show is the gap that exists between the total number of children in each group and the number of them who are enrolled in nursery or preschool programs. For example, of the slightly more than 8 million three and four year olds in 2008, 50.6 percent were enrolled in nursery or preschool programs. By comparison, of the approximately 2 million three and four year old Latino children that year, 39.7 percent were enrolled in nursery or preschool programs, while the rate for the 4.4 million non-Hispanic Whites was 54.8 percent, and for the 1.2 million African Americans it was 50.6 percent.[4]

As might be expected, very young Latino children are likely to come from families that cannot afford to place them in preschools or are not integrated into our societal institutions well enough to do so. It may also be that the traditional family emphasizes early socialization within the family. Overall, one thing is for sure, the nation's education systems must find ways to effectively retain and educate all children, but especially Latinos, who experience the greatest decline from elementary to high schools levels.

Table 1.5 presents the average percentage of Latino children under the age of 18 attending school by grade level, group origin, and birth origin for the years 2005 to 2007. Among the native born, Cubans have the highest percentage of participation at the preschool level; Mexicans have the

Table 1.5

Percent of Latino Children Ages 0–17 Attending School by Grade Level, Group Origin, and Foreign-Born Status

	Grade Level Attending				
Group Origin	Nursery School/ Preschool	Kinder-garten	Grade 1 to Grade 4	Grade 5 to Grade 8	Grade 9 to Grade 12
Natives					
Mexican	8.6	9.2	32.6	28.7	20.8
Puerto Rican	8.4	8.0	29.5	30.2	23.9
Cuban	11.2	7.5	29.3	28.3	23.7
Other Latino	9.6	8.5	30.4	29.0	22.5
Foreign-Born					
Mexican	2.4	4.4	27.4	34.7	31.2
Puerto Rican	5.1	5.0	16.4	26.8	46.7
Cuban	2.2	4.2	22.7	34.1	36.8
Other Latino	3.1	3.7	23.4	33.7	36.2

Source: American Community Survey, 2005–2007.

highest percentages at the kindergarten and elementary levels; Puerto Ricans have the highest percentages at the middle and high school levels. Mexican-origin students experience the greatest decrease from the elementary to the high school level (11.8 percentage points), while Puerto Ricans and Cubans have much lower decreases (approximately 5.6 percentage points).

Among the foreign born, all groups have lower percentages of students at the preschool, kindergarten and elementary school levels than their native-born counterparts. Interestingly, all of them have greater percentages at the middle (except Mexicans) and high school levels than their native-born counterparts. These particular distributions may reflect the age at which Latino immigrant youth came to the United States, immigration waves that may have occurred, or other factors that influence their shape. While they reflect the dropout phenomenon, they do not represent it as strongly as do the figures among the native born because of the factors just mentioned.

Although the enrollment numbers are improving, Latino children are the least likely among the major population groups to be enrolled in preschool or early education programs. In terms of high school completion, a similar pattern is evident. While there have been improvements over time, Latino youth are still the least likely to complete high school (Federal Interagency Forum on Child and Family Statistics, 2009). Moreover, Latino youth, like their African American counterparts, are the most likely to be "neither enrolled in school nor working" (Ibid., p. 54). Enrollment rates are lower among foreign-born Latino children than their native-born counterparts, especially among those of Mexican origin. Low educational attainment has long-term consequences for Latinos and their children, as it is one of the primary factors contributing to upward social mobility. Not only does low educational attainment close off opportunities for postsecondary education, particularly for a high quality college education, but it reproduces low socio-economic status from one generation to the next.

Addressing the educational achievement gap will require multiple approaches, including expansion of after-school programs (especially those that provide academic support), policies that link teacher salaries to student performance and that increase educational opportunities for undocumented immigrant students at the postsecondary level, improvement of low-performing schools, transformation of school cultures into multicultural environments that address the learning needs of all children, and expansion of effective dropout prevention and recovery programs (Fleischman & Heppen, 2009; Stern, 2009; Tyler & Lofstrom, 2009).

HEALTH

The health status of Latino children is greatly impacted by traditional culture, socio-economic status, and organizational cultures (Flores et al., 2002; Mendoza 1994; Rodriguez-Triás & Ramirez de Arellano, 1994). Traditional culture, which emphasizes traditional gender roles and collectivism rather than individualism, seems to serve as a protective factor against risk behaviors such as smoking and drug abuse, while poverty impacts the quality of diet and health care, and organizational cultures, whether because of racism or the lack of cultural competence, hinder the delivery of health care provided to Latinos. For instance, more-acculturated Latinos with diabetes are more likely to adopt less desirable dietary habits than their less-acculturated counterparts (Mainous, Diaz, & Geesey, 2008). Quality of health care is impacted by several factors, including language barriers, cultural differences, lack of health insurance, transportation problems, and so on (Flores, Abreu, Oliva, & Kastner, 2009). In addition, obesity and diabetes have reached epidemic proportions across the country, but their prevalence is particularly high among Latinos. Moreover, it may be that sons of immigrants may have higher obesity rates than those of native-born Latinos (Van Hook, Balistreri, & Baker, 2009).

Finally, puzzling researchers is the phenomenon dubbed the "Hispanic paradox," which refers to favorable Mexican immigrant mortality rates relative to Whites with higher socio-economic status and better than expected birth weight and infant mortality rates among the Mexican origin population given its relatively low socio-economic status. Although some may view the Hispanic Paradox as an ecological fallacy (Scribner, 1996), or the result of faulty logic using group-level data to interpret individual-level outcomes, evidence continues to support a mortality advantage even in old age (Markides & Eschbach, 2005). In terms of infant mortality, for example, in 2005, Latinos had a rate of 5.8 deaths per 1,000 live births, while non-Hispanic Whites had one of 5.8, and African Americans had one of 13.6. Only Asian Americans had a lower rate (4.9). Among Latino subgroups, Puerto Ricans had the highest rate (8.3), while Cuban Americans had the lowest (4.4) (Federal Interagency Forum on Child and Family Statistics, 2009).

Figure 1.7 presents the average percentage of children less than 18 years of age in fair/poor health by race/ethnicity for 2007 to 2009. While the overall percentages of children in fair/poor health are relatively low (ranging from 1.6% to 3.0%), Latinos (2.9%), and non-Latino Blacks (3.0%) have the highest percentages in this health category, with non-Latino Whites and Asian/Pacific Islanders having the lowest rates (1.6%).

Figure 1.8 presents the average percentage of Latino children under the age of 18 in fair/poor health by group origin for 2007 to 2009. Puerto Rican children have the highest percentage (3.8%) of children with fair/poor health, followed by Cuban Americans (2.9%), Mexican origin (2.8%), and Other Latinos (2.5%).

Figure 1.7
Average Percent of Children Ages 0–17 in Fair/Poor Health by Race/Ethnicity, 2007–2009

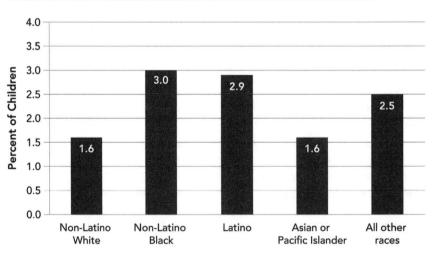

Source: CPS, Annual, Social, and Economic (ASEC) Supplement, 2007-2009

Figure 1.8
Average Percent of Latino Children Ages 0–17 in Fair/Poor Health by Group Origin, 2007–2009

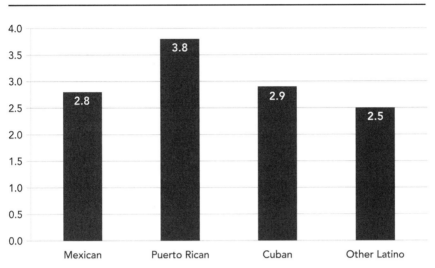

Source: CPS, Annual, Social, and Economic (ASEC) Supplement, 2007-2009

An important indicator of health care is preschool immunizations. Data are collected annually through the National Immunization Survey by the Centers for Disease Control and Prevention, but are limited to children ages 19 to 35 months whose immunization history can be verified. Although race/ethnic disparities have been found (Chu, Barker, & Smith, 2004; Herrera, Zhao, & Klevens, 2001), they may have closed over time between Latinos and Whites, and prevail primarily between Whites and African Americans. Zhao and Luman (2010), for example, found that Whites were less likely to have coverage with the 4:3:1:3:3:1 vaccination series in 2001 and in 2008 than Latinos.[5] Given the limitations of the data, which are based on a telephone survey, the actual reality of coverage may still not be well understood. Additionally, it may be that disparities still prevail among the Latino subgroups (Herrera, Zhao, & Klevens, 2001).

A major health concern regarding Latino children is obesity (Odgen et al., 2006). Since 1980, the prevalence of overweight has increased among all age groups, including children (Hedley, 2004), although it appears to have slowed in recent years (Federal Interagency Forum on Child and Family Statistics, 2009; Anderson & Butcher, 2006). Obesity rates are higher among Latino and African American children than White children. In general, male Mexican American children (24.7%) have higher rates of obesity than their African American (18.7%) and White (14.8%) counterparts. Female

Mexican American children (19.6%) tend to have lower rates of obesity than their African American (25.6%) counterparts, but higher than their White (12.7%) counterparts (Kumanyika & Grier, 2006). Variability among Latino subgroups and across generations may also exist (Taverno, Rollins, & Francis, 2010). Obesity remains one of the nation's major health challenges because it is linked to several diseases and health problems, not the least of which is diabetes. It also tends to have psychosocial consequences.

Although studies show that Latino children tend to have lower rates of emotional and behavioral difficulties, because poverty, which is high among Latinos, is associated with having such difficulties (Federal Interagency Forum on Child and Family Statistics, 2009), especially among boys, service delivery systems must nonetheless develop the capacity to address these issues among Latinos (Arya et al., 2009; Simpson et al., 2005). This is particularly the case given that the educational and juvenile systems are particularly harsh on Latino youth (Arya, Villarruel, Villanueva, & Augarten, 2009). Additionally, it may be the case that there are more unmet mental health needs among Latino children than their White counterparts (Kataoka, Zhang, & Wells, 2002). Not only do these difficulties impact the family relative to finances and relationships, the lack of systematic attention by professionals may lead to misplacement in special education programs or, given the racialized nature of society, in our juvenile and criminal justice systems.

In sum, although the rates are low, Latino children, like their African American counterparts, are more likely to be in fair to poor health than their White and Asian counterparts. Among Latinos, Puerto Rican children are more likely to be in fair to poor health, followed by Cuban Americans, Mexican origin, and Other Latino children. Moreover, there may be more unmet mental health needs among Latino children than their White counterparts. While there seems to be little difference in immunization coverage between Latino young children and their White counterparts, more detailed studies are needed. Additionally, obesity remains a major challenge for Latinos and the nation. Overall, there are substantial gaps in our understanding of the health needs of Latino children generally (Flores et al., 2002).

VALUES, IDENTITY, AND PERCEPTIONS OF THEIR FUTURES

The Pew Hispanic Center (2009) recently released findings from a telephone survey of a representative sample of Latinos (2,012) with an over-sample (1,240) of those between the ages of 16 and 25. While young Latinos report satisfaction with their lives, optimism about their futures, and tend to value education, hard work, and career success, they are also more likely than their counterparts from other groups to drop out of school and to become teen parents. They also are more likely than their White and Asian counterparts to live in poverty, and they have higher levels of exposure to gangs and their activities (Pew Hispanic Center, 2009). Additionally, although native-born Latino youth do better than their foreign-born counterparts, on some indicators, such as education, household income, and so on, they are more likely to have ties to gangs and to be incarcerated (3% versus 2%, respectively). Young Latinos with Mexican ancestry are more likely (56%) than other young Latinos (40%) to report experience with gangs.

In terms of identity, young Latinos tend to place strong emphasis on their family's country of origin over being American. They also say that their parents encourage them to speak Spanish, and tend to perceive more cultural differences than commonalities within the Latino community, although they report that Latinos from different countries tend to get along here in the United States. Interestingly, young Latinos do not perceive themselves within the racial categories of the U.S. Census Bureau, responding that their race is "some other race" or asserting that their race is "Hispanic or Latino." Unlike their older counterparts (30%), those 26 years of age and older, they are less likely (16%) to view themselves as White.

Young Latinos are more likely (38%) than their older counterparts (31%) to report having close friends or relatives who have been the targets of ethnic or racial discrimination. Moreover, perceptions of discrimination are more likely among native-born (41%) young Latinos than their foreign-born (32%) counterparts.

In terms of education, the overwhelming majority (87%) of young Latinos view the college degree as important for success in life, however, less than half of them say they plan to obtain one. The reasons given by those who end their formal education before college are financial pressures to support their family, poor English skills, a dislike of school, and no need for further education in the career they have chosen for themselves. This gap between their subjective view of the importance of education and the reality of their relatively low educational attainment requires systematic attention both by researchers and educators.

CONCLUSION

The status of Latino children reflects the status of the overall Latino population in the United States. It is growing rapidly at the same time that it remains marginal to the nation's institutions. For example, they are more likely than their White counterparts to live in poverty and to drop out of school. In a context in which their rapid growth has become more and more evident, Latinos and their children become increasingly vulnerable to the dynamics of institutional exclusion based on established patterns of racism. Consequently, nativistic movements engendered by globalization, fear of immigrants, and the rapid growth of the Latino population have converged to limit their life chances. As a result, recent immigrants are not experiencing the upward mobility across generations that became a tradition for earlier waves of European immigrants (North, 2009). In particular, the patterns for Latino immigrants are as follows: educational success declines from the first to the third generation; violence and drug abuse rises across these generations; risky sexual behavior increases; health among children worsens; and, earnings and home ownership remain flat for the second through the fourth generations, especially among Mexican Americans (Ibid.). Despite all of these negative indicators, Latino children and youth remain resilient and hopeful of a better future. And, given the demographic shift that continues to occur, the nation will sooner or later have to address their needs if it is to position itself for a competitive future in a global economy.

The United States is at a major crossroads relative to the social, economic, and political incorporation of Latinos, both native-born and foreign-born. Latinos are positioned with the greatest demographic potential to contribute to the rebuilding of the nation and its economy as it moves into the future (Martinez, 2009). However, it is such a marginalized population group, from the young to the elderly, that it cannot possibly realize its potential unless dramatic steps are taken to incorporate it into the core of the nation's institutions. Educational systems, in particular, must transform themselves into organizations with the capacity to educate Latinos (Cisneros, 2009; Tienda & Mitchell, 2006). Overall, the incorporation of Latinos remains one the nation's greatest challenges at the same time that it is one about which very little public consciousness exists, except, of course, as part of ideological discourses that fail to grasp the issues in rational terms. How this paradox is resolved will determine the future of the nation and its Latino children.

NOTES

Thanks to Jean Kayitsinga for his assistance in the construction of the tables and figures, and to Jennifer Tello Buntin for her constructive comments on earlier versions of this chapter.

1. While this fact holds for the two population groups in general, it may not hold for higher SES Latinos who are more likely to attend colleges and universities than their lower SES counterparts.

2. Unless otherwise indicated, the numbers and statistics for this section come from calculations based on figures taken from several tables provided by the U.S.

Census Bureau, including the Hispanic Population in the United States, 2008; U.S. Population Projections, National Population Projections Released 2008 (Table 4); and Census 2000 Population Briefs.

3. The figures provided in this section for income, poverty, and health insurance are from the DeNavas-Walt et al., report on *Income, Poverty and Health Insurance in the United States: 2008*.

4. These figures were calculated using information from Tables 1 and 2 of the School Enrollment—Social and Economic Characteristics of Students: October 2008, available through the U.S. Census Bureau webpage at http://www.census.gov/population/www/socdemo/school/cps2008.html.

5. The 4:3:1:3:3:1 vaccine series includes at least 4 doses of diphtheria-tetanus-pertussis vaccine, three doses of poliovirus vaccine, one dose of measles-mumps-rubella vaccine, three doses of hepatitis B vaccine, three doses of *Haemophilus influenzae* type B vaccine, and one dose of varicella vaccine.

REFERENCES

Abreu, M., & Hynes H. P. (2009). The Latino Health Insurance Program: A pilot intervention for enrolling Latino families in health insurance programs, East Boston, Massachusetts, 2006–2007. *Preventing Chronic Disease 6*(4): 1–9.

Anderson, P. M., & Butcher K. F. (2006). Childhood obesity: Trends and potential causes. *The Future of Children 16*(1): 19–45.

Arnett, J. J. (2003). Conceptions of the transition to adulthood among emerging adults in American ethnic groups. *New Directions for Child and Adolescent Development 100*:63–75.

Arnett, J. J. (1994). Are college students adults? Their conceptions of the transition to adulthood. *Journal of Adult Development 1*(4): 213–224.

Arya, N., Villarruel, F., Villanueva, C., & Augarten, I. (2009). *America's invisible children: Latino youth and the failure of justice*. Policy Brief, Race and Ethnicity Series, v. 3. Washington, DC: National Council of La Raza.

Castañeda, X., & Ojeda, G. (2008). *Health insurance coverage of Latinos in the United States*. Heath Policy Fact Sheet. Berkeley, CA: Health Initiative of the Americas, UC Berkeley School of Public Health.

Center for Labor Market Studies. (2009). *Left behind: The nation's dropout crisis*. Boston, MA: Northeastern University.

Chu, S. Y., Barker, L. E., & Smith, P. J. (2004). Racial/Ethnic disparities in preschool immunizations: United States, 1996–2001. *American Journal of Public Health 94*(6): 973–977.

Cisneros, H. G. (Ed.), (2009). *Latinos and the nation's future*. Houston, TX: Arte Público Press.

Crowley, M., Lichter, D. T., & Qian, Z. (2006). Beyond gateway cities: Economic restructuring and poverty among Mexican immigrant families and children. *Family Relations 55*:345–360.

DeNavas-Walt, C., Proctor, B. D., & Smith, J. C. (2009). *Income, poverty, and health insurance coverage in the United States: 2008.* Current Population Reports, P60-236. Washington, DC: U.S. Census Bureau.

Durand, J., Massey, D. S., & Parrado, E. A. (1999). The new era of Mexican emigration to the United States. *The Journal of American History 86*(2): 518–536.

Federal Interagency Forum on Child and Family Statistics. (2009). *America's children: Key national indicators of well-being.* Washington, DC: U.S. Government Printing Office.

Fleischman, S., & Heppen, J. (2009). Improving low-performing high schools: Searching for evidence of promise. *The Future of Children 19*(1): 105–133.

Flores, G., et al. (2002). The health of Latino children: Urgent priorities, unanswered questions, and a research agenda. *JAMA 288*(1): 82–90.

Flores, G., Abreu, M., Olivar, M. A., & Kastner, B. (1998). Access barriers to health care for Latino children. *Archives of Pediatrics & Adolescent Medicine. 152*(11): 1119–1125.

Frankenberg, E., Lee, C., & Orfield, G. (2003). *A multiracial society with segregated schools: Are we losing the dream?* Cambridge, MA: The Civil Rights Project, Harvard University.

Frey, W. H. (2005). *Immigration and domestic migration in US metro areas: 2000 and 1990 Census findings by race and education.* Report 05-572. Ann Arbor, MI: Population Studies Center, Institute for Social Research, University of Michigan.

Fry, R., & Passel, J. S. (2009). *Latino children: A majority are U.S.-born offspring of immigrants.* Washington, DC: Pew Hispanic Center.

Grieco, E. M. (2009). *Race and Hispanic-origin of the foreign born population in the United States, 2007.* American Community Survey Reports, ACS-11. Washington, DC: U.S. Census Bureau.

Guzmán, B. (2001). *The Hispanic population.* Census 2000 Brief, C2KBR/01-3. Washington, DC: US Census Bureau.

Hamilton, B. E., Martin, J. A., & Ventura, S. J. (2009). *Births: Preliminary data for 2007.* National vital statistics reports, Web release. Vol. 57 no. 12. Hyattsville, MD: National Center for Health Statistics.

Hedley, A. A., et al. (2004). Prevalence of overweight and obesity among US children, adolescents, and adults, 1999–2002. *Journal of the American Medical Association 291*(23): 2847–2850.

Hernandez, D. J., Denton, N. A., & Macartney, S. E. (2007). Young Hispanic children in the 21st Century. *Journal of Latinos and Education 6*(3): 209–228.

Hernandez, D. J., & Macartney, S. E. (2008). *Racial-ethnic inequality in child well-being from 1985–2004: Gaps narrowing, but persist.* FDC Policy Brief no. 9. NY, NY: Foundation for Child Development.

Herrera, G. A., Zhen, Z., & Klevens, R. M. (2001). Variation in vaccination coverage among children of Hispanic ancestry. *American Journal of Preventive Medicine. 20*(4S): 69–74.

Hirschman, C. (2001). The educational enrollment of immigrant youth: A test of the segmented-assimilation hypothesis. *Demography 38*(3): 317–336.

Johnson, K. M., & Lichter, D. T. (2008). Natural increase: A new source of population growth in emerging Hispanic destinations. *Population and Development Review 34*:327–346.

Kataoka, S. H., Zhang, L., & Wells, K. B. (2002). Unmet need for mental health care among U.S. children: Variation by ethnicity and insurance status. *American Journal of Psychiatry 159*(9): 1548–1555.

Kumanyika, S., & Grier, S. (2006). Targeting interventions for ethnic minority and low-income populations. *The Future of Children 16*(1): 187–207.

Liaw, L.-L., & Frey, W. H. (2007). Multivariate explanation of the 1985–1990 and 1995–2000 destination choices of newly arrived immigrants in the United States: The beginning of a new trend? *Population, Space and Place 13*:377–399.

Mainous, III, A. G., Diaz, V. A., & Geesey, M. E. (2008). Acculturation and healthy lifestyle among Latinos with diabetes. *Annals of Family Medicine 6*(2): 131–137.

Markides, K. S., & Eschbach, K. (2005). Aging, migration and mortality: Current status of research on the Hispanic paradox. *Journal of Gerontology 60B* (Special Issue II): 68–75.

Martin, P. (2009). *Report on immigration reform: Implications for farmers, farm workers and communities*. Conference held in Washington, DC, May 21–22.

Martinez, R. (2009). Demographic shifts, Latinos and social justice. *PA Times 32*(8): 5.

McDaniel, P. N., & Drever, A. I. (2009). Ethnic enclave or International corridor? Immigrant businesses in a New South city. *Southeastern Geographer 49*(1): 3–23.

Mendoza, F. S. (1994) The health of Latino children in the United States. *The Future of Children 4*(3): 43–72.

Mooney, A., Oliver, C., & Smith, M. (2009). *Impact of family breakdown on children's well-being: Evidence review*. Research Report No. DCSF-RR113. London: Institute of Education, University of London.

Niner, D. A., & Rios, M. (2009). *Hispanics in the United States, Puerto Rico, and the U.S. Virgin Islands: 2000*. Working Paper No. 84. Washington, DC: U.S. Census Bureau.

North, D. S. (2009). The immigrant paradox: The stalled progress of recent immigrants' children. *Backgrounder*. Washington, DC: Center for Immigration Studies.

Ogden, C. L. et al. (2006). Prevalence of overweight and obesity in the United States, 1999–2004. *Journal of the American Medical Association 295*(13): 1549–1555.

Pew Hispanic Center. (2009). *Between two worlds: How young Latinos come of age in America*. Washington, DC: Pew Research Center.

Rodriguez-Triás, H., & Ramírez de Arellano, A. B. (1994). The health of children and youth. In C. W. Molina & M. Aguirre-Molina (Eds.), *Latino health in the US: A growing challenge* (pp. 115–133). Washington, DC: American Public Health Association.

Ryan, S., Franzetta, K., & Manlove, J. (2005). *Hispanic teen pregnancy and birth rates: Looking behind the numbers*. Child Trends Research Brief No. 2005-01. Washington, DC: Child Trends.

Rytina, N. (2002). *IRCA legalization effects: Lawful permanent residence and naturalization through 2001*. Paper presented at the Effects of Immigrant

Legalization Programs on the United States, NIH Main Campus, Bethesda, MD, October 25.

Scribner, R. (1996). Paradox as paradigm—The health outcomes of Mexican Americans. *American Journal of Public Health 86*(3): 303–304.

Simpson, G. A. et al. (2005). *U.S. children with emotional and behavioral difficulties: Data from the 2001, 2002, and 2003 National Health Interview Surveys*. Advance Data from Vital and Health Statistics, no. 360. Hyattsville, MD: National Center for Health Statistics.

South, S. J., Crowder, K., & Chavez, E. (2005). Migration and spatial assimilation among U.S. Latinos: Classical versus segmented trajectories. *Demography 42*(3): 497–521.

Stern, D. (2009). Expanding policy options for educating teenagers. *The Future of Children 19*(1): 211–239.

Taverno, S. E., Rollins, B. Y., & Francis, L. A. (2010). Generation, language, body mass index, and activity patterns in Hispanic children. *American Journal of Preventive Medicine 38*(2): 145–153.

Tienda, M. (2009). *Hispanicity and educational inequality: Risks, opportunities and the nation's future*. The 25th Tomás Rivera Lecture presented at the annual conference of the American Association of Hispanics in Higher Education, San Antonio, TX.

Tienda, M., & Mitchell, F. (Eds.). (2006). *Multiple origins, uncertain destinies: Hispanics and the American future*. Washington, DC: National Academies Press.

Tyler, J. H., & Lofsrom, M. (2009). Finishing high school: Alternative pathways and dropout recovery. *The Future of Children 19*(1): 77–103.

U.S. Census Bureau. (2009a). *Statistical abstract of the United States, 2009*. Washington, DC: U.S. Census Bureau.

U.S. Census Bureau. (2009b). Census Bureau estimates nearly half of children under age 5 are minorities. U.S. Census Bureau News. Retrieved August 2, 2010 from http://www.census.gov/newsroom/releases/archives/population/cb09-75.html.

U.S. Census Bureau. (2008) National population projections, table 4. U.S. population projections. *Projections of the population by sex, race, and Hispanic origin for the United States: 2010 to 2050*. Retrieved October 10, 2009 from http://www.census.gov/population/www/projections/files/nation/summary/np2008-t4.xls.

Van Hook, J., Balistreri, K. S., & Baker, E. (2009). Moving to the land of milk and cookies: Obesity among the children of immigrants. *Migration Information Source*. Retrieved August 2, 2010 from http://media.timesfreepress.com/docs/2009/09/Children_of_immigrants_and_obesity.pdf.

Zhao, Z., & Luman, E. T. (2010). Progress toward eliminating disparities in vaccination coverage among U.S. children, 2000–2008. *American Journal of Preventive Medicine 38*(2): 127–137.

Chapter 2

SOCIAL ADAPTATION AND POSITIVE ADJUSTMENT OF YOUNG LATINO CHILDREN

Natasha J. Cabrera, Daniela Aldoney, Brianne Kondelis, Tracy W. Kennedy, and Karen M. Watkins-Lewis

Overall, children constitute the fastest growing sector of the population in many western industrialized countries (Hernandez, Denton, & Macartney, 2008). Children of Latino origin constitute the largest and fastest growing ethnic group, comprising 20 percent of the total population of all children, yet account for approximately 34 percent of young children living in poverty (Hernandez et al., 2008). By 2050, it is projected that there will be approximately 101 million Latinos in the United States (Suro & Passel, 2003). Latino families in the United States face many challenges and difficulties. Twenty-one percent of Latino families live below the poverty line compared to 6 percent of non-Latino European Americans and 14 percent of non-Latino Blacks (Lichter & Landale, 1995). Although almost one-third of Latino mothers and fathers participate in the labor force, they are almost twice as likely as working African American parents to be poor and almost four times as likely to be poorer than European American working parents (Lichter & Landale, 1995). Reasons for this disparity include low levels of education, language proficiency, job and pay discrimination and gender wage inequalities (Lichter & Landale, 1995). Being poor and an immigrant means having less access to federal or state social and economic supports (e.g., welfare, food stamps, public housing, the Special Supplemental Nutrition Program for Women, Infants, and

Children [WIC], and unemployment insurance) that other low-income families in the United States are entitled. Immigrants who are socially excluded from utilizing services also lack recourse to remuneration or retribution when they are denied services they have purchased. In short, limited human capital, poverty, and stress are risk factors that may result in maladaptive parenting and suboptimal child functioning.

Researchers and policymakers interested in improving the lives of Latino children and their families, generally, have focused on how risk factors influence children's adjustment. This research, while helpful in identifying the negative impact of risk on children's lives, suffers from some limitations. It has been mostly conducted from a deficit model that compares Latinos to a European American "standard" and it has not included protective factors (e.g., two-parent families) that might reduce some of the negative effects of risk on children's outcomes. Extant research has also not recognized the ethnic and cultural diversity within Latino subgroups and, therefore, has not focused on within-group variability that can highlight the reasons why some Latino children succeed and others do not.

Research that has focused on risk factors has not always considered that Latino children also live in families with many strengths, including living in two-parent families and being surrounded by a social network that may include extended kin and *comadres* and *compadres*, typically the child's godparents, who, in this role, coparent or help to guide the child through the *good path of life*. These strengths or protective factors enable individuals to deal with severe adversity and show positive adaptation in the presence of difficult circumstances (Rutter, 1990). A robust body of research shows that children fare better in two-parent families than in single-parent families (McLanahan & Sandefur, 1994). Although the majority of Latino children are born in the United States, their parents are more likely to be first generation immigrants with ties to their families and friends in their country of origin (García & Jensen, 2009; Hernandez et al., 2008). Children who live in two-parent households with parents who have access to social support are more likely to be better adjusted than are children in single-parent households (Morgan et al., 2008). In this context, Latino children live in families with many protective factors that can promote their well-being.

Latino families have other strengths that can benefit their children's adjustment. For example, Latinos' strong work ethic, high motivation regarding their children's success, and potential for bilingualism and biculturalism can be important predictors of children's success (Dinan, 2006). Given the heterogeneity of this population due to their immigration history, cultural practices, and reasons for immigration to the United States, there is considerable variability in the degree to which protective factors play out in families. Although a significant proportion of immigrant Latino children live with families who face economic disadvantage, there are many immigrant children who have highly educated and economically secure parents (Hernandez et al., 2008). This economic diversity is rarely included in research studies that explore within-group variability giving the impression that all Latino children in the United States are poor.

The dominant focus of research on risk factors is problematic because it not only emphasizes a deficit approach, but, more importantly, it also has the unintended consequence of obscuring or neglecting the conditions that can promote social adaptation. Consequently, there are few studies that examine normative and positive development of minority children as well as within-group differences (Raffaelli, Carlo, Carranza, & Gonzalez-Kruger, 2005). The purpose of this chapter is to highlight research that has shed light on the strengths of protective family factors that may lead to positive social adaptation among Latino children. Because this research is limited, we do not focus on any particular Latino ethnic group and, at times, we draw from studies examining social adaptation in other groups as a way to understand how these processes might develop in Latino children. The chapter is organized as follows: First, we start with a brief description of the socialization process and the theories and methods used to study this phenomenon during the first five years of life, a critical and fundamental period that has long-term implications for child functioning over time. Second, we discuss research that has focused on the socialization of Latino children. Third, we review the research on parenting beliefs and behaviors and the factors that promote positive parenting. We conclude the chapter with future directions for research and practice.

SOCIALIZATION: THEORETICAL/METHODOLOGICAL AND MEASUREMENT CONSIDERATIONS

An important milestone in early childhood social development occurs at about twelve months of age when attachment formation becomes critical for the developing child and parent. Attachment theory suggests that individual differences in later-life functioning and personality are shaped by a child's early experiences with his/her caregivers (Ainsworth, 1969). The quality of those early attachments (or lack of) is thought to act as a model for future patterns in relationships with peers and adults. For example, during the preschool years, children begin to develop friendships with other children of their same age. These early relationships at first lack perspective taking, but between the ages of 5 and 9, children begin to develop enduring friendships, engage in social comparison, and are able to take the perspective of others thus sharing and taking turns in peer and play interactions (Smith & Hart, 2004).

Children develop and reach these social milestones when they interact with their environments in dynamic, stimulating, and complex ways (Smith & Hart, 2004). This developmental dance between a child and his/her environment results in the most significant socialization experiences in a child's life. The "science of relationships" (Hinde, 1979) include interactions with various aspects of children's environmental ecology, including fathers, mothers, siblings, peers, and the community at large composed of social and macro institutions. These adult-child interactions unfold in a dynamic cultural context (Rogoff, 2003).

According to Rogoff (2003), culture is composed of the ways in which people process and make sense of their experiences. Culture also influences a wide array of family processes including roles, decision-making patterns, and cognitions and practices about childrearing and child development. Rogoff (2003) has argued that human development must be understood as a cultural process. One's "cultural participation" is determined by our cultural and biological heritage that enables us to use language and to learn from others (Rogoff, 2003). That is, "development can be understood only in light of the cultural practices and circumstances of their communities—which also change" (Rogoff, 2003, p. 3). From this perspective, all children, regardless of ethnicity, develop in a dynamic cultural context. For immigrant children, their cultural context might be a combination of the practices and customs of the sending society as well as of the practices and norms of the receiving society. Both sets of beliefs/practices will change over time, providing a dynamic and complex environment for children's development.

The notion that culture underlies development is also a dominant aspect of sociological and developmental theories. For example, the ecocultural niche framework, in the tradition of Vygotsky's sociocultural theory, has been used to examine children's participation in culturally structured activities and families' efforts to sustain daily routines over time (Weisner, 1996). This theory highlights the role of settings and routines (e.g., cultural scripts, tasks and activities, motivations, and cultural goals and beliefs) of daily life as a mechanism of cultural transmission and the measure of family adaptation (Harkness, Hughes, Muller, & Super, 2004; Rogoff, 1982). Thus, *all* parents aim to shape sustainable and meaningful daily routines that are compatible with family member and community competencies (Weisner, Matheson, & Bernheimer, 1996). These routines are embedded in practices and beliefs that are central to how children are socialized in families. Beyond the family influence, children develop friendships and peer relationships and are also influenced by other contextual characteristics such as parents' employment, culture, and childcare or school experiences, and the neighborhood they live in. Together, this comprises the developmental niche of the child (Super & Harkness, 1997). As with the ecocultural framework, from the child's perspective, the developmental niche consists of the physical and social settings (e.g., sibling social interactions) of the child's daily life, culturally regulated customs of childcare and rearing (e.g., daily routines), and the caretakers' cultural beliefs and "ethnotheories" (e.g., beliefs and views on what promotes development) (Harkness et al., 2004).

Social development begins during infancy in the context of an ecological network of social and reciprocal relationships, which unfold in a particular cultural context and have enduring imprint on the developing child. In this sense, theorists have argued that human development must be understood as a cultural process during which parents' ethnotheories—parenting values and practices of a particular cultural group—help them shape daily routines, which are instrumental in how children are socialized to meet the expectations and norms of their cultural group. As children grow up, the ecological niche expands to include peers, friends, and other adults operating in the larger society, which influences the development of the child through parents' employment patterns, cultural expectations, and childcare or school experiences. Thus, Latino children, as all children, are socialized in particular physical and social settings by parents, peers, and other adults who use their views about child rearing to transmit particular cultural values through daily routines.

LATINO CHILDREN'S SOCIALIZATION

With few exceptions (Halgunseth, Ispa, & Rudy 2006; Harwood, Miller, & Lucca Irizarry, 2002; Parke et al., 2004; Domenech Rodríguez, Donovick, & Crowley, 2009), research on the social adaptation of Latino children within theoretical frameworks is rarely conducted. One of the challenges for researchers has been to conduct studies that capture the fact that immigrant children, as do all children, develop and grow in a cultural context that is dynamic and changes over time due to normative sources of change as well as to the acculturation process. Scholars have argued that to fully understand the adaptation of immigrant children, theoretical models need to include acculturation and enculturation and developmental theories (García Coll & Magnuson, 1997; Laosa, 1997). As children acculturate, they also develop and change a process that is marked by age and time (Sam & Berry, 2006). For example, from a developmental perspective, younger children adapt to new situations easier than do older children. From an acculturation perspective, the longer one stays in the host country the higher the likelihood of learning social skills such as the acquisition of language (Berry, 1997). While age-related changes in cognition (younger children think and behave differently from older children) arise from the dynamic interaction between biological maturational processes and environmental learning experiences, change in acculturation, marked by time, is a function of learning adaptive and functional coping skills (Sam & Berry, 2006). That is, acculturation includes learning *or* adaptation and development includes both learning *and* maturation. In this sense, acculturation is embedded in development, which confounds acculturation; development continues as acculturation occurs (Phinney, Berry, Vedder, & Liebkind, 2006).

Therefore, as immigrant children develop and acculturate simultaneously, this process is intermingled and difficult to disentangle (Sam & Berry, 2006). Although some researchers have provided descriptive accounts on the acculturation gaps between parents and children (Fuligni, 1998; Portes & Rumbaut, 1996) and of the mechanisms that might explain it (White, Roosa, Weaver, & Nair, 2009), only few have offered an overarching model that includes acculturation and developmental experiences (Sam & Berry, 2006). To date, most acculturation research does not include developmental theory. For example, research focusing on intergenerational conflict between immigrant children and their parents suggests that immigrant children acculturate faster than their parents do to cultural values and norms of the host society (Buriel & de Ment, 1997; White et al., 2009). As a result, children and parents develop an acculturative gap over time and experience value discrepancies, which, in turn, can result in psychological maladaptation. However, a cross-sectional study of two cohorts (parents and their children) of immigrant and host families found no differences between the intergenerational value discrepancy of immigrants and host national families (Virta, Sam, & Westin, 2004). Similarly, Phinney, Ong, and Madden (2000) did not find larger intergenerational value discrepancies in immigrant families compared to European American families. Although these studies are cross-sectional and do not speak to causality, they suggest that value discrepancies between parents and their children might be more the result of developmental processes/change than of the acculturation process, or at the very least a combination of the two.

Notably, most of the research on cultural adaption has focused on how families acculturate to the values and norms of the host society, rather than on how families *enculturate* or maintain their own cultural norms and values (Calzada, Miller Brottman, Huang, Bat-CHava, & Kingston, 2009). In their study of urban preschoolers of four ethnicities (i.e., Latino, Black, European American, Asian), Calzada and her colleagues (2009) found that families who were bicultural, or had indicated high levels of ethnic *and* U.S. identity, had children with positive social, academic, and emotional functioning. This suggests that embracing one's cultural values and ethnic identity as well as those of the host society can be a protective factor because it provides children with adaptive skills with which to navigate the mainstream culture.

Studies on the socialization process of Latino children have paid little attention to describing their developmental niche and examining how it might be linked to social development. This research has focused mainly on how children and families adapt to two often-opposing cultures and the challenges they face at home and within the larger society rather than on normative developmental processes. For example, the bulk of the early research on Latino parents, focused primarily on mothers, was dominated by studies on the immigration experiences as well as children's vulnerability to the stresses of migration, which may result in psychological difficulties (Bashir, 1993). A small-scale study from Central America and Mexico examined the impact of cultural, financial, and familial factors on the incidence of children's behavioral and emotional problems (Weiss, Goebel, Page, Wilson, & Warda, 1999). Findings suggest that the majority of children in this study fell within the normal range of behavioral and emotional behaviors for their age group, and only 21 percent of the children exhibited symptoms of mental problems either in the "at risk" or "clinical concern" range (Weiss et al., 1999). Internalizing behaviors, however, were found to be most common. Although results showed no association between acculturation-related variables (income, adaptability, and cohesiveness) and emotional problems, parents' immigration status, the family's use of coping strategies (e.g., passive appraisal), and family satisfaction ratings were predictive of children's internalizing problems. Immigration status predicted externalizing problems but there were within-group differences. Immigration from Central America was more predictive of externalizing behaviors than was immigration from Mexico. Weiss and colleagues suggest that perhaps Central American immigrants' immigration to the United States was more fraught with physical and/or emotional trauma than the more voluntary immigration of Mexicans. Parental stress due to the immigration experience, even as much as nine years earlier, may have long-term impact on their interactions with their children (Weiss et al., 1999).

The few studies that focused on positive normative development have shown that despite the harrowing conditions of immigration, many immigrant children and adolescents show remarkably high levels of adaptation, ranging from good school adjustment to strong academic performance (Fuligni, 1998, 2003) through few problem behaviors and comparable psychological adjustment (Harris, 1999). Not surprisingly, there is little research on the process of adaptation as well as on the paradox of good adaptation in the context of the hardships of immigration. Part of the reason for this is the fact that there is a dearth of theories that can account for immigrant children's successful adaptation under these conditions. Moreover, this research is plagued by methodological and measurement shortcomings, including using measures that are rarely designed with the Latino population in mind and are often not validated for use with this population (García Coll & Magnuson, 1997; Knight, Roosa, & Umaña-Taylor, 2009; Sam & Berry, 2006).

In summary, there is limited research on the process of social adaptation of immigrant children in the context of development and acculturation. Studies on the developmental niche of immigrant children as well as the cultural and developmental factors that promote social competencies are rare. The little research that exists suggests that in order to understand Latino children's adjustment and adaption, researchers need to use a broader ecological lens that includes reasons for immigration (refugee vs. economic opportunity) and its consequences on both parents' and children's well-being. There is a lack of adequate research on the complex nature of the process of adaptation, as well as reliable and valid methodology designed with the Latino population in mind.

PARENTING BELIEFS

Parents' beliefs and practices reflect the norms, expectations, and value systems of the cultural groups, defined by nationality, race, or ethnicity and small sub-cultural communities (e.g., middle-class), in which they are embedded and are important mechanisms for propagating "systems of cultural priorities" (Kagitcibasi, 1996; Keller, 2003). Parents transmit values, rules, and standards about ways of thinking and acting, and provide an interpretive lens through which children view social relationships and structures (McGillicuddy-De Lisi, & Sigel, 1995; Ogbu, 1988; Super & Harkness, 2002). The *socialization strategies* parents adopt emphasize the development of particular instrumental competencies needed to succeed in certain environments. Although transmission of beliefs and practices from parents to children is universal, the content of such beliefs and practices and the beliefs that are transmitted (or not) varies widely across cultures (Harwood et al., 2002). Research on parents' beliefs among Latino families suggests that the value of interdependence is manifested in three important goals parents use to socialize their children: familism, *respeto*, and *educación*.

Familism among Latino families encompasses feelings of closeness, allegiance, and mutuality with family members, as well as notions of the self as an extension of the family (e.g., Gonzales-Ramos, Zayas, & Cohen, 1998; Sabogal, Marín, Otero-Sabogal, & Marín, 1987). Overall, Latinos tend to report higher levels of family cohesion than European Americans (e.g., Knight, Virdin, & Roosa, 1994; Rumbaut, 2005; Sabogal et al., 1987). Intergenerational stability in *familismo* tends to be high, regardless of country of origin (e.g., Fuligni, Tseng, & Lam; 1999; Phinney, Ong, & Madden, 2000; Procidano & Rogler, 1989) or level of acculturation (Rueschenberg & Buriel, 1989).

Research on familism suggests that some aspects of familism decline over generations. For example, Portes and Rumbaut (2001) found that predominantly English-speaking immigrant children were less familistic than their bilingual and native speaking peers. Rumbaut concludes that consistent with cultural change theory that conceptualizes familism as a multidimensional concept, Latinos may elect to keep only some aspects of their cultural heritage. Ethnographic accounts (Delgado-Gaitan, 1992), interventions (Goldenberg & Sullivan, 1994), and recent interviews conducted with Latino immigrant families reveal that most Latinos retain a value system that includes an identification with and attachment to the family (i.e., familism) and strong connection to the community (Lieber, Davis, Weisner, Farver, & Lonigan, 2004).

Research on familism has been conducted in the context of traditional family roles where fathers are heads of the households and women are subservient and obedient to men. In this cultural context, children would learn gender roles that are more traditional than egalitarian. Recent research on family roles not only in the United States, but also in Latin American countries has challenged the view that despite the heterogeneity among Latino families, they are generally traditional in value orientation with fathers enjoying absolute authority, mothers subservient to the will of their partners, and children socialized to be obedient and unquestioning (Buriel & de Ment, 1997; Cabrera & García Coll, 2004). New findings suggest that Latino families in the United States may be more egalitarian, less traditional, and more adaptive than previously believed (Behnke, Taylor, & Parra-Cardona, 2008; Cabrera & García Coll, 2004).

However, there is a dearth of research on how these familistic values and beliefs are linked to children's social adaptation.

Another aspect of familism that is less well understood, but that may play an important role in children's socialization, is the role of siblings. Families socialize their children to feel obligation and cohesion toward all family members including siblings, aunts, uncles, and grandparents. Latinos are more likely to grow up in families with more siblings and spend more time together than American children (U.S. Census Bureau, 2000; Updegraff, McHale, White, Thayer, & Delgado, 2005). A study of 246 adolescent Mexican American sibling pairs revealed that they spend approximately 17 hours a week in shared activities compared to 10 hours per week reported by a sample of European American siblings (Tucker, 2004). Given the amount of time siblings spend together, they can play a key role in the maintenance of ethnic values, providing access to cultural traditions, and functioning as emotional support for younger children. One special way in which older siblings can help their parents is through language brokering (Buriel, Perez, De Ment, Chavez, & Moran, 1998). Children who language broker for their parents have strong connections to their parents and may have strong cognitive skills, which can result in increased social competence (Cooper, Denner, & Lopez, 1999; Buriel et al., 1998; this volume).

Older siblings can also serve as socializing agents for younger children. Although the study of the sibling relationships among Latino families is relatively new, emerging evidence shows a strong association between the quality of siblings' relationships and children's behavioral problems. Studies with Latino and African American samples have reported significant associations between sibling interactions and measures of relationship quality during the preschool years and behavior problems during early adolescence (Brody, 1998; Dunn, Slomkowski, Beardsall, & Rende, 1994; Modry-Mandell, Gamble, & Taylor, 2007; Volling, 2003). For example, Modry-Mandell and her colleagues found that sibling warmth was significantly higher than sibling antagonism/competition and sibling relationships that were characterized by warmth were more likely to exhibit significantly better behavioral adjustment outcomes than sibling relationships that were less warm (Modry-Mandell et al., 2007). Similarly, a small-scale study of Mexican families with young children enrolled in the Head Start program found that sibling relationships characterized as warm were significantly and negatively correlated with behavioral problems (internalizing and externalizing) reported by mothers and positively with emotional and peer adjustment reported by teachers (Cooper et al., 1999). Other researchers have studied the time of transition from elementary to middle school in Mexican immigrant families and found that the companionship and guidance offered by older siblings may help to enhance motivation and achievement for younger children in the family (Gamble et al., 2007). These findings suggest that sibling relationships, an important aspect of familism, are an important source of variation in the socialization of children and should be integral to this type of research.

Respect, obedience, and orientation to the larger group (sociocentrism) are considered central to the harmony of the group, which is attained when the young respect and obey the decisions of parents and elders in the community (Keller, 2003). A goal of Latino families is to raise a child who is *bien educado*, thus they socialize their children to have *respeto* for parents and elders or figures of authority (Gonzalez-Ramos et al., 1998; Harwood et al., 1995). Latino mothers of various ethnicities participating in a focus group revealed that *respeto* is the core value they teach their children and they believe it is an essential foundation of their children's development, suggesting that *respeto* might be a pan-Latino value (Calzada & Cortes, 2010). These mothers expected their children to show *respeto* in all contexts, and viewed the teaching of this value as not optional. In another study, Puerto Rican mothers described ideal children as those who were obedient to elders, calm in order to attend to the needs of others, polite, and kind (Harwood et al., 1995). In contrast, an investigation of European American mothers showed that they emphasized qualities that highlighted self-maximization. Another study found that by the age of four, Latino children were taught the verbal and nonverbal rules of respect such as politely greeting elders, not challenging an elder's point of view, and not interrupting conversations between adults (Valdés, 1996). The emphasis on good manners and respect for others are important skills that encourage social competence in various settings, including school, and hence can be an important aspect of Latino children's academic success. However, there is little research linking *respeto* to children's social behaviors as well as the factors that predict the degree to which *respeto* is valued as a socialization goal by children and parents.

Educación

Studies have shown that immigrant Latino parents hold high aspirations for their children's educational attainment and believe in their children obtaining a good *educación* (Goldenberg & Gallimore, 1995). The term *educación*, unlike the English translation of the word, includes moral development, basic beliefs about right and wrong, school achievement, and general developmental outcomes (Reese, Balzano, Gallimore, & Goldenberg, 1995). It refers to the goal of rearing a moral, responsible, and socially competent child, who will become *una persona de bien* (a good person) who is *bien educado* (has manners and is well brought up), respectful of adults, and is on *el buen camino* (following the good path) (Delgato-Gaitan, 1992; Reese et al., 1995; Reese, 2001; Reese & Gallimore, 2000). "Following the *good path of life*" involves a network of beliefs including *respeto* toward parents and elders and responsibility to the family, a central aspect of the value of familism (Azmitia & Brown, 2002; Reese et al., 1995). Azmitia and Brown (2002) used qualitative methodology to examine parents' beliefs about the meaning of the *good and bad* path of life, how parents judged their children's progress on the path of life, the challenges they faced, and the strategies they used to support their children. They found that parents believed that peers, especially of their older children, whom they did not know well, were the greatest challenge to their children to stay on the good path of life. These findings, although preliminary, suggest the importance of understanding the strategies parents use to guide their children in the context of developmental and social change.

Research has also shown that parents' beliefs about the importance of education are stable over time. A small study of Latino immigrants and their kindergarteners found that Latino parents' educational aspirations (i.e., hope: How far do you want your child to go in his/her formal schooling?) are high throughout the elementary school years, but *expectations* (i.e., actual beliefs: How far do you think your child will go in his/her formal schooling?), which may be influenced by child's performance, fluctuate (Goldenberg, Gallimore, Reese, & Garnier, 2001). Immigrant Latino parents maintain a strong belief in the value of formal schooling even in light of acculturation and perceived discrimination (Goldenberg et al., 2001).

The Latino value of *educación* emphasizes not only learning to read and write, but also being respectful, socially competent, and well mannered (Delgado-Gaitan, 1992; Greenfield, Quiroz, & Raeff, 2000). The extent to which Latino families emphasize education and the importance of being *bien educado* is a key source of variation that is associated with children's language and social skills (Farver et al., 2004). *Educación* has been found to be an important indicator of Latino children's achievement (Suárez-Orozco & Suárez-Orozco, 2002, Valenzuela & Dornbusch, 1994). Parents who encourage their children to do well in school, but also to develop social competencies might have children who will develop positive peer relationships and perform well academically. Unfortunately, there is little research with Latino children linking parents' socialization strategies, social competencies, and school success.

Despite the emphasis on the value of formal schooling, and *educación* more generally, Latino children are underrepresented in both early childhood and after-school programs. If not cared for by kin or older siblings, they become latchkey children, spending their afternoon hours alone in the home. Only 15 percent of Latino children attended after-school programs in the United States, compared to 23 percent of European American children and 30 percent of all children (Afterschool Alliance, 2004). Participation in after-school programs may serve as a protective factor, particularly for minority, urban, and rural children (Riggs & Greenberg, 2004). Riggs and Greenberg (2004) found that rural first- through sixth-grade children's participation in an academically intensive after-school enrichment program benefitted them positively through academic gains as well as increased social competence and decreased behavior problems. In a follow up study, Riggs (2006) found that for first- through sixth-grade rural Latino students high program dosage (in a quality program) was related to increased social competence and decreased behavior problems compared to children who did not attend the after-school program as often. This is perhaps due to the skills and competencies taught through the program, as well as providing children with a safe environment in which to spend their after-school hours. It is unclear, however, why Latino children are less likely than other children to be enrolled in after-school programs. Although the cost might be a barrier, many of these programs are free. A possible explanation, consistent with the value of familism, and the role of siblings and extended families in the socialization of children, might be that families may need their older children to look after younger children, for whom care is often unavailable or too expensive. Further research is needed to understand how Latino children can obtain this important opportunity for increased social and academic functioning.

In summary, research on Latino parents' beliefs, including familism, *respeto*, and *educación* suggests that these are important strategies used by parents to socialize their children into being respectful, socially competent, and well mannered. Although there is little research on within-group variation, and little research exists linking values of *respeto* and *educación* to children's social development, the existing evidence suggests that having strong family links, including warm relationships with siblings, is an important predictor of children's adjustment.

PARENTING BEHAVIORS

The most important environmental influence on children's outcomes is the home environment, in particular parenting behaviors and resources available to the child (Guo & Harris, 2000; von Figueroa-Moseley, Ramey, Kellner, & Lanzi, 2006). A robust body of research shows that while maternal sensitivity and responsiveness are consistently associated with young children's cognitive and social behaviors in European American families and minority families (Ainsworth, Blehar, Waters, & Wall, 1978; Cabrera, Shannon, West, & Brooks-Gunn, 2006; DeWolff & Van IJzendoorm, 1997; Tamis-LeMonda, Shannon, Cabrera, & Lamb, 2004), negative parenting behaviors such as maternal intrusiveness and controlling behaviors are linked to children's negative socio-emotional and academic functioning in non-Latino families (Barber, 2002; Egeland, Pianta, & O'Brian, 1993). In this section, we examine research on three types of parenting behaviors: responsiveness, non-punitive control (i.e., physical guidance and directing and modeling), and punitive control (i.e., physical and verbal punishment and psychological control).

Responsive Parenting

The bulk of research on responsive parenting in Latino families has been conducted primarily with mothers, with few exceptions (Cabrera et al., 2006; Gamble, Sri Ramakumar, & Diaz, 2007). Early research found that Latino fathers reported more emphasis on children's control of emotions (not crying, hiding anger) than European American mothers or fathers (Durrett, O'Bryant, & Pennebaker, 1975). More recent research has challenged the traditional stereotypes of Latino fathers as being authoritarian and emotionally uninvolved with their children and Latino mothers as being high on warmth and high on control or low in autonomy granting. A recent study of Mexican American fathers found that fathers used parenting strategies associated with authoritative parenting, endorsed coaching on emotions, and were observed to be supportive and responsive to their children during discussions of emotions (Gamble et al., 2007). A national study of 9-month-old Latino babies and their parents showed that Mexican American mothers, compared to other Latinas, had lower mother-infant interaction scores; these were related to levels of acculturation rather than to SES (Cabrera et al., 2006).

There is also some evidence that Latino parents socialize their daughters differently from their sons. A study of first generation Latinos and their young children found that Latino parents scored high on warmth and demandingness and medium to low on autonomy granting (Domenech Rodríguez et al., 2009). Although parental expressions of warmth were equal across gender, parents were lower in autonomy granting for girls and higher on demandingness when compared with boys (Domenech Rodríguez et al., 2009).

Parents' responsiveness and nurturance have been directly linked to child well-being. Mirroring findings with non-Latino samples, evidence suggests that positive parenting is related to positive child adjustment. Several studies have shown that mothers who are closely attached to their children, and are warm and sensitive toward them, have children who are well adjusted (Gamble & Modry-Mandell, 2008; Howes, Wishard, & Zucker, 2007). For example, a small-scale study examining the peer interactions in low-income Mexican American mothers and their young children found that children with a more secure mother-child attachment relationship also had more concurrent complex play and more rapid growth of complex play. Children who engaged in more social pretend play at 54 months were more likely to engage in more language interaction when younger (Howes, Wishard, & Zucker, 2008). Using a nationally representative sample of infants born in 2001, Cabrera and her colleagues (2006) found that after controlling for SES, acculturation, and levels of depression, mother-infant interactions (but not paternal engagement) were positively related to infant cognition. As with research on the influence of father involvement on children's development, research with Latino samples has found few direct effects of father involvement on children's social and cognitive outcomes with infants and toddlers. There is little research, however, on the influence of Latino father involvement on older children's outcomes. This is an important avenue for future research as research with non-Latino samples show that father involvement is related to better outcomes for older children (Amato, 2001).

Although most of this research is correlational and does not establish causality, some studies have begun to explore the mechanisms by which maternal sensitivity is linked to child outcomes. A small-scale study of low income Mexican American and European American families showed that mothers with high levels of warmth and acceptance, who were consistent in their use of discipline and enforcing rules, and had low levels of conflict and hostility had children with fewer conduct problems (Hill, Bush, & Rosa, 2003). Moreover, the effect of Mexican American maternal acceptance on children's conduct problems was moderated by mothers' language preference. That is, maternal language preference may serve as a protective factor against conduct problems (Hill et al., 2003).

Non-Punitive Control

In this section, we describe the strategies Latino parents use to shape their children's behavior. Specifically, we focus on physical guidance, direct modeling, monitoring, rule setting, and decision making because these have been used in studies with young children.

Physical Guidance

Cross-cultural studies of young children (0–2 years of age) reveal that Mexican American and Puerto Rican parents exercise more physical guidance than European American mothers, regardless of level of acculturation or SES (Carlson & Harwood, 2003; Ispa et al., 2004). However, the use of physical guidance, which is defined in multiple ways in the literature, has been found to vary by cultural group.

Researchers have noted that despite Latino mothers being more intrusive and physically controlling than European American mothers (Carlson & Harwood, 2003; Leyendecker, Harwood, Lamb, & Scholmerich, 2002; Richman, Miller, & Levine, 1992), Latino children do not always exhibit negative outcomes. For example, several studies have shown that maternal physical control predicted secure attachment in Puerto Rican, Dominican, and Mexican infants and toddlers (Carlson & Harwood, 2003; Fracasso, Busch-Rossnagel, & Fisher, 1994). Maternal intrusiveness with 14-month-olds was not negatively linked to child engagement at 24 months in either more or less acculturated Mexican American families (although it was for European Americans) (Halgunseth et al., 2006). In another study, no association between hostile parenting and children's adjustment was found in a Mexican American sample (Parke et al., 2004). One possible explanation is that if particular behaviors are normative for a particular ethnic group, then they have different emotional connotations and meanings by both parent and child, as evidenced by the lack of negative effects on children's development (Grusec, Rudy, & Martini, 1997; Martinez, 1988). For example, Latino mothers who display high levels of controlling intrusive behavior are also warm and sensitive toward their children (Carlson & Harwood, 2003). Another explanation put forth is that Latina mothers' controlling behaviors stem from efforts to teach children to act in accordance with cultural goals or values (e.g., *familismo*), and that the fostering of these goals may be more consonant with physical control than the fostering of independence (Carlson & Harwood, 2003). Moreover, when there is low parental stress, children may perceive parental controlling behaviors as a form of caring rather than an act of rejection (Grusec & Goodnow, 1994).

Directing, Modeling, and Rule Setting

Studies suggest that modeling (e.g., parental performance of a task and the intention that children observe and imitate) and directing (e.g., parent's verbal commands to pursue a given course of action) predict negative child outcomes in families of Mexican ethnicity (Bronstein, 1994; Halgunseth et al., 2006; Laosa, 1980; Martinez, 1988). A study found that poorly educated Mexican American mothers of kindergarteners used a higher number of directives and amount of modeling than did their European American counterparts (Laosa, 1980). After controlling for education, these differences disappeared. Laosa suggests that because more-educated mothers have greater access to parenting resources than less-educated mothers, their parenting models have integrated new goals, strategies, and values that enable them to use positive ways of parenting (Laosa, 1980). However, this study did not control for the effects of acculturation on parenting behaviors. It is possible that parents with high acculturative stress are more likely to use directives and modeling and are less likely to use cognitive strategies for inquiry and praise (Laosa, 1980).

A small study of middle-school ethnically diverse children found that differential knowledge of display rules was related to children's social competence with peers (McDowell & Park, 2000). Children who endorsed more display-rule use for both negative as well as positive emotions were rated as more socially competent by both teachers and peers. Results suggest that parents influence children's social competence through the socialization of rules for emotion expression and regulation. Children whose parents are more controlling of emotion expression were rated as less socially competent (McDowell & Parke, 2000).

Punitive Control

Research shows that Latino families use physical and psychological control to socialize children. In a review of the literature, Halgunseth and her colleagues (2006) note that there is fairly consistent evidence that regardless of child age, SES is a strong predictor of the use of physical and verbal punishment in Latino families and that these forms of punishment are associated with adolescent anxiety and depression (Hill et al., 2003) and negativity toward or conflict with parents (Barber, 1994; Laosa, 1980; Martinez, 1988). Most of this research has been conducted with older children and thus there is less information on young children.

Another strategy used by Latino parents to influence their children's behavior is the use of *consejos* (advice), a type of psychological control. Parents use *consejos*, or spontaneous homilies, to influence children's moral behaviors and attitudes. *Consejos* are not always perceived as a form of punishment and are not used independent of other forms of behavioral control. A study of Mexican American children and their parents found that although the most frequently used strategy to help their children was by giving them advice, they also said that they restricted and monitored their children's activities to help them stay on the good path of life (Azmitia & Brown, 2002). The effectiveness of *consejos* on children's behavior is difficult to discern given the little research on this area. There is a clear need for research to disentangle the various forms of psychological control and its effects on children's socialization.

Another similar socialization strategy used by Latino parents is the use of *dichos* (proverbs). Even though *dichos* are not unique to the Latino culture, there are especially prevalent in Spanish speaking countries, which are characterized by a strong oral tradition (Burciaga, 1997). Through *dichos*, parents intergenerationally transmit cultural beliefs and values related to the socializing processes. For example, Mexican families use *dichos* as an important tool for socializing younger children, especially when the extended kin are involved in child rearing (Chahin, Villarruel, & Viramontez, 1999). Although the use of *dichos* is most frequently used among earlier rather than later generations of Mexican families, *dichos* are used for monitoring children's whereabouts (Arora, 1982). For example, *"Dime con quién andas, y te diré quién eres"* (Tell me who your friends are and I will tell you who you are) is commonly used by parents in efforts to monitor their children's friendships. Although *dichos* appear to be an important aspect of socialization in Latino children, additional research is needed in order to better understand their influence on children's social development (Chahin et al., 1999).

In summary, maternal responsiveness among Latino families is associated with young children's cognitive development. Despite Latino mothers' higher intrusiveness and physical control, Latino children do not always exhibit negative outcomes possibly due to this type of parental control being more normative in Latino culture. The use of physical and verbal punishment is associated with parents' SES and is related to future negative outcomes in their children. *Consejos* and *dichos* are also used as a strategy to guide children through the good path of life.

FACTORS PROMOTING POSITIVE PARENTING

The study of the factors that promote positive parenting has been conducted within several theoretical frameworks, including human capital (Coleman, 1990), Belsky's (1984) model of parenting, and sociocultural theories. From a human capital perspective, parents' human capital includes measures of employment, income, and education, which enable parents to invest in their children. Parents who have high levels of human capital are more likely to be responsive to the developmental needs of their children. Parents with human capital can provide a supportive home environment, engage in literacy activities in the home, provide literacy materials, and exhibit positive attitudes and beliefs toward literacy that can strengthen children's oral language skills (Moon & Wells, 1979), particularly among low-income Latino preschoolers (Farver, Xu, Epe, & Lonigan, 2005). Studies show that accounting for SES differences, low-income mothers are generally less responsive than other mothers (Ispa et al., 2004). Parents' education is also related to the frequency with which parents engage in reading to their children, which has been found to be of lower frequency compared to European Americans (Barrueco, López, & Miles, 2007). Although employment is generally linked to parent involvement, it can have both negative and positive effects. A large scale study of urban fathers with young children found that under-the-table work and hustling have more negative effects on paternal engagement for African American fathers than for Latino fathers. In general, participation in the formal economy has a positive effect on father involvement, but if parents do not earn a living wage then employment may have a deleterious effect on families (Woldoff & Cina, 2007). However, there is also some evidence showing that immigrant families provide opportunities and experiences that support their children's early skill development (Delgado-Gaitan, 1992; Reese & Gallimore, 2000).

Belsky's (1984) parenting model suggests that the characteristics of parents (e.g., mental health, education), children (e.g., temperament), and the context in which children develop (e.g., marital quality, employment, etc.) are important predictors of parenting behaviors, which in turn, influence children's outcomes. Studies of Latino families using Belsky's model have shown that parenting characteristics have an effect on children's outcomes through parenting behaviors, especially maternal sensitivity (Cabrera et al., 2006).

Sociocultural theories, most often used in studying Latino parenting, have generally focused on how parent's beliefs and behaviors change as a function of the acculturation process as well as the influence of adults' illiteracy and lack of English skills on parenting behaviors (Marín, Van Oss Marín, Otero-Sabogal, Sabogal & Perez-Stable, 1989; Walker, Greenwood, Hart, & Carter, 1994). More recently, Halgunseth and her colleagues (2006) have proposed using social information processing theory (SIP) (Crick & Dodge, 1994) to study Latino parenting. SIP posits that parents make attributions and develop goals and behavior repertoires in a particular cultural context (Crick & Dodge, 1994). Parents' attributions, goals, and behaviors are influenced by parent's characteristics and other contextual factors such as acculturative process, racism and discrimination, and economic hardship (Halgunseth et al., 2006). Parents experiencing higher levels of stress might assess/judge their children's behavior more negatively than parents who are less stressed (Halgunseth et al., 2006).

Although the findings are inconsistent, a growing literature suggests that level of acculturation may directly influence parenting behaviors (Cabrera et al., 2006; Halgunseth et al., 2006). Less acculturated Mexican Americans tend to engage in more controlling or harsh parenting with their young children than do more acculturated parents, but this style of parenting has weaker links with children's social outcomes in less acculturated Mexican families (Halgunseth et al., 2006). The meaning of directive, often harsh, parenting and its impact on development may differ for less acculturated Mexican Americans to the extent that it reflects normative beliefs about parenting rather than emotional distress as might be the case for non-Latino families. On the other hand, harsh parenting by second-generation Mexican parents may have negative effects on children's outcomes that parallel the effects of this type of parenting in other groups in the United States.

In summary, parents' human capital affects the acculturation process by determining the context (e.g., parent involvement, home environment and neighborhood quality) in which the children will develop. Parent behaviors may also vary by level of acculturation, as well as the consequences of specific parent practices on children's development.

CONCLUSION

In this chapter, we highlighted research that focused on positive and some negative factors that promote social competences in Latino children. Given that Latinos are the largest ethnic group in the United States and as such constitute an "urgent demographic" (García & Jensen, 2009), it is imperative that we understand not only the challenges Latino families face, but also the strengths and protective factors that might reduce the harmful effects of risk factors on children's well-being. The bulk of the research on Latino children's socialization has used a deficit model and consequently little is known about the protective processes that might reduce or buffer the influence of risk on families' well-being. Further, extant research has not recognized ethnic and cultural diversity within Latino subgroups and therefore has not focused on within-group variability that can highlight the reasons why some Latino children succeed and others do not.

This has resulted in an incomplete view of Latino children's adaptation and a lack of understanding on the positive factors that can promote different pathways to children's social development. For example, Latino families' sense of familism, strong cultural ties to their country of origin, and social support from *comadres*, *compadres*, and extended kin are important protective processes that can counter the negative influence of poverty and stress on children's development.

Theoreticians have argued that to fully understand the adaptation of immigrant children, theoretical models need to include acculturation/enculturation and developmental theories. Extant research has focused mainly on how children and families adapt to two often-opposing cultures and the challenges they face at home and within the larger society rather than on normative developmental processes. For example, early research on Latino parents, focused primarily on mothers, was dominated by studies on the immigration experiences as well as children's vulnerability to the stresses of migration, which may result in psychological difficulties. Additionally, extant research is plagued by methodological and measurement shortcomings, including using measures that are not particularly designed with the Latino population in mind and are often not validated for use with this population. The challenge is, then, to conduct scientifically rigorous studies that capture the fact that immigrant children, as do all children, develop and grow in a cultural context that is dynamic and changes over time due to normative sources of change as well as to the acculturation process. This type of research is needed to capitalize on the fact that compared to other minority children, Latino children's social skills as reported by teachers and parents are positive and adaptive. Latino children are more likely to follow directions, listen to teachers' instruction, and develop positive relationships with peers. If social skills are important for academic performance, the question is why are Latino children still falling behind their peers in academic achievement? This type of research is urgently needed if we are going to mount interventions during the early years to improve learning opportunities and outcomes for Latino children (García & Jensen, 2009).

A major hurdle in this area of research has been the lack of attention given to how acculturation and enculturation unfold in the context of development. Latino parents' beliefs and parenting behaviors develop in a cultural context that is new and different from their own, which creates the developmental niche in which their children are reared. Thus, Latino children's-development of social competencies occurs in a bi-cultural context. Research to date has not examined normative patterns of children's development in a social context that while it may be economically disadvantaged, it is also characterized by protective factors such as two-parent families, social support, socialization strategies that emphasize respect for others, educational aspirations, and strong family ties. More research is needed to understand the effects of protective factors on the normative development of young Latino children's social competencies. This type of research direction is needed as research that only emphasizes deficits and limitations is likely to further marginalize these families and, more importantly, ignore and neglect the strengths of these families that are likely to promote child well-being.

Another area ripe for research is the need for studies that not only describe and document Latino parent's beliefs and values, but also examine how these are linked to children's outcomes. For example, siblings play an important role in the socialization of Latino children, yet there is virtually no research on how this occurs and what are the costs and benefits for both siblings. Research is needed that links specific socialization practices to specific child outcomes. Moreover, there is a dearth of information on how fathers' beliefs and values influence their children's development. Given that the majority of Latino children live in two-parent families, the lack of research on family functioning and adaptation that includes both parents is sorely noticeable. This research is critical to understand the aspects of the home environment, including parenting, that need to be supported and encouraged by programs and policies and which aspects need to be shaped and improved upon. To be clear, this call for research that focuses on positive adaptation and protective factors does not minimize in any way the real and difficult challenges faced by Latino families. The effects of poverty and perceptions of economic hardship on family functioning, especially on children's development, are robust and well established in the literature. In this sense, low-income Latino families face the same challenges that other poor families do. However, what we need is a balanced, comprehensive research agenda that while addressing poverty-related challenges also considers the many unique and important ways that Latino families promote the physical, cognitive, and mental well-being of their children.

REFERENCES

Afterschool Alliance (2004). America after 3 PM: A household survey on afterschool in America. Washington, D.C. Retrieved from http://www.after schoolalliance.org/press_archives/america_3pm/Executive_Summary.pdf.

Ainsworth, M. D. (1969). Object relations, dependency, and attachment: A theoretical review of the infant-mother relationship. *Child Development, 40*, 969–1025.

Ainsworth, M. D. S., Blehar, M. C., Waters, E., & Wall, S. (1978). *Patterns of attachment: A psychological study of the strange situation*. Mahwah, NJ: Erlbaum.

Amato, P. R. (2001). Children of divorce in the 1990s: An update of the Amato and Keith (1991) meta-analysis. *Journal of Family Psychology 3*, 355–370.

Arora, S. L. (1982). Proverbs in Mexican-American traditions. *Aztlán: International Journal of Chicano Studies Research 13*, 43–69.

Azmitia, M., & Brown, J. R. (2002). Latino immigrant parents' beliefs about the "path of life" of their adolescent children. In J. M. Contreras, K. A. Kerns and A. M. Neal-Barnett (Eds.), *Latino children and families in the United States: Current research and future directions* (pp. 77–105). Westport, CT: Greenwood Publishing Group.

Barber, B. L. (1994). Support and advice from married and divorced fathers: Linkages to adolescent adjustment. *Family Relationships 43*, 433–438.

Barber, B. K. (Ed.) (2002). Intrusive parenting: How psychological control affects children and adolescents (pp. 15–52). Washington, DC, US: American Psychological Association. XV.

Barrueco, S., López, M. L., & Miles, J. C. (2007). Parenting behaviors in the first year of life: A national comparison of Latinos and other cultural communities. *Journal of Latinos and Education 6*(3), 253–265.

Bashir, M. R. (1993). Issues of immigration for the health and adjustment of young people. *Journal of Pediatrics and Child Health 29*, Supplement 1, 42–45.

Behnke, A. O., Taylor, B. A., & Parra-Cardona, J. R. (2008). "I hardly understand english, but . . .": Mexican origin fathers describe their commitment as fathers despite the challenges of immigration. *Journal of Comparative Family Studies 39*(2), 187–205.

Belsky, J. (1984). The determinants of parenting. *Child Development 55*(1), 83–96.

Berry, J. W. (1997). Immigration, acculturation, and adaptation. *Applied Psychology 46*(1), 5–34.

Berry, J. W., Phinney, J. S., Sam, D. L., & Vedder, P. (Eds.) (2006). *Immigrant youth in cultural transition: Acculturation, identity and adaptation across national contexts.* Mahwah, NJ: Lawrence Erlbaum Associates, Publishers.

Brody, G. H. (Ed.) (1998). Sibling relationship quality: Its causes and consequences. *Annual Review Psychology 49*, 1–24.

Bronstein, P. (1994). Patterns of parent-child interaction in Mexican families: A cross-cultural perspective. *International Journal of Behavioral Development 17*, 423–466.

Burciaga, J. A., Christensen, C., & Christense, T. (1997). *In few words: A compendium of Latino folk wit and wisdom: A bilingual collection (1997).* San Francisco: Mercury House.

Buriel, R., & De Ment, T. (1997). Immigration and sociocultural change in Mexican, Chinese and Vietnamese American families. In A. Booth, A. C. Crouter, & N. Landale (Eds.), *Immigration and the family*: Research and policy on U.S. immigrants (pp.165–200). Mahwah, NJ: Lawrence Erlbaum Associates.

Buriel, R., Perez, W., De Ment, T., Chavez, D. V., & Moran, V. R. (1998). The relationship of language brokering to academic performance, biculturalism, and self-efficacy among Latino adolescents. *Hispanic Journal of Behavior Sciences 20*, 283–297.

Cabrera, N., & García Coll, C. (2004). Latino Fathers: Unchartered territory. In M. E. Lamb (Ed.), *The role of the father in child development* (pp. 98–120) (4th Ed.), New York: Wiley.

Cabrera, N., Shannon, J., West, J., & Brooks-Gunn, J. (2006). Parental interactions with Latino infants: Variation by country of origin and English proficiency. *Child Development 74*, 1190–1207.

Calzada, E., Miller Brottman, L., Huang, K., Bat-CHava, J., & Kingston, S. (2009). Parent cultural adaptation and child functioning in culturally diverse, urban families of preschoolers. *Journal of Applied Developmental Psychology 30*, 515–524.

Calzada, E. J., & Cortes, D. E. (2010). Incorporating the cultural value of *respeto* into a framework of Latino parenting. *Cultural Diversity and Ethnic Minority Psychology 16*(1), 77–86.

Carlson, V. J., & Harwood, R. L. (2003). Attachment, culture, and the caregiving system: The cultural patterning of everyday experiences among Anglo and Puerto Rican mother-infant pairs. *Infant Mental Health Journal 24*, 53–73.

Chahin, Villarruel, and Viramontez (1999). Dichos y refranes: the transmission of cultural values and beliefs. In H. P. McAdoo (Ed.), *Family ethnicity. Strength in diversity* (153–167). Thousand Oaks: Sage Publications.

Coleman, J. S. (1988). Social capital in the creation of human capital. *The American Journal of Sociology 94*, 95–120.

Coleman, J. S. (1990). *Foundations of social theory*. Cambridge: Belknap Press of Harvard Univ. Press.

Cooper, C. R., Denner, J., & Lopez, E. M. (1999). Cultural brokers: Helping Latino children on pathways toward success. *The Future of Children 9*(2), 51–57.

Crick, N. R., & Dodge, K. A. (1994). A review and reformulation of social information processing mechanisms in children's adjustment. *Psychological Bulletin 115*, 74–101.

Delgado-Gaitan, C. (1992). School matters in the Mexican-American home: Socializing children to education. *American Educational Research Journal 29*(3), 495–513.

DeWolff, M. S., & Van IJzendoorm, M. H. (1997). Sensitivity and attachment: A meta-analysis on parental antecedents on parental antecedents of infant attachment. *Child Development 68*, 571–591.

Dinan, K. A. (2006). *Young children in immigrant families: The role of philanthropy*. New York: National Center for Children in Poverty.

Domenech Rodríguez, M., Donovick, M. R., & Crowley, S. L. (2009). Parenting styles in a cultural context: Observations of "protective parenting" in first-generation Latinos. *Family Process 48*, 195–210.

Dunn, J., Slomkowski, C., Beardsall, L., & Rende, R. (1994). Adjustment in middle childhood and early adolescence: Links with earlier and contemporary sibling relationships. *Journal of Child Psychology and Psychiatry 35*(3), 491–504.

Durrett, M. E., O'Bryant, S., & Pennebaker, J. W. (1975). Child rearing reports of White, Black and Mexican-American families. *Developmental Psychology 11*(6), 871–901.

Egeland, B., Pianta, R., & O'Brien, M. (1993). Maternal intrusiveness in infancy and child maladaptation in early school years. *Development and Psychopathology 5*, 359–370.

Farver, J. M., Lonigan, C. J., Weisner, T., Lieber, E., & Davis, H. (2004). Helping parents support their children's pre-literacy skills. Symposium presented at NAEYC, Anaheim, CA.

Farver, J. M., Xu, Y., Eppea, S., & Lonigan, C.J. (2005). Home environments and young Latino children's school readiness. *Early Childhood Research Quarterly 21*, 196–212.

Fracasso, M. P., Busch-Rossnagel, N. A., & Fisher, C. B. (1994). The relationship of maternal behavior and acculturation to the quality of attachment in Hispanic infants living in New York City. *Hispanic Journal of Behavioral Sciences 16*(2), 143–154.

Fuligni, A. J. (1998). The adjustment of children from immigrant families. *Current directions in psychological science 7*, 99–103.

Fuligni, A. J. (2003). The adaptation of children from immigrant families. *International Society for the Study of Behavioral Development Newsletter 44*, 9–11.

Fuligni, A. J., Tseng, V., & Lam, M. (1999). Attitudes toward family obligations among American adolescents from Asian, Latin American, and European backgrounds. *Child Development 70*, 1030–1044.

Gamble, W. C., & Modry-Mandell, K. (2008). Family relations and the adjustment of young children of Mexican descent: Do family cultural values moderate these associations? *Social Development 17*, 358–379.

Gamble, W. C., Ramakumar, S., & Diaz, A. (2007). Maternal and paternal similarities and differences in parenting: An examination of Mexican-American parents of young children. *Early Childhood Research Quarterly 22*, 72–88.

García, E., & Jensen, B. (2009). Early educational opportunities for children of Hispanic origins. *Social Policy Report*, Society for Research in Child Development, XXIII, 2, 3–11.

García Coll, C. T., & Magnuson, K. (1997). The psychological experience of immigration: A developmental perspective. In A. Booth, A. C. Crouter, & N. Landale (Eds.), *Immigration and the family: Research and policy on U.S. immigrants* (pp. 124–167). Mahwah, NJ: Erlbaum.

Goldenberg, C., Gallimore, R., Reese, L., & Garnier H. (2001). Cause or effect? A longitudinal study of immigrant Latino parents' aspirations and expectations, and their children's school performance. *American Educational Research Journal 38*(3), 547–582.

Goldenberg, C., & Sullivan, J. (1994). "Making change happen in a language minority school: A search for coherence." Santa Cruz, CA: National Center for Research on Cultural Diversity and Second Language Learning.

Goldenberg, C. N., & Gallimore, R. (1995). Immigrant Latino parents' values and beliefs about their children's education: Continuities and discontinuities across cultures and generations. In P. Pintrich & M. Maehr (Eds.), *Advances in Motivation and Achievement* (Vol. 9, pp. 183–227). Greenwich, CT: JAI Press.

Gonzalez-Ramos, G., Zayas, L., & Cohen, E. (1998). Values of low-income, urban Puerto Rican mothers of preschool children. *Professional Psychology: Research and Practice 29*, 377–382.

Greenfield, P., Quiroz, B., & Raeff, C. (2000). Cross-cultural conflict and harmony in the social construction of the child. In S. Harkness, C. Raeff, & C. M. Super (Eds.), *Variability in the social construction of the child. New directions in child and adolescent development* (Vol. 87, pp. 93–108). San Francisco: Jossey-Bass.

Grusec, J. E., & Goodnow, J. J. (1994). Impact of parental discipline methods on the child's internalization of values: A reconceptualization of current points of view. *Developmental Psychology 30*, 4–19.

Grusec, J. E., Rudy, D., & Martini, T. (1997). Parenting cognition and child outcomes: An overview and implications for children's internalization of values. In J. E. Grusec and L. Kuczynski (Eds.), *Parenting and children's internalization of values: A handbook of contemporary theory* (pp. 259–282). New York: Wiley.

Guo, G., & Harris, K.M. (2000). The Mechanisms Mediating the Effects of Poverty on Children's Intellectual Development. *Demography 37*(4), 431–447.

Halgunseth, L., Ispa, J. M., & Rudy, D. (2006). Parental control in Latino families: An integrated review of the literature. *Child Development 77*, 1282–1297.

Harkness, S., Hughes, M., Muller, B., & Super, C. M. (2004). Entering the developmental niche: Mixed methods in an intervention program for inner city children. In T. Weisner (Ed.), *Discovering successful pathways in children's development: New methods in the study of childhood and family life* (pp. 329–358). Chicago: Univ. of Chicago Press.

Harris, K. M. (1999). The health status and risk behavior of adolescents in immigrant families. In D. J. Hernandez (Ed.), *Children of immigrants: Health adjustment and public assistance* (pp. 286–315). Washington, DC: National Academy Press.

Harwood, R.L., Leyendecker, B., Carlson, V.J., Asencio, M., & Miller, A.M. (2002). Parenting among Latino families in the U.S. In M.H. Bornstein (Ed.), *Handbook of parenting, Vol. 4: Social conditions and applied parenting* (pp. 21–46), 2nd Ed. Mahwah, NJ: Erlbaum.

Harwood, R. L., Miller, A. M., Carlson, V. J., & Leyendecker, B. (2002). Parenting beliefs and practices among middle-class Puerto Rican mother-infant pairs. In J. M. Contreras, K. A. Kerns, & A. M. Neal-Barnett (Eds.), *Latino children and families in the United States: Current research and future directions* (pp. 133–153). Westport, CT: Praeger.

Harwood, R. L., Miller, J. G., & Lucca Irizarry, N. (1995). *Culture and attachment: Perceptions of the child in context.* New York: The Guilford Press.

Henderson, R. W. (1997). Educational and occupational aspirations and expectations among parents of middle school students of Mexican descent: Family resources for academic development and mathematics learning. In R. D. Taylor & M. C. Wang (Eds.), *Social and emotional adjustment and family relations in ethnic minority families* (pp. 99–131). Mawah, NJ: Erlbaum.

Hernandez, D. J., Denton, N. A., & Macartney, S. E. (2008). Children in Immigrant Families: Looking to America's Future, *Social Policy Report*, Society for Research in Child Development, XXII, 3, 1–24.

Hill, N. E, Bush, K. R., & Rosa, M. W. (2003). Parenting and family socialization strategies and children's mental health: Low-income Mexican-American and Euro-American mothers and children. *Child Development 74*(1), 189–204.

Hinde, R. A. (1979). Towards understanding relationships. *London and New York: Published in cooperation with European Association of Experimental Social Psychology by Academic Press.*

Howes, C., Wishard, A., & Zucker, E. (2007). Cultural communities and parenting in Mexican-heritage families. *Parenting: Science and Practice 7*, 235–270.

Howes, C., Wishard, A. G., & Zucker, E. (2008). Migrating from Mexico and sharing pretend with peers in the United States. *Merrill-Palmer Quarterly 54*, 256–288.

Ispa, J.M., Fine, M.A., Halgunseth, L.C., Harper, S., Robinson, J., Boyce, L., Brooks-Gunn, J., & Brady-Smith, C. (2004). Maternal intrusiveness, maternal warmth, and mother-toddler relationship outcomes: Variations across low-income ethnic and acculturation groups. *Child Development 75*(6), 1613–1631.

Kagitcibasi, C. (1996). *Family and human development across cultures: A view from the otherside.* Mahwah, NJ: Erlbaum.

Keller, H. (2003). Socialization for competence: Cultural models of infancy. *Human Development 46*, 288–311.

Knight, G. P., Roosa, M. W., & Umaña-Taylor, A. J. (2009). *Studying Ethnic Minority and Economically Disadvantaged Populations.* Washington, DC: American Psychological Association.

Knight, G. P., Virdin, L. M., & Roosa, M. (1994) Socialization and Family Correlates of Mental Health Outcomes Among Hispanic and Anglo American Children: Consideration of Cross-Ethnic Scalar Equivalence. *Child Development 65*, 212–224.

Laosa, L. M. (1980). Maternal teaching strategies in Chicano and Anglo-American families: The influence of culture and education on maternal behavior. *Child Development 51*, 759–765.

Laosa, L. M. (1997). Research perspectives on constructs of change: Intercultural migration and developmental transitions. In A. Booth, A. Crouter, & N. Landale (Eds.), *Immigration and the family: Research and policy on U.S. immigrants* (pp. 133–148). Mahwah, NJ: Erlbaum.

Leyendecker, B., Harwood, R. L., Lamb, M. E., & Schoelmerich, A. (2002). Mothers' socialization goals and evaluations of desirable and undesirable everyday situations in two diverse cultural groups. *International Journal of Behavioral Development 26*, 248–258.

Lichter, D. T., & Landale, N. S. (1995). Parental work, family structure, and poverty among Latino children. *Journal of Marriage and the Family 57,* 346–354.

Lieber, E., Davis, H. M., Weisner, T. S., Farver, J. M., & Lonigan, C. J. (2004). *Pre-literacy practices in head start families: Qualitative and mixed methods in the study of children's literacy preparedness.* Prepared for symposium, Helping parents support their young children's emergent literacy skills, J. M. Farver, organizer. Annual Conference of the National Association for the Education of Young Children (NAEYC), November, 10–13.

Marín, G., Van Oss Marín, B., Otero-Sabogal, F., Sabogal, F., & Pérez-Stable, E. J. (1989). The role of acculturation in the attitudes, norms, and expectancies of Hispanic smokers. *Journal of Cross-Cultural Psychology 20,* 399–415.

Martinez, C., Jr. (1988). Mexican-Americans. In L. Comas-Díaz & E. E. H. Griffith (Eds.), *Clinical guidelines in cross-cultural mental health* (pp. 182–232). New York: Wiley.

McDowell, D. J., & Parke, R. D. (2000). Differential knowledge of display rules for positive and negative emotions: Influences from parents, influences on peers. *Social Development 9,* 415–432.

McGillicuddy-De Lisi, A. V., & Sigel, I. E. (1995). Parental beliefs. In M. H. Bornstein (Ed.), *Handbook of parenting* (Vol. 3, pp. 333–358). Mahwah, NJ: Lawrence Erlbaum.

McLanahan, S., & Sandefur, G. (1994). *Growing up with a single parent: What hurts, what helps.* Cambridge, MA: Harvard University.

Modry-Mandell, K. L., Gamble, W. C., & Taylor, A. R. (2007). Family emotional climate and sibling relationship quality: Influences on behavioral problems and adaptation in preschool-aged children. *Journal of Child and Family Studies 16,* 61–73.

Moon, C., & Wells, G. (1979). The influence of home on learning to read. *Journal of Research in Reading 2*(1), 53–62.

Morgan, S. P., Beldsoe, C., Bianchi, C., Chase-Landsale, P. L., DiPrete, T. A., Hotz, V. J., & Thomas, D. (2008). Designing new models for explaining family change and variation. *Recommendations to the Demographic and Behavioral Sciences Branch of the National Institute of Child Health and Human Development.* NICHD Report.

Ogbu, J. U. (1988). Cultural identity and human development. *New Directions for Child Development 42,* 11–28.

Parke, R. D., Coltrane, S., Duffy, S., Buriel, R., Dennis, J. Powers, J., French, S., & Widaman, K.F. (2004). Economic stress, parenting, and child adjustment in Mexican American and European American families. *Child Development 75*(6), 1632–1656.

Phinney, J. S., Berry, J. W., Vedder, P., & Liebkind, K. (2006). The acculturation experience: Attitudes, identities and behaviors of immigrant youth. In J. W. Berry, J. S. Phinney, D. L. Sam, & P. Vedder (Eds.). *Immigrant youth in cultural transition: Acculturation, identify, and adaptation across national contexts* (pp. 71–116). Mahwah, NJ: LEA.

Phinney, J. S., Ong, A., & Madden, T. (2000). Cultural values and intergenerational value discrepancies in immigrant and non-immigrant families. *Child Development 71*(2), 528–539.

Portes, A., & Rumbaut, R. G. (1996) *Immigrant America: A Portrait*. Berkeley, CA: University of California Press.

Portes, A., & Rumbaut, R. G. (2001). *Legacies: The Story of the Immigrant Second Generation*. Berkeley, CA: University of California Press.

Procidano, M. E., & Rogler, L. H. (1989) Homogamous assortative mating among Puerto Rican families: Intergenerational processes and the migration experience. *Behavior Genetics 19*, 343–354.

Raffaelli, M., Carlo, G., Carranza, M. A., & Gonzalez-Kruger, G. E. (2005). Understanding Latino children and adolescents in the mainstream: Placing culture at the center of developmental models. *New Directions for Child and Adolescent Development 109*, 23–32.

Reese, L. (2001). Morality and identity in Mexican immigrant parents' visions of the future. *Journal of Ethnic and Migration Studies 27*(3), 455–472(18).

Reese, L., Balzano, S. Gallimore, R., & Goldenberg, C. (1995). The concept of educacion: Latino family values and American schooling. *International Journal of Educational Research 23*(1), 57–81.

Reese, L., & Gallimore, R. (2000). Immigrant Latinos' cultural model of literacy development: An evolving perspective on home-school discontinuities. *American Journal of Education 108*(2), 103–134.

Richman, A. L., Miller, P. M., & LeVine, R. A. (1992). Cultural and educational variations in maternal responsiveness. *Developmental Psychology 28*(4), 614–621.

Riggs, N. R. (2006). *After-school program* attendance and the social development of rural *Latino* children of immigrant families. *Journal of Community Psychology 34*(1), 75–87.

Riggs, N. R., & Greenberg, M. T. (2004). Moderators in the academic development of migrant Latino children attending after-school programs. *Applied Developmental Psychology 25*, 349–367.

Rogoff, B. (2003). *The cultural nature of human development*. New York: Oxford University Press.

Rueschenberg, E., & Buriel, R. (1989). Mexican American family functioning and acculturation: A family systems perspective. *Hispanic Journal of Behavioral Sciences 11*, 232–244.

Rumbaut, R. G. (2005). Sites of belonging: Acculturation, discrimination, and ethnic identity among children of immigrants. In T. S. Weisner (Ed.), *Discovering successful pathways in children's development: Mixed methods in the study of childhood and family life* (pp. 111–162). Chicago, IL: University of Chicago Press.

Rutter, M. (1990). Psychosocial resilience and protective mechanisms. In J.Rolf, A.S. Masten, D. Cicchetti, K.H. Nuechterlein, & S. Weintraub (Eds.), *Risk and protective factors in the development of psychopathology* (pp. 181–214). New York: Cambridge University Press.

Sabogal, F., Marín, G., Otero-Sabogal, R., & Marín, B. V. (1987). Hispanic familism and acculturation: What changes and what doesn't? *Hispanic Journal of Behavioral Sciences 9*, 397–412.

Sam, D. L., & Berry, J.W. (2006). Introduction to psychology of acculturation. In D. L. Sam & J. Berry (Eds.), *Cambridge handbook of acculturation psychology* (pp. 1–7). Cambridge, England: Cambridge University Press.

Smith, P. K., & Hart, C. H. (Eds.) (2004). *Blackwell handbook of social development.* Oxford: Blackwell.

Suárez-Orozco, C., & Suárez-Orozco, M. M. (2002). *Children of immigrants.* Cambridge, MA: Harvard University Press.

Suárez-Orozco, M. M., & Suárez-Orozco, C. (1995). The cultural patterning of achievement motivation: A comparison of Mexican, Mexican immigrant, Mexican American, and non-Latino White American students. In Rúben G. Rumbaut and Wayne Cornelius (Eds.), *California's immigrant children: Theory, research, and implications for educational policy* (pp. 161–190). La Jolla, CA: Center for U.S.–Mexican Studies.

Super, C. M., & Harkness, S. (1997). The cultural structuring of child development. In J. Berry,P. Dasen & T. S. Saraswathi (Eds.), *Handbook of cross-cultural psychology*, Vol. 2: Basic processes and developmental psychology (pp. 1–39). Boston: Allyn & Bacon.

Super, C. M., & Harkness, S. (2002). Culture structures the environment for development. *Human Development 45*, 270–274.

Suro, R., & Passel, J. (2003). *The rise of the second generation: Changing patterns in Hispanic population growth.* Washington, DC: Pew Hispanic Center.

Tamis-LeMonda, C. S., Shannon, J. D., Cabrera, N. J., & Lamb, M. E. (2004). Fathers and mothers at play with their 2- and 3-year-olds: Contributions to language and cognitive development. *Child Development 75*, 1806–1820.

Tucker, C. J. (2004, March). *Sibling shared time: An important context for adolescent well-being.* Poster session presented at the biennial meeting of the Society for Research on Adolescence, Baltimore.

Updegraff, K., McHale, S., Whiteman, S., Thayer, S., & Delgado M. (2005). Adolescents' sibling relationships in Mexican American families: Exploring the role of familism. *Journal of Family Psychology (Special Issue on Siblings).*

U.S. Census Bureau. (2000). *Projections of the total resident population by 5-year age groups, race, and Hispanic origin with special age categories: Middle series, 2001 to 2005.* Retrieved January 2004, from http://www.census.gov/population/projections/nation/summary/np-t4-b.pdf.

U.S. Department of Education. National Center for Education Statistics, 1999, NCES 2000-031.

Valdés, G. (1996). *Con Respeto: Bridging the distances between culturally diverse families and schools. An ethnographic portrait.* New York: Teachers College Press.

Valenzuela, A., & Dornbusch, S. M. (1994). Familism and social capital in the academic achievement of Mexican origin and Anglo adolescents. *Social Science Quarterly 75*(1), 18–36.

Virta, E., Sam, D. L., & Westin, C. (2004). Adolescents with Turkish background in Norway, and Sweden: A comparative study of their psychological adaptation. *Scandinavian Journal of Psychology 45*, 15–25.

Volling, B. L. (2003). Sibling relationships. In M. H. Bornstein, L. Davidson, C. L. M. Keyes, K. A.Moore, & the Center for Child Well-being (Eds.) *Well-being: Positive development across the lifecourse* (pp. 205–220). Mahwah, NJ: Erlbaum.

Von Figueroa-Moseley, C. D., Ramey, C. T., Kellner, B., & Lanzi, R. G. (2006). Variations in Latino parenting practices and their effects on child cognitive developmental outcomes. *Hispanic Journal of Behavioral Sciences 28*, 102–114.

Walker, D., Greenwood, C., Hart, B., & Carter, J. (1994). Prediction of school outcomes based on early language production and socioeconomic factors. *Child Development 65*, 606–621.

Weisner, T. S. (1996) Why ethnography should be the most important method in the study of human development. In R. Jessor, A. Colby, & R. Sweder (Eds.), *Ethnography and human development: Context and meaning in social inquiry* (pp. 305–324). Chicago: University of Chicago Press.

Weisner, T. S., Matheson C., & Bernheimer, L. (1996). American cultural models of early influence and parent recognition of developmental delays: Is earlier always better than later? In S. Harkness, C. M. Super, & R. New (Eds.), *Parents' cultural belief systems* (pp. 496–531). New York: Guilford Press

Weiss, S. J., Goebel, P., Page, A., Wilson, P., & Warda, M. (1999). The impact of cultural and familial context on behavioral and emotional problems of preschool Latino children. *Child Psychiatry and Human Development 29*(4), 287–301.

White, R. M. B., Roosa, M. W., Weaver, S. R., & Nair, R. L. (2009). Cultural and contextual influences on parenting in Mexican American families. *Journal of Marriage and Family 71*, 61–79.

Woldoff, R. A., & Cina, M. G. (2007). Regular work, underground jobs, and hustling: An examination of paternal work and father involvement. *Fathering 5*(3), 153–173.

Chapter 3

THE ROLE OF EARLY CARE AND EDUCATION IN THE DEVELOPMENT OF YOUNG LATINO DUAL LANGUAGE LEARNERS

Tamara G. Halle, Dina C. Castro, Ximena Franco, Meagan McSwiggan, Elizabeth C. Hair, and Laura D. Wandner

The term "dual language learners" refers to children who are learning two or more languages at the same time, as well as those learning a second language while continuing to develop their first (or home) language (Administration for Children and Families, 2009). The population of young dual language learners (DLLs) is large and continues to grow within the United States, reflecting recent immigration patterns (Hernandez, Denton, & Macartney, 2007; Wolf et al., 2008). While there is certainly overlap in the populations, dual language learners and children of immigrants are distinct groups (Castro, 2009). Nevertheless, many children of immigrants are dual language learners. Among immigrant parents of children under age 6, the largest percentage come from Mexico and other Latin American countries and the Caribbean (64%) (Capps et al., 2005; Hernandez, Denton, & Macartney, 2008). Dual language learners constituted approximately 5.5 million of the students in U.S. schools during the 2003–04 school year (Lazarin, 2006). The largest proportion of dual language learners in the United States are individuals whose home language is Spanish (Shin & Bruno, 2003). Furthermore, it is projected that Latino children will be one-third of the entire population of children under age 18 by the year 2050 (U.S. Department of Health and Human Services, 2001).

Despite their growing presence in the United States, Latino dual language learners are an under-studied population. Nevertheless, there is increased awareness that being bilingual presents both challenges and benefits to these young children. The majority of the available research on Latino dual language learners has focused on patterns of their language acquisition and academic success (Bialystok, 2001; Espinosa, 2006; Garcia & Jensen, 2007; Oller & Jarmulowicz, 2007; Tabors, 2008; Tabors, Paez, & Lopez, 2003; Tabors & Snow, 2002). Much of this research suggests that these children are not as well prepared for school as their monolingual English-speaking peers, and continue to lag behind in academic-related outcomes in later schooling. Because of the increased emphasis on accountability within schools, policymakers are particularly interested in strategies that support all learners that may be struggling academically. In comparison, the social-emotional well-being of young Latino dual language learners tends to receive less attention in the literature, but some research suggests that these children demonstrate strengths in this area, which can be an important aspect of school success.

Both the challenges and benefits of being a dual language learner has focused the attention of researchers, policymakers, and educators to identify specific supports for the comprehensive development of the dual language learner population in general, and the large and growing population of Latino dual language learners in particular. One avenue for providing this support is early childhood education. This chapter highlights issues related to the cognitive, linguistic, and social-emotional development of young Latino dual language learners and the early care and education contexts that support their development. The chapter begins with a brief overview of the concept of school readiness and the important role that social-emotional development plays in children's school readiness. We then look at the context of being a dual language learner and how that may affect a child's early learning experiences. In particular, we examine the role of early care and education settings as important contexts for socialization of Latino children, especially those who are dual language learners. Furthermore, we take a critical look at the literature on Latino children's school readiness and attempt to provide a context within which to understand the findings in the field thus far. To foreshadow our conclusions, we contend that much of the existing research in this area is hampered by methodological/design constraints, or has not adequately controlled for confounding factors, such as socioeconomic status. We conclude that early care and education settings and early school experiences could do more to support young Latino dual language learners cognitively, linguistically, and socially, and we provide some suggestions for how to strengthen these settings. We also provide suggestions on how to expand future research of this important and growing population.

THE IMPORTANCE OF SOCIAL-EMOTIONAL DEVELOPMENT TO SCHOOL READINESS

The National Education Goals Panel identified five domains of development that were essential for children's school readiness, including physical well-being and motor development, social and emotional development, approaches toward learning, language development, and cognition and general knowledge (Kagan, Moore, & Bradekamp, 1995). Although all of these aspects of development are important and mutually influence one another, many practitioners and researchers believe that social-emotional development may be one of the most important factors in children's school readiness (McClelland, Morrison, & Holmes, 2000; Raver, 2002). Teachers and parents repeatedly cite factors such as cooperation, respect for others, and paying attention as more important than reading and mathematics skills for children's success in kindergarten (Kim, Murdock, & Choi, 2005; Knudsen-Lindauer & Harris, 1989; Lin, Lawrence, & Gorrell, 2003; O'Donnell, 2008; Piotrkowski, Botsko, & Matthews, 2000; Wesley & Buysse, 2003).

Indeed, social-emotional development is a critical component of young children's overall well-being (Damon & Eisenberg, 1998; Fabes, Gaertner, & Popp, 2006; Halle, 2002; Thompson & Lagattuta, 2006). Being able to regulate one's own emotional states and recognize and respond to others' emotional states are necessary skills for functioning successfully in social situations (Saarni, 1990). Other important components of social-emotional competency include being able to initiate social interactions, reciprocate appropriately to social gestures made by others, share with others, resolve conflicts, and take turns (Denham, 1998; Hubbard & Coie, 1994). The early childhood years provide the foundation for the development of social-emotional competency. Parents and caregivers are some of the first social partners that infants and young children encounter. As such, the attachment relationship developed between parents and children, and caregivers and children, set the stage for later patterns of social interactions. In addition, interactions with peers provide opportunities for experimenting with and practicing joint play/interaction, turn taking, sharing, and conflict resolution (Rubin, Bukowski, & Parker, 1998).

Recent research on a nationally representative sample of first-time kindergartners indicates that social-emotional development at the beginning of formal schooling is an important factor associated with later cognitive and behavioral outcomes in first grade (Hair, Halle, Terry-Humen, Lavelle, & Calkins, 2006). Hair and colleagues identified children who shared different "profiles" of school readiness across four domains of readiness: language, cognition, health, and social-emotional development. They found that having a profile of "social-emotional risk" (i.e., being two standard deviations below the mean in social-emotional development at the start of kindergarten, in addition to having below-average scores in other domains of development), puts children at much greater risk for poor cognitive and behavioral outcomes at the end of first grade compared to children with a profile of "social-emotional and health strengths" (i.e., being about half a standard deviation above the mean on social-emotional and health outcomes at kindergarten entry but below average on cognition and language outcomes). Similar patterns were found for children who had a profile identified as "health risk" (i.e., more than one standard deviation below the mean on indicators of health at kindergarten entry, in addition to being below average in the domains of cognition and language development). In contrast, children with a "social-emotional and health strengths" profile performed as well as children with a "compre-hensive positive development" profile (i.e., above average on all domains of development at kindergarten entry) on behavioral assessments at the end of first grade. Children with a comprehensive positive development profile performed best on cognitive outcomes at the end of first grade. These patterns emerged even when controlling for a host of child, family, and school characteristics. Thus, having poor social-emotional (and health) status at the start of kindergarten is associated with ongoing poor academic and behavioral performance. Other longitudinal studies confirm that there are important linkages between early social and emotional development and later cognitive achievement (Raver & Knitzer, 2002).

However, in addition to the competencies that children bring with them to school, children's school readiness also depends on the contexts in which learning occurs—including the home and school environments and the larger community. Experts assert that school readiness is the prod-uct of complex interactions between a child's inherent characteristics and past and present environmental and cultural contexts (Carlton & Winsler, 1999; May & Kundert, 1997). Especially for children who may be more at risk for difficulties in the transition to school, such as low-income chil-dren and children whose home language is not English, it becomes par-ticularly important to identify those aspects of the home, school, and community environments that can provide the supports needed to sustain these children through the transition to school and throughout the later years of schooling (Administration for Children and Families, 2010). For example, the high prevalence of working fathers among Latino families may serve as one potential familial support for young Latino children who see men in their lives modeling a strong work ethic (National Task Force on Early Childhood Education for Hispanics, 2007). Furthermore, most Latino parents have a strong commitment to their children's education, including not only their academic success but also their moral and social development (Halgunseth, Ispa, & Duane, 2006). The chapter by Cabrera and colleagues (this volume) provides an in-depth discussion of the familial factors that influence young Latino children's social adaptation. In this chapter, we focus on the context of the early care and education setting and how it plays a role in preparing and supporting young Latino dual language learners for ongoing success.

But first, we need to understand the factors associated with second language learning and how these may influence young Latino children's experiences in early care and education settings. Because these factors are universal to all dual language learners, this particular discussion encompasses dual language learners from any home language background.

THE PROCESS OF LEARNING A SECOND LANGUAGE AND IT'S RELATION TO SOCIO-EMOTIONAL DEVELOPMENT AND SCHOOL SUCCESS

Regardless of when a second language is introduced, all young dual language learners undergo four sequential phases of language development. According to Tabors (2008), these four phases begin with the children speaking their home language even in a setting where the new language is being used. Secondly, they use a non-verbal method of communication in the setting(s) where the new language is present. During this non-verbal stage, the children's understanding of spoken words in the new language is developing, although they themselves do not use the spoken language. The third phase is characterized by the dual language learners using common words or phrases in the new language in what is often called telegraphic speech, which involves short phrases (e.g., two- or three-word utterances), often without the use of all speech parts. Finally, children develop enough fluency in the new language to become productive users of it (Tabors, 2008). Although it is argued that all children go through this developmental sequence, there will likely be individual differences in dual language learners' rate of second-language acquisition (Tabors & Snow, 2002).

Indeed, there is evidence for individual differences in the speed and manner of second language acquisition among dual language learners. For example, Krashen (2005) found that dual language learners with high levels of self-confidence and high levels of motivation were more likely to become proficient in English, whereas DLL children with low self-esteem and children who generally did not feel good about themselves struggled with acquiring English. Besides personality characteristics, other factors that may influence second language learning include how well the child has developed oral and written language skills in the first language, socio-economic status, immigrant status, unique features of the second language, and the degree to which the typologies of the first and second language differ (Genesee, Geva, Dressler, & Kamil, 2006). In fact, it has been argued that dual language learning is a product of complex interactions between family and child characteristics as well as school policies, and classroom and teacher characteristics (Garcia & Jensen, 2007). More research is needed in this area. For example, it will be important for future research to examine within-group variability among the dual language learner population more thoroughly, rather than just look at differences by language or geographic location (Tharp, 1997).

Learning a second language involves linguistic skills and also sophisticated social cognition skills that help the dual language learner to determine when it is appropriate to use one language or another with a speech partner. Indeed, "code switching" is a complex skill that can be used by Latino children as an indicator of social group membership (Zentella, 1997). But learning a second language also includes negotiating social situations with a variety of speech partners, and acceptance into a social group often hinges on the ability to speak the language (Tabors, 2008). Consequently, acquiring a second language is a process that may generate anxiety and tension among children. Being under pressure to learn a new language in an unfamiliar environment, where often the teacher does not speak the child's home language, and where the environment lacks familiar cultural characteristics, will likely be a stressful situation for a child.

The limited research on this topic suggests that the process of learning a second language might be related to children's social-emotional development. For example, dual language learners who are in the first stage of second language acquisition (that is, using their home language exclusively) may become frustrated with the inability to communicate their thoughts and needs to teachers and peers, and feel a sense of isolation. Furthermore, when dual language learners are in the non-verbal stage of second language development, as noted above, teachers and peers may misinterpret their silence as being shy or disengaged with the activities presented around them (Restrepo, 2008, January). Peers may ignore or exclude a dual language learning classmate who does not use normal verbal cues. In addition, a dual language learner's silence does not align with teachers' typical expectations for class participation; as such, a teacher may assume that the dual language learning child is disengaged or has low cognitive ability. It has been argued that if educators were better informed about the typical progression of second language acquisition, teachers might adopt more effective practices for working with DLL students. In turn, changes in classroom practices would help reduce dual language learners' social isolation and lead to improvements in the social interactions between dual language learners, their teachers, and their peers (Castro, Espinosa, & Paez, in press; Tabors, 2008).

Dual language learners are at risk of losing their home language, especially once they become more immersed in a new language and culture. Maintaining one's home language in addition to a second language helps to support cultural identity and boost both self-concept and metalinguistic abilities (Bialystok, 2001; Espinosa, 2006; Gudykunst & Ting-Toomey, 1990; Oller & Jarmulowicz, 2007). It also helps to maintain cultural and familial ties (Espinosa, 2006). In addition, research has shown that positive psychological outcomes for immigrants tend to be related to strong identification with both their ethnic group and the larger society (Phinney, Horenczyk, Liebkind, & Vedder, 2001). Furthermore, becoming a fluent bilingual can be a benefit in the increasingly global economy. Indeed, learning a second language is something that middle-class and upper middle-class families in the United States see as a benefit and seek out such opportunities for their children. For all these reasons, supporting the maintenance of a dual language learner's home language while also supporting the child's acquisition of English (in the United States) should be a priority among family members and educators (Garcia & Jensen, 2007).

A CRITICAL EXAMINATION OF EXISTING RESEARCH ON LATINO DUAL LANGUAGE LEARNERS' SCHOOL READINESS AND ONGOING DEVELOPMENT

As stated at the beginning of this chapter, much of the existing research on dual language learners' school readiness, and that of Latino dual language learners in particular, seems to indicate that they are at a disadvantage compared to their peers and continue to lag behind in later schooling. Here, we summarize the existing research on Latino dual language learners' cognitive and social development as they enter school and progress through later schooling. We follow this summary by highlighting some important methodological considerations for interpreting the current set of findings. These methodological concerns also have implications for the direction of future research.

Latino Dual Language Learners' Cognitive Development Throughout Schooling

U.S. children whose first language is not English are at greater risk than native English-speaking children for physical, social-emotional, and learning problems (Fujiura & Yamaki, 2000; Fujiura, Yamaki, & Czechowicz, 1998; Margai & Henry, 2003; Martinez, DeGarmo, & Eddy, 2004; Stanton-Chapman, Chapman, & Bainbridge, 2002), all of which have implications for future success. For example, children who are non-native English speakers are at risk for reading difficulties in elementary school, becoming a high school drop out, and for low college attendance (Committee on the Prevention of Reading Difficulties in Young Children, 1998; Espinosa, 2007; Fitzgerald, 1993; Snow, Burns, & Griffin, 1998). While children who are dual language learners are at higher risk overall, there is also substantial variation, with some children showing more and some children less positive development.

For the Latino population in particular, a good portion of the research on school readiness and ongoing development has shown that Latino children do not perform as well on reading and mathematics assessments at the beginning of kindergarten compared to their non-Latino White and Asian American peers, and continue to perform at lower rates throughout primary and secondary school (Hampden-Thompson, Mulligan, Kinukawa, & Halle, 2008, December; Lee, Grigg, & Donahue, 2007; National Task Force on Early Childhood Education for Hispanics, 2007, June; Princiotta, Flanagan, & Germino-Hausken, 2006; Reardon & Galindo, 2006). Furthermore, Latino children who are not proficient in English have lower academic performance than Latino children who are proficient in English (Hampden-Thompson et al., 2008, December).

An in-depth examination of the differences in reading and mathematics scores between Latino children and other racial/ethnic groups from kindergarten through third grade based on the Early Childhood Longitudinal Study—Kindergarten Class of 1998–99 (ECLS-K), a nationally representative sample of kindergartners who were followed longitudinally through eighth grade, found that the gaps between Latinos and Whites in math and reading persisted from kindergarten through third grade, but the gaps were largest for children from Mexican, Central American, and

Puerto Rican origins; children who were first or second generation immigrants rather than third generation; and for children whose English language fluency was lower at the start of kindergarten (Reardon & Galindo, 2006).

Latino Dual Language Learners' Social-Emotional Development throughout Schooling

The research on dual language learners' social-emotional development is not as vast as the research on their linguistic development and academic outcomes. Some research suggests young children from Latino backgrounds (regardless of their home language status) may be at a disadvantage for developing optimally in the social-emotional domain. Analyses of a nationally representative sample of infants born in the year 2000 and followed longitudinally (the Early Childhood Longitudinal Study—Birth Cohort, ECLS-B) indicate that, when these children were approximately two years old, Latino and African American children were less likely than young children from White and Asian backgrounds to have secure attachments to their mothers (Chernoff, Flanagan, McPhee, & Park, 2007). It should be noted here that other attachment relationships (i.e., with fathers, grandparents) were not measured. In addition, researchers have found that, compared to native European American, native African American and immigrant Asian Indian preschoolers, Latino preschoolers who are immigrants perceive themselves to be lower on peer acceptance (Jambunathan & Burts, 2003). The effects of these disadvantages in the social-emotional domain in early childhood may have negative implications for young Latino children's successful functioning in early education environments.

However, not all of the research findings indicate negative social-emotional outcomes for dual language learners in general or Latino dual language learners in particular. Halle and colleagues (2009, April) recently examined whether a child's dual language learner status influenced developmental trajectories from kindergarten through fifth grade. The ECLS-K dataset, the nationally representative sample of children who started kindergarten in the 1998–99 school year, was used for these analyses. One indicator of dual language learner status was that the child's home language was not English, and the majority (76%) of these dual language learners spoke Spanish at home. Halle and colleagues found that children whose home language was not English tended to start kindergarten with more social-emotional competencies, and grew in these competencies at a faster rate than did native English speakers. Specifically, students who were native English speakers scored lower on measures of approaches to learning and self-control at kindergarten entry and grew more slowly in these areas than students whose home language was not English. Furthermore, students who were native English speakers scored higher on externalizing behaviors at kindergarten entry and grew faster than students whose home language was not English. In addition, Halle and colleagues found that although dual language learners started kindergarten at lower levels of competency in reading and mathematics at the start of kindergarten compared to their native English-speaking peers, they grew at a similar rate in reading skills and grew at a faster rate in math skills compared to native English speakers (Halle et al., 2009, April). Taken together, these findings suggest particular social-emotional strengths among non-native English speaking children, and the ability to "catch up" to native speakers in important academic skills over the elementary school years.

Halle and colleagues also recently examined school readiness profiles among native Spanish-speaking low-income preschoolers attending Head Start. Specifically, Halle, Hair, and Wandner (2010, June) examined the subset of Spanish-speaking four-year-olds in two cohorts of Head Start children gathered as part of the Head Start Family and Child Experiences Survey (FACES 1997 and FACES 2000), a nationally representative sample of Head Start programs, families, and children. Halle et al. (2010, June) found that almost two-thirds of the Spanish-speaking subsample of children in the FACES 1997 dataset was characterized by either "cognitive risk" or "social-emotional risk" in the fall of their four-year-old Head Start year; this was a larger percentage than in the FACES 1997 sample as a whole. A similar pattern was found for the FACES 2000 dataset. However, when examining whether Head Start children for whom Spanish is the primary language moved or stayed in their profiles between the fall and spring of the Head Start year, Halle and colleagues (2010, June) found that a majority of the Spanish-speaking children in the 1997 (62%) and 2000 (68%) cohorts stayed or moved to the "On Track" developmental profile by the spring of the four-year-old Head Start year. A final set of analyses examined whether child, home, and/or classroom characteristics predicted movement in developmental profiles. Findings indicated that receiving more social services was predictive of moving to a positive developmental profile by the spring. In addition, being in a full-day rather than part-day program and having a higher adult-child ratio in the classroom were associated with moving to a positive profile. The FACES 1997 data did not find classroom characteristics to be associated with movement to or retention in a positive profile over the four-year-old Head Start year.

In sum, this study found that although Spanish-speaking four-year-old Head Start children are less likely than the average Head Start student to be characterized by a positive developmental profile in the fall of the Head Start year, the vast majority of these children move to a positive profile (relative to their peers) by the end of the year. Furthermore, classroom characteristics may be important in helping Spanish-speaking Head Start children make positive gains in their development over the four-year-old Head Start year. However, the only factors that were found to be predictive were primarily structural components of the program (e.g., ratio, number of services received). In the section later in this chapter on contexts that support young dual language learners' development we argue that, in addition to structural features of an early care environment, there may be specific features of teacher-child relationships and instructional practices that may support the dual language learner population as well.

Methodological Concerns with Existing Research on Young Latino Dual Language Learners

Several factors should be considered when interpreting the results summarized above. These include potential confounds between unanalyzed factors such as socioeconomic status, immigrant status, or country of origin; or a failure to measure the full cognitive and social competencies of dual language learners because of a lack of adequate measures or techniques.

Failure to Take into Account Confounding Sociodemographic Characteristics

It is important to note that the findings reported above on disparities in reading and mathematics outcomes at kindergarten entry and in later grades, while based on national population estimates,[1] are descriptive in nature and compare racial/ethnic groups without controlling for other factors such as socioeconomic status (SES). Latino children, on average, tend to differ from their White peers on sociodemographic factors such as parental education and household income, which might explain some of the achievement gaps between the groups. For example, Latino children are more likely than non-Latino Whites to live in low-income households and to have a mother with low educational attainment (Hernandez, 2006). Indeed, according to the National Poverty Center, 23 percent of Latinos were living in poverty in 2008, compared to less than 9 percent of non-Latino Whites (DeNavas-Walt, Proctor, & Smith, 2009). When SES is taken into account, disparities based on racial/ethnic background often disappear (Fryer & Levitt, 2006). It is therefore important to account for potentially confounding factors such as SES when examining differences in school readiness outcomes among multiple racial/ethnic groups.

Poverty and low parental education are two prominent risk factors among the dual language learner population in general. In 2000, almost seven out of ten dual language learners in elementary school lived in low-income households, and almost four out of ten of these students had parents with less than a high school degree (Capps et al., 2005; The Urban Institute, 2006). Furthermore, of the many ethnic groups that comprise the dual language learner student population, Latino children are the most likely to live in poverty and to have the least educated parents (Capps et al., 2005; Larsen, 2004; Lopez & Cole, 1999). Nevertheless, there is still variation among the Latino population in socioeconomic status based on country of origin. According to Census 2000 data, Latino children come from a variety of cultural and national origins including Mexico (65%), Puerto Rico (9%), Central America (7%), South America (6%), the Dominican Republic (3%), and Cuba (2%) (Hernandez, 2006). The distribution by country of origin within the ECLS-K dataset is quite similar (Reardon & Galindo, 2006).[2] It is clear, then, that the largest subpopulation of Latinos in the United States is of Mexican heritage. However, what might not be as clear is that Mexican Latinos tend to be of lower income than Latinos from other origins, such as Cuba. Therefore, when interpreting the findings from the ECLS-K or other national data, it is important to bear in mind that the income distribution of the sample of Latinos is truncated and likely is more representative of a low-income population. Thus, it is important to keep in mind within-group variations when examining national data on Latino children. Not all findings may be appropriate to generalize to all Latinos; neither would it be appropriate to compare all Latinos with children from other racial/ethnic backgrounds who, as a group, might be of higher income without controlling for this confounding factor.

In sum, socioeconomic disadvantage, racial/ethnic minority status, immigrant status, and country of origin have each been linked with poorer development in young children (Capps et al., 2005; Denton & West, 2002; Halle, Forry et al., 2009; National Research Council & Institute of Medicine, 2000; Reardon & Galindo, 2006; West, Denton, & Germino-Hausken, 2000; Zill & West, 2001). It is possible, then, that multiple sociodemographic risk factors may compound, in addition to partially explain, the difference between young Latino dual language learners' academic and social-emotional well-being and that of their more advantaged peers (Gutman, Sameroff, & Cole, 2003). At the very least, there are confounds between Latino dual language learner status and other sociodemographic factors that are not fully taken into account by the analyses of reading and mathematics disparities noted above.

Lack of Adequate Measurement of Dual Language Learners' Competencies

An additional limitation of existing studies of children who are dual language learners is that they rarely capture these children's competencies as assessed in the child's home language. For example, we may know children's proficiency level in English, but we do not know their level of proficiency or comprehension in their home language. To date, there are few—if any—assessments of cognitive or social-emotional abilities that have been normed and validated on a representative sample of English-Spanish dual language learners. Rather, most assessments are developed with monolingual speakers of either English or Spanish (Espinosa & Lopez, 2007b; Pena & Halle, in press). In some cases, measures have been translated into Spanish without proper investigation into whether the measure is comparable for Spanish-speaking children. Such translations may call into question construct validity of the measure, because a word in one language may translate into a different level of complexity or difficulty (e.g., in terms of morphology) in another language (Pena, 2007). Further, issues around cultural bias and finding qualified people to conduct the assessment also come into play (Castro, 2009). For example, we need to consider the potential "mismatch" between the home and school culture that could result in young Latino dual language learners' abilities being misinterpreted or not fully realized by the teacher or school system (Greenfield, 1997). In sum, methodological concerns surrounding the use of valid and reliable measures may thwart the ability of Latino dual language learners to demonstrate their full academic and social capabilities.

It should be noted that new research, some happening at the state level (e.g., Florida, California), is beginning to look at the school readiness skills of the Spanish-speaking preschool population in a more comprehensive way. For example, a study of children's school readiness in Los Angeles county is employing "conceptual scoring" to determine children's understanding of concepts in either their home language (Spanish) or English. This approach involves developing test items simultaneously in both languages and allowing the child to respond in either language. Simultaneous development of test items, as well as other possible accommodations (such as oral directions in the child's primary language and small group administration), are important techniques that might increase the chance of validly assessing the capabilities of children within this population (Castro, 2009). Findings from state studies are still mostly in process, but will surely be helpful in better understanding the particular competencies of Latino dual language learners and the supports that will be most helpful across school readiness domains.

Summary and Implications

It is likely that socioeconomic factors such as household income and parental education are accounting for much of the differences now noted by race/ethnicity and/or home language in education disparities data (Fryer & Levitt, 2006; Halle, Forry et al., 2009). One way to explore this directly would be to conduct multivariate analyses including multiple factors of interest. Unfortunately, the distribution of some factors may be so skewed that the full distribution may not be able to be included in analyses because of small sample sizes in some categories (e.g., country of origin). In addition, several factors may be so highly correlated that they cannot be included in the same analysis due to multicollinearity. Consequently, careful selection of variables to include in multivariate analyses is needed.

An alternative analytic method would be to ensure that the comparison group is a true comparison group and does not differ on multiple factors. For instance, researchers find that the school contexts that low-income Latino children experience are often different than those of non-Latino Whites (Reardon & Galindo, 2006), but they may not disentangle income or school characteristics from race/ethnicity in the comparison group of non-Latino Whites. It would be informative, for example, to compare Latino children from middle-class socioeconomic backgrounds with middle-class children from other racial/ethnic backgrounds. To date, very few studies have examined Latino children (or dual language learners) who are not primarily low-income. There is a need to understand within group variation, but there is also a need to have a better-specified and more appropriate comparison group. Otherwise, results can be misleading. The analyses presented in this chapter that compare low-income Latino dual language learners attending Head Start with the full group of low-income children attending Head Start begins to provide a more appropriate comparison group. Nevertheless, the field could improve on the methodologies and statistical techniques used to examine Latino dual language learners. Future research should (1) include sociodemographic factors that may provide additional explanatory power in analyses, (2) make use of more appropriate comparison groups, and (3) make use of valid and reliable assessments and assessment techniques with dual language learners to capture their full capabilities.

Finally, as noted in the research reviewed above, very few studies have taken into account when examining young Latino dual language learners' school readiness the characteristics of the classroom environments that these children experience (Halle et al., 2010, June; Reardon & Galindo, 2006). Given the full conceptual framework of school readiness that includes not only the child's readiness for school but also the school's readiness for children and family and community supports, it is important to examine the features of the early care and education environments that aim to support and prepare children for success in kindergarten and beyond. In the next section, we examine the context of early care and education and how it might best support young Latino dual language learners' development.

EARLY CARE AND EDUCATION AS A CONTEXT TO SUPPORT YOUNG LATINO DUAL LANGUAGE LEARNERS' DEVELOPMENT

Children whose home language is not English are more often cared for by relatives in their own home or in another's home than in center-based care, especially during the early years of life (Halle, Hair et al., 2009). Latino children are the least likely of all racial/ethnic groups to attend pre-school programs (Espinosa, 2007). Some researchers suggest that children of immigrants, and Latinos in particular, are less likely to use center-based care because of cultural preferences (Hernandez et al., 2007). However, others suggest that the decision to use relatives rather than center-based care is reflective of lack of affordability and access to center-based care rather than cultural factors (Espinosa, 2007; Hernandez et al., 2007).

Regardless of the setting, early care and education environments that are of high quality will optimally support children's growth and development. Castro, Espinosa, and Paez (in press) have outlined the elements of high-quality early care and education for dual language learners. These elements include: (1) Creating an organized and supportive early childhood environment; (2) Positive educator-child interactions; (3) Increased opportunities for peer interactions; (4) Strategic use of the child's first language; (5) Explicit vocabulary instruction; (6) Ongoing and frequent-assessment of the child's first and second language development and other developmental domains; (7) Small group and one-on-one activities; (8) Structural program characteristics; (9) Educator knowledge and skill; and (10) Family engagement. Below, we highlight some of the elements of high-quality early care and education most relevant for the positive development of social-emotional skills among young Latino children.

Classroom Environment and Practices

The National Literacy Panel on Language Minority Children and Youth suggests that a key step in promoting the literacy skills of dual language learners is providing intentional instruction of the key components of reading, as identified by the National Reading Panel: phonological and phonemic awareness, phonics, fluency, vocabulary, and text comprehension. Also critical is supporting the oral language skills of young dual language learners, including expressive vocabulary and listening comprehension (August & Shanahan, 2006; National Reading Panel, 2000). In addition, Castro, Espinosa, and Paez (in press) identify several specific features of the classroom environment and classroom practices that appear to be critical for optimal development of dual language learners, particularly for supporting both languages. Specifically, they mention the use of research-based curricula, instructional practices that support both the first and second language and literacy development of the dual language learner, intentionally incorporating elements of the child's home language and culture into the curriculum, building on the child's prior knowledge to support the learning of new concepts, and maintaining a classroom environment that supports and values bilingualism. As noted earlier, supporting fluent bilingualism for dual language learners can enhance their self-esteem as well as help maintain their cultural and familial connections, all of which are important factors that contribute to their overall emotional well-being. Supporting fluent bilingualism among young children learning English will also ultimately help them compete in an increasingly global work environment.

With regard to instructional practices that support both the first and second language, the National Literacy Panel on Language Minority Children and Youth conducted a meta-analysis of 15 studies that seemed to point to bilingual instruction as more beneficial to dual language learners' English reading development than English-only instruction (August & Shanahan, 2006). The Panel suggested that receiving instruction in the child's home language may serve as a "bridge" to learning the linguistic principles of the new language. In addition, a model called "English plus Spanish" (EPS) may be promising for supporting both English language acquisition and fluency in Spanish for Latino dual language learners (Espinosa, 2010; Garcia & Jensen, 2007). However, the majority of studies in the meta-analysis included children in elementary school rather than children in early childhood programs. More rigorous research comparing the different models of language of instruction within early childhood settings is needed (Espinosa, 2010).

Regardless of language of instruction, some specific classroom practices that may make dual language learners more comfortable emotionally in a classroom include using pictures as well as words to label objects in the classroom, using word labels on objects in English and the home language, modeling behaviors for the child, pairing the dual language learner with a classmate who wants to help him/her, displaying and using books and other resources (e.g., posters) that include representations of the child's home culture and language, using bilingual books in the classroom, and making use of an interpreter in the classroom, if needed.

Beyond the work on language and literacy development, little research currently focuses on what additional features of the early childhood context best support dual language learners' school readiness skills, broadly defined, and social-emotional development in particular. A recent study of state-funded pre-kindergarten classrooms across 11 states indicates that dual language learners may not require a different set of classroom practices to facilitate their optimal development than do other children. Downer and colleagues (2009) found that teacher-child interactions look similar across pre-kindergarten classrooms with varying levels of dual language learners in the classrooms. Furthermore, this study found that classrooms characterized by emotional support, organizational support, and instructional support were associated with positive cognitive and social development for all children, regardless of their dual language learner status. These findings seem to indicate that high-quality classrooms will benefit all children, and that teacher-child interactions are not moderated by the dual language learner status of the child or the classroom as a whole in relation to positive child outcomes. The authors caution, however, that their findings may not be generalizable beyond state-funded pre-kindergarten programs. Certainly more research is needed to determine the specific classroom practices that may benefit dual language learners' social-emotional development specifically.

Teacher-Child Relationship

Learning is facilitated through joint, productive activities among teachers and students. Howes and Ritchie (2002) indicated that teachers can enhance their teacher-child relationships when they are involved in learning with children, are consistent and firm, support children's positive behaviors, use classroom organization and predictable classroom routines, and use cooperative learning and peer-assisted instruction. Taking a proactive role in creating positive teacher-child relationships becomes especially important when monolingual English-speaking teachers work with children who are dual language learners because of the language barriers. As suggested by a study conducted by Gillanders (2007), effective teacher-child relationships can have implications in terms of the social status of children who are dual language learners and, in turn, can positively affect these children's inclusion in the classroom community.

An important aspect of the teacher-child relationship is teachers' interpretation of challenging behaviors in children who are dual language learners (e.g., periods of silence, inability to follow oral instruction). In order for teachers to establish positive relationships with these children, they need to understand the process of second language acquisition and learn effective strategies for dealing with challenging behaviors (Santos & Ostrosky, 2002). However, few early childhood educators receive explicit pre-service or in-service training in working with dual language learners (Maxwell, Lim, & Early, 2006; Menken, Antunez, Dilworth, & Yasin, 2001). Another goal for the field is to improve professional development of early childhood educators regarding the optimal development of (and educational support for) dual language learners.

Peer Relationships

Just as teacher-child interactions can facilitate the learning and social-emotional well-being of dual language learners, so too can peer interactions. Peer relationships can facilitate the social integration of a dual language learning child into the classroom. However, reports from the ECLS-K raise concerns that Latino children may have difficulty engaging in prosocial behavior, such as joining others, making friends, and comforting their peers (Araujo & Williams, 2008). These difficulties, if left unattended, represent a potentially significant barrier to successful peer relations and adaptation to a new environment.

Teachers should monitor and support peer interactions within an early childhood setting. Small group or one-on-one activities may be a less threatening venue for a dual language learning student to interact with peers and learn than in a large group activity. Researchers caution, however, that instructors need to put care and thought into how they pair dual language learners with other, more fluent English speakers (Santos & Ostrosky, 2002). For example, teachers are encouraged to select a clearly defined activity and prepare both the dual language learning child and the fluent English-speaking child for the activity so that it is a positive experience for both students (Castro et al., 2010).

The Home-School Connection

An abundance of research shows that engagement of parents and extended family in supporting the child's academic success is key for students to have better social skills, significant improvement in their behavior, and ease of adaptation to school (Henderson & Mapp, 2002). Research indicates that families can make a difference in their child's success by being active partners in their children's life at school (Birman & Espino, 2007; Henderson & Mapp, 2002). It is important to begin to build partnerships between the school staff and parents in order to establish positive relationships that will support Latino children's social-emotional development. "By knowing how the family is socializing the child, what aspirations the parents have for the child, common styles of interaction, and family values and customs, the program staff can design instructional activities that capitalize on and extend the strengths and abilities of [dual language learning] children" (Espinosa, 2010, p. 154). It is important to understand and recognize the different needs of these families and to engage the entire family in addressing these needs in order to build strong home-school partnerships. Research in this area with Latino children and families is very scarce and further research is necessary to develop appropriate interventions that will support positive outcomes within the Latino child population.

CONCLUSION

Young Latino dual language learners are a large and growing segment of the dual language learner population in the United States. However, they are not a monolithic group. Among Spanish-speaking dual language learners, there is diversity in language, culture, and geographic location. There are many factors that influence risk and resilience among this population, including how long they have been in the United States, what generation of immigrant they are, English-language fluency, fluency in their home language, socioeconomic status, parents' educational level, and country of origin.

As a group, dual language learners lag behind monolinguals in academic outcomes (Oller & Jarmulowicz, 2007). In particular, Latino students lag behind their Asian and White peers at kindergarten entry in academic outcomes and continue to lag behind as they progress through school (Hampden-Thompson et al., 2008, December; Lee et al., 2007; National Task Force on Early Childhood Education for Hispanics, 2007, June; Princiotta et al., 2006). However, there is some indication that

Latino dual language learners may start school with better social-emotional capabilities, and grow in these capabilities at a faster rate than monolinguals. They also appear to catch up to monolinguals in their math skills over the elementary school years (Halle et al., 2009, April). Research indicates that there are supports that can be put in place in the early care and education environments that can aid young dual language learners in their social-emotional development as well as their cognitive and language development. For example, recommendations of the National Task Force on Early Childhood Education for Hispanics (2007) include increasing the access to high-quality early care and education programs for Latino children and increasing the number of Spanish-speaking teachers and language acquisition specialists.

In light of the paucity of research in the area of Latino dual language learners' social-emotional development, a more systematic and rigorous research agenda should focus on this topic. One hindrance to pursuing this research endeavor is the limited number of measures that are available for use with the bilingual or multilingual population. Clearly, measurement tools and methodological techniques need improvement. For example, current measures of child care quality may not adequately capture all the practices within an early childhood setting that likely support the development of young dual language learners (Castro et al., 2010). In addition, few assessments of children's language, cognitive, or social-emotional development have been validated for use with young dual language learners (Espinosa & Lopez, 2007a; Pena & Halle, in press). The lack of appropriate school readiness measures poses a challenge for educational policies and programs, many of which require assessments of children's academic skills. These policy and practice issues make the study of school readiness and social-emotional well-being among young Latino dual language learners complex. Without valid and reliable ways to assess these children's language development and overall academic progress, it is impossible to gain an accurate picture of their strengths and weaknesses, and therefore impossible to know how to best support their development.

Current research is also lacking the inclusion of sociodemographic factors necessary for better explanatory power within analyses. Including such measures in multivariate analyses would permit the disentanglement of confounding factors such as dual language learner status, SES, and country of origin. Many national datasets (i.e., Census, ECLS-K, and the National Assessment of Educational Progress, NAEP), while representative of the Latino population in the United States, should be examined in a way to illuminate variations within groups rather than just to make cross-group comparisons. Further, research in this area has tended to focus on low-income

Latino dual language learners, and has not always included appropriate comparison groups. We cannot gather meaningful information from studies on low-income Latino dual language learners when the comparison groups differ by both race/ethnicity and SES.

In addition, intervention research should focus on helping teachers learn about the importance of establishing positive relationships with children who are dual language learners and the consequences of these relationships in the social milieu of the classroom; examine their own beliefs about dual language learners and how these beliefs might influence the way they establish relationships with children who are dual language learners; learn to interpret and respond to children's challenging behaviors in the context of the process of second language acquisition; be sensitive that some young immigrants and refugees may be suffering from social-emotional stress; and learn to use strategies to build positive relationships with these children and their parents. In an effort to provide support to Latino children and their families, professionals should focus on going beyond recognizing the risk factors associated with this population to identify their strengths and build on their previous knowledge and belief systems to promote healthy development.

In general, the literature on Latino dual language learners has not adequately examined these children's social and emotional well-being. Furthermore, it is our contention that research in this area has not taken into account enough positive aspects of being a dual language learner for poor Latino children, such as the cognitive benefits of bilingualism and the benefits of belonging to two or more cultures. Future research should focus more on these benefits as well as additional supports (e.g., positive teacher interactions, developing more valid and reliable assessments) in order to better understand these young children's experiences and capabilities. If the above-mentioned supports were in place, better social-emotional and academic outcomes may be possible for this population. In sum, we argue for looking not only at whether Latino dual language learners are "ready for school," but also at whether early care and education settings and schools are ready to receive and support young Latino dual language learners.

NOTES

1. Estimates come from the Early Childhood Longitudinal Study—Kindergarten Class of 1998–99 (ECLS-K) (Hampden-Thompson et al., 2008, December; Halle et al., 2009, April; Princiotta, Flanagan, & Germino-Hausken, 2006; Reardon& Galindo, 2006), the National Assessment of Educational Progress (NAEP)

(Lee, Grigg, & Donahue, 2007) and Census 2000 (National Task Force on Early Childhood Education for Hispanics, 2007, June).

2. Of the Latino children in the ECLS-K whose country of origin is known, the distribution is as follows: Mexico (46%), Puerto Rico (7%), Central America (7%), South America (4%), Cuba (3%) and other (5%) (Reardon & Galindo, 2006).

REFERENCES

Administration for Children and Families. (2009). OHS Definition of Dual Language Learners. Retrieved January 24, 2010 from http://eclkc.ohs.acf.hhs.gov/hslc/Dual%20Language%20Learners/DLL_%20Resources/OHSDefinitionof.htm

Administration for Children and Families. (2010). *Head Start Impact Study. Final report*. Washington, DC: U.S. Department of Health and Human Services.

Araujo, B., & Williams, S. (2008). The impact of language status as an acculturative stressor on internalizing and externalizing behaviors among Latino/a children: A longitudinal analysis from school entry through third grade. *Journal of Youth Adolescence 37*, 399–411.

August, D., & Shanahan, T. (Eds.). (2006). *Developing literacy in second-language learners: Report of the National Literacy Panel on Language-Minority Children and Youth*. Mahwah, NJ: Erlbaum.

Bialystok, E. (2001). *Bilingualism in development: Language, literacy & cognition*. Cambridge, England: Cambridge University Press.

Birman, D., & Espino, S. R. (2007). The relationship of parental practices and knowledge to school adaptation for immigrant and non-immigrant high school students. *Canadian Journal of School Psychology 22*, 152–166.

Capps, R., Fix, M. E., Murray, J., Ost, J., Passel, J., & Herwantoro Hernandez, S. (2005). *The new demography of America's schools: Immigration and the No Child Left Behind Act*. Washington, DC: The Urban Institute.

Carlton, M. P., & Winsler, A. (1999). School readiness: The need for a paradigm shift. *School Psychology Review 28*(3), 338–352.

Castro, D. (2009). *Assessing dual language learners and children of immigrant families in early care and education*. Paper presented at the Child Care Policy Research Consortium Meeting, Washington, DC.

Castro, D., Espinosa, L. M., & Paez, M. (in press). Defining and measuring quality early childhood practices that promote dual language learners' development and learning. In M. Zaslow, I. Martinez-Beck, K.Tout & T. Halle (Eds.), *Quality measurement in early childhood settings*. Baltimore, MD: Brookes Publishing.

Chernoff, J. J., Flanagan, K. D., McPhee, C., & Park, J. (2007). *Preschool: First findings from the Third Follow-up of the Early Childhood Longitudinal Study, Birth Cohort (ECLS-B) (No. NCED 2008-025)*. Washington, DC: National Center for Educational Statistics, Institute of Education Sciences, U.S. Department of Education.

Committee on the Prevention of Reading Difficulties in Young Children. (1998). *Preventing reading difficulties in young children*: National Academy of Sciences.

Damon, W., & Eisenberg, N. (Eds.). (1998). *Handbook of child psychology: Vol. 3. Social, emotional, and personality development*. New York: Wiley.

DeNavas-Walt, C., Proctor, B.D., & Smith, J. C. (2009). Income, poverty, and health insurance coverage in the United States: 2008, Current Population Reports, P60–236, Washington, DC: U.S. Census Bureau. http://www.census.gov/prod/2009pubs/p60-236.pdf.

Denham, S. (1998). *Emotional development in young children*. New York: Guilford Press.

Denton, K., & West, J. (2002). *Children's reading and mathematics achievement in kindergarten and first grade* (NCES 2002-125). Washington, DC: U.S. Department of Education, National Center for Education Statistics.

Downer, J. T., Lopez, M. L., Hamagami, A., Pianta, R., & Howes, C. (2009). Addressing the learning needs of dual language learners: The role of teacher-child interactions within a multi-state study of preschool programs. *Paper submitted to Child Development on October 23, 2009.*

Espinosa, L. (2010). Classroom teaching and instruction "best practices" for young English language learners. In E. E. Garcia & E. Frede (Eds.), *Young English-language learners: Current research and emerging directions for practice and policy (Chapter 8)* (pp. 143–164). New York: Teacher's College Press.

Espinosa, L. M. (2006). *Young English language learners in the U.S.* Parents as Teacher News. Fall 2006.

Espinosa, L. M. (2007). English-language learners as they enter school. In R. Pianta, M. Cox & K. Snow (Eds.), *School readiness and the transition to kindergarten in the era of accountability* (pp. 175–196). Baltimore, MD: Paul H. Brookes.

Espinosa, L. M., & Lopez, M. (2007a). *Assessment consideration for young English language learners across different levels of accountability.* Paper presented at the Paper prepared for the National Early Childhood Accountability Task Force and First 5 LA.

Espinosa, L. M., & Lopez, M. L. (2007b). *Assessment consideration for young English language learners across different levels of accountability.* Paper presented at the National Early Childhood Accountability Task Force and First 5 Los Angeles and the Pew Charitable Trusts' National Early Childhood Accountability Task Force.

Fabes, R. A., Gaertner, B. M., & Popp, T. K. (2006). Getting along with others: Social competence in early childhood. In K. McCartney & D. Phillips (Eds.), *Blackwell handbook of early childhood development* (pp. 297–316). Malden, MA: Blackwell Publishing.

Fitzgerald, J. (1993). Literacy and students who are learning English as a second language. *The Reading Teacher 46*(8), 638–647.

Fryer, R. G., & Levitt, S. D. (2006). *Testing for racial differences in the mental ability of young children.* NBER Working Paper.

Fujiura, G. T., & Yamaki, K. (2000). Trends in demography of childhood poverty and disability. *Exceptional Children 66*(2), 187–199.

Fujiura, G. T., Yamaki, K., & Czechowicz, S. (1998). Disability among ethnic and racial minorities in the United States: A summary of economic status and family structure. *Journal of Disability Policy Studies 9*(2), 111–130.

Garcia, E., & Jensen, B. (2007). *Language development and early education of young Hispanic children in the United States.* Working paper.

Genesee, F., Geva, E., Dressler, C., & Kamil, M. (2006). Synthesis: Cross-linguistic relationships. In D. August & T. Shanahan (Eds.), *Report of the National Literacy Panel on language minority youth and children* (pp. 153–174). Mahwah, NJ: Lawrence Erlbaum Associates.

Gillanders, C. (2007). An English-speaking prekindergarten teacher for young Latino children: Implications of the teacher–child relationship on second language learning. *Early Childhood Education Journal 35*(1), 47–54.

Greenfield, P. M. (1997). You can't take it with you: Why ability assessments don't cross cultures. *American Psychologist, 52*(10), 1115–1124.

Gudykunst, W., & Ting-Toomey, S. (1990). Ethnic identity, language and communication breakdowns. In *Handbook of language and social psychology* (pp. 309–327). Oxford, England: John Wiley & Sons.

Gutman, L. M., Sameroff, A. J., & Cole, R. (2003). Academic growth curve trajectories from 1st grade to 12th grade: Effects of multiple social risk factors and preschool child factors. *Developmental Psychology 39*(4), 777–790.

Hair, E., Halle, T., Terry-Humen, E., Lavelle, B., & Calkins, J. (2006). Children's school readiness in the ECLS-K: Predictions to academic, health, and social outcomes in first grade. *Early Childhood Research Quarterly 21*(4), 431–454.

Halgunseth, L. C., Ispa, J. M., & Duane, R. (2006). Parental control in Latino families: An integrated review of the literature. *Child Development 77*(5), 1282–1287.

Halle, T. (2002). Emotional development and well-being. In M. Bornstein, L. Davidson, C. Keyes & K. Moore (Eds.), *Well-being: Positive development across the lifespan* (pp. 125–138). Hillsdale, NJ: Lawrence Erlbaum.

Halle, T., Forry, N., Hair, E., Perper, K., Wandner, L., & Vick, J. (2009). *Disparities in early learning and development: Lessons from the Early Childhood Longitudinal Study—Birth Cohort (ECLS-B).* Washington, DC: Child Trends.

Halle, T., Hair, E., & Wandner, L. (2010, June). *School readiness of Spanish-speaking students: Predictors of changes in developmental profiles over the Head Start year. Poster Symposium.* Paper presented at the Head Start's 10th National Research Conference, Washington, DC.

Halle, T., Hair, E. C., Nuenning, M., Weinstein, D., Vick, J., Forry, N., et al. (2009). *Primary child care arrangements of U.S. infants: Patterns of utilization by poverty status, family structure, maternal work status, maternal work schedule, and child care assistance.* OPRE Research Brief #1. Washington, DC: Child Trends.

Halle, T., Hair, E. C., Zaslow, M., McNamara, M., Nuenning, M., Kinukawa, A. et al. (2009, April). *Factors predicting early versus later English proficiency among English language learners in the ECLS-K.* Paper presented at the Biennial Meeting of the Society for Research in Child Development, Denver, CO.

Hampden-Thompson, G., Mulligan, G., Kinukawa, A., & Halle, T. (2008, December). *Mathematics achievement of language minority students during the elementary years.* Washington, DC. U.S. Government Printing Office: U.S. Department of Education, National Center for Education Statistics. NCES 2009-036.

Henderson, A. T., & Mapp, K. L. (2002). *A New Wave of Evidence: The impact of school, family, and community connections on student achievement. Annual synthesis, 2002*: National Center for Family & Community Connections with Schools, Southwest Educational Development Laboratory.

Hernandez, D. J. (2006). *Young Hispanic children in the U.S.: A demographic portrait based on Census 2000. A report to the National Task Force on Early Childhood Education for Hispanics*: University of Albany, State University, New York.

Hernandez, D. J., Denton, N. A., & Macartney, S. E. (2007). *Children in immigrant families—The U.S. and 50 States: National origins, language, and early education. Publication #2007–11.* Washington, DC: Child Trends and The Center for Social and Demographic Analysis.

Hernandez, D. J., Denton, N. A., & Macartney, S. E. (2008). Children in immigrant families: Looking to America's future. *Social Policy Report 22*(3).

Howes, C., & Ritchie, S. (2002). *A matter of trust: Connecting teachers and learners in the early childhood classroom.* New York, London: Teacher College Press.

Hubbard, J. A., & Coie, J. D. (1994). Special issue: Children's emotions and social competence. *Merrill-Palmer Quarterly 40*(1), 1–20.

Jambunathan, S., & Burts, D. C. (2003). Comparison of perception of self-competence among five ethnic groups of preschoolers in the U.S. *Early Child Development and Care 173*(6), 651–660.

Kagan, S. L., Moore, E., & Bradekamp, S. (1995). *Reconsidering children's early development and learning: Toward common views and vocabulary.* Washington, DC: National Education Goals Panel Goal 1 Technical Planning Group.

Kim, J., Murdock, T., & Choi, D. (2005). Investigation of parents' beliefs about readiness for kindergarten: An examination of National Household Education Survey. *Educational Review Quarterly 29*(2), 3–17.

Knudsen-Lindauer, S. L., & Harris, K. (1989). Priorities for kindergarten curricula: Views of parents and teachers. *Journal of Research in Childhood Education 4*, 51–61.

Krashen, S., & Brown, C. L. (2005). The ameliorating effects of high socioeconomic status: A secondary analysis. *Bilingual Research Journal 29*(1), 185–196.

Larsen, L. J. (2004). *The foreign-born population in the United States: 2003 (Population characteristics).* Washington, DC: U.S. Census Bureau.

Lazarin, M. (2006). Improving assessment and accountability for English language learners in the No Child Left Behind Act [Electronic Version]. *National Council of La Raza, 16* Retrieved January 22, 2010 from www.nclr.org.

Lee, J., Grigg, W., & Donahue, P. (2007). *The nation's report card, Reading 2007. (NCES 2007-496).* Washington, DC: National Center for Education Statistics, Institute of Education Sciences, U.S. Department of Education.

Lin, H., Lawrence, F. R., & Gorrell, J. (2003). Kindergarten teachers' views of children's readiness for school. *Early Childhood Research Quarterly, 18*, 225–237.

Lopez, A., & Cole, C. L. (1999). Effects of a parent-implemented intervention on the academic readiness skills of five Puerto Rican Kindergarten students in an urban school. *School Psychology Review 28*(3), 439–447.

Margai, F., & Henry, N. (2003). A community-based assessment of learning disabilities using environmental and contextual risk factors. *Social Science & Medicine 56*(5), 1085.

Martinez, C. R., DeGarmo, D. S., & Eddy, J. M. (2004). Promoting academic success among Latino youths. *Hispanic Journal of Behavioral Sciences 26*(2), 128–151.

Maxwell, K. L., Lim, C.-I., & Early, D. M. (2006). *Early childhood teacher preparation programs in the United States: National report.* Chapel Hill, NC: The University of North Carolina, FPG Child Development Institute.

May, D. C., & Kundert, D. K. (1997). School readiness practices and children at-risk: Examining the issues. *Psychology in the Schools 34*(2), 73–84.

McClelland, M. M., Morrison, F. L., & Holmes, D. L. (2000). Children at risk for early academic problems: The role of learning-related social skills. *Early Childhood Research Quarterly 15*, 307–329.

Menken, K., Antunez, B., Dilworth, M. E., & Yasin, S. (2001). *An overview of the preparation and certification of teachers working with limited English proficient (LEP) students.* Retrieved December 14, 2003, from http://www.ncbe.gwu.edu

National Reading Panel. (2000). *Teaching children to read: An evidence-based assessment of the scientific research literature on reading and its implications for reading instruction.* Washington, DC: National Institute for Literacy.

National Research Council & Institute of Medicine. (2000). *From neurons to neighborhoods: The science of early childhood development.* Washington, DC: National Academy Press.

National Task Force on Early Childhood Education for Hispanics. (2007). Para nuestros ninos: Expanding and improving early education for Hispanics. Retrieved January 22, 2010, from www.ecehispanics.org

National Task Force on Early Childhood Education for Hispanics. (2007, June). *The school readiness and academic achievement in reading and mathematics of young Hispanic children in the United States.* Tempe, AZ: The National Task Force on Early Childhood Education for Hispanics.

O'Donnell, K. (2008). *Parents' reports of the school readiness of young children from the National Household Education Surveys Program of 2007. (NCES 2008-051).* Washington, DC: National Center for Education Statistics, Institute of Education Science, U.S. Department of Education.

Oller, D. K., & Jarmulowicz, L. (2007). Language and literacy in bilingual children in the early school years. In E. Hoff & M. Shatz (Eds.), *Blackwell Handbook of Language Development* (pp. 368–386). Malden, MA: Blackwell Publishing.

Pena, E. D. (2007). Lost in translation: Methodological considerations in cross-cultural research. *Child Development 78*(4), 1255–1264.

Pena, E. D., & Halle, T. G. (in press). Assessing preschool English learners: Traveling a multi-forked road. *Child Development Perspectives.*

Phinney, J., Horenczyk, G., Liebkind, K., & Vedder, P. (2001). Ethnic identity, immigration, and well-being: An interactional perspective. *Journal of Social Issues 57*(3), 493–510.

Piotrkowski, C. S., Botsko, M., & Matthews, E. (2000). Parents' and teachers' beliefs about children's school readiness in a high-need community. *Early Childhood Research Quarterly 15*(4), 537–558.

Princiotta, D., Flanagan, K. D., & Germino-Hausken, E. (2006). *Fifth grade: Findings from the fifth-grade follow-up of the Early Childhood Longitudinal Study, Kindergarten Class of 1998–99 (ECLS-K). (NCES 2006-038).* Washington, DC: National Center for Education Statistics, Institute of Education Sciences, U.S. Department of Education.

Raver, C. C. (2002). Emotions matter: Making the case for the role of young children's emotional development for early school readiness. In *Social Policy Reports, 16*(3). Ann Arbor, MI: Society for Research in Child Development.

Raver, C. C., & Knitzer, J. (2002). *Ready to enter: What research tells policymakers about strategies to promote social and emotional school readiness among three- and four-year-old children.* New York: NY: National Center for Children in Poverty, Columbia University Mailman School of Public Health.

Reardon, S. F., & Galindo, C. (2006). *K–3 academic achievement patterns of Hispanics and other racial/ethnic groups.* Paper presented at the American Educational Research Association Meeting.

Restrepo, A. (2008, January). Personal Communication at Quality Measures Roundtable. Washington, DC.

Rubin, K. H., Bukowski, W., & Parker, J. G. (1998). Peer interactions, relationships, and groups. In W. Damon & N. Eisenberg (Eds.), *Handbook of child psychology: Vol. 3. Personality and social development* (pp. 619–700). New York: Wiley.

Saarni, C. (1990). Emotional competence: How emotions and relationships become integrated. In R. Thompson (Ed.), *Nebraska symposium on motivation 1988: Socioemotional development* (pp. 115–182). Lincoln, NB: University of Nebraska Press.

Santos, R., & Ostrosky, M. (2002). *Understanding the impact of language differences on classroom behavior. What Works Briefs.*

Shin, H. B., & Bruno, R. (2003). *Language use and English-speaking ability: 2000 (Census 2000 Brief).* Washington, DC: U.S. Census Bureau.

Snow, C. E., Burns, M. S., & Griffin, P. (1998). *Preventing reading difficulties in young children.* Washington, DC: National Academy Press.

Stanton-Chapman, T. L., Chapman, D., & Bainbridge, N. L. (2002). Identification of early risk factors for language impairment. *Research in Developmental Disabilities, 23*(6), 390–405.

Tabors, P. (2008). *One child, two languages: A guide for early childhood educators of children learning English as a second language* (2nd ed.). Baltimore, MD: Paul H. Brookes Publishing.

Tabors, P., Paez, M., & Lopez, L. M. (2003). Dual language abilities of Spanish-English bilingual four-year olds: Initial finding from the Early Childhood Study of Language and Literacy Development of Spanish-speaking children. *NABE Journal of Research and Practice 1*, 70–91.

Tabors, P., & Snow, C. E. (2002). Young bilingual children and early literacy development. In S. B. Neuman & D. K. Dickinson (Eds.), *Handbook of Early Literacy Research* (pp. 159–178). New York: NY: The Guilford Press.

Tharp, R. (1997). *From at-risk to excellence: Research, theory, and principles for practice*. UC Berkeley: Center for Research on Education, Diversity, and Excellence. Retrieved January 20, 2010 from http://www.escholarship.org/uc/item/8nc0979r.

Thompson, R., & Lagattuta, K. H. (2006). Feeling and understanding: Early emotional development. In K. McCartney & D. Phillips (Eds.), *Blackwell handbook of early childhood development* (pp. 317–337). Malden, MA: Blackwell Publishing.

The Urban Institute. (2006). *Children of immigrants: Facts and figures*. Washington, DC: The Urban Institute.

U.S. Department of Health and Human Services. (2001). *Mental health: Culture, race, and ethnicity (Supplement to Mental health: A report of the Surgeon General)*. Rockville, MD: U.S. Department of Health and Human Services.

Wesley, P. W., & Buysse, V. (2003). Making meaning of school readiness in schools and communities. *Early Childhood Research Quarterly, 18*, 351–375.

West, J., Denton, K., & Germino-Hausken, E. (2000). *America's kindergartners. Working Paper No. 2000-070*. Washington, DC: National Center for Education Statistics.

Wolf, M. K., Kao, J., Griffin, N., Herman, J. L., Bachman, P. L., Chang, S. M., et al. (2008). *Issues in assessing English Language Learners: English language proficiency measures and accommodation uses*. Los Angeles, CA: National Center for Research on Evaluation, Standards, and Student Testing.

Zentella, A. C. (1997). *Building on Strengths: Language and Literacy in Latino Families and Communities*. New York: Teachers College Press.

Zill, N., & West, J. (2001). *Entering kindergarten: Findings from the Condition of Education 2000 (NCES 2001-035)*. Washington, DC: U.S. Department of Education, Office of Educational Research and Development.

Chapter 4

LANGUAGE BROKERING IN LATINO IMMIGRANT FAMILIES: DEVELOPMENTAL CHALLENGES, STRESSORS, FAMILIAL SUPPORTS, AND ADJUSTMENT

Raymond Buriel, Julia A. Love, and
Christina M. Villanueva

I had many students pose as language brokers in my classroom this past year. Many times the oldest child is used for this purpose, but I taught kindergarten. This means some of my five year olds were carrying a very important responsibility. I would have been lost without their help.
—D. D., English monolingual Latina kindergarten teacher

The children of Latino immigrants are usually the first members of their families to attend school in the United States, and to learn English. Prior to entering school, these children learn Spanish as their native language, and use it to communicate with parents and members of their community. As these children learn English, they are also able to communicate with teachers and other English-speaking agents of the larger U.S. society. Most Latino children in newcomer families speak English very well (Hernandez, Denton, & Macartney, 2008). Schooling also introduces these children to diverse aspects of U.S. culture, such as customs and social norms, many of which are unfamiliar to their parents. Thus, in the normal course of their early development, many children of immigrants become bilingual and bicultural (Buriel, 1993a). Because these children's parents have usually completed the extent of their schooling in their native country prior to immigrating, and devote most of their time in the United States to work, they are very limited in their opportunities to learn English and American culture (Suro, 2005). As a result, children are often called upon to serve as Spanish/English interpreters and translators for their immigrant parents, and serve as mediators between their families and American society. Not only do they interpret cultural and linguistic information, they are often also responsible for making adult-like decisions for themselves and their families. Children who fulfill this role have been labeled "language brokers" (Tse, 1995; Buriel, Perez, De Ment, Chavez, & Moran, 1998; Weisskirch & Alva, 2002). Language brokers interpret for their parents at schools, banks, stores, car dealerships, and medical settings, and handle disputes with creditors and landlords. They also translate documents such as job applications, business forms, and letters from school. Language brokers even interpret English language movies and TV programs for parents and family members. At school, language brokers assist their English monolingual teachers communicate with their Spanish monolingual students.

It is only within the past 15 years that behavioral scientist have begun to study the unique developmental challenges faced by language brokers (Morales and Hanson, 2005). Within the United States, these studies have focused on Asians and Latinos, the two fastest growing immigrant groups. As the size of the immigrant population grows, so does the number of potential language brokers. For the total U.S. population, as of 2005, approximately one in four children lived in homes where one or both parents were immigrants (Hernandez et al., 2008). The percentage is even higher among Latinos, where 63 percent of all children of this group live in immigrant families (Fry & Passel, 2009). It is not surprising, therefore, that in some studies, a majority of children from immigrant families who were sampled reported serving as language brokers at some time (De Ment, Buriel, & Villanueva, 2006; Love, 2006; McQuillan & Tse, 1995; Tse, 1995). In some Latino families, there are multiple language brokers. Love (2006) identified primary language brokers, who were chosen first when parents needed a language broker, and non-primary language brokers who were *not* chosen first when parents needed a language broker. Among foreign-born children of immigrants, language brokering begins one to five years after arriving in this country (McQillian & Tse, 1995; Tse 1995). Many native-born children of immigrants start language brokering between the ages of eight and ten years (Buriel et al., 1998; De Ment et al., 2005; Tse, 1995). Moreover, many children's language-brokering responsibilities continue through adolescence, and even into adulthood (De Ment et al., 2005; Mercado, 2003; Sy, 2006). These language-brokering activities are varied and complex, and include family and non-family members (see Figure 4.1), in many different settings (see Figure 4.2), and involving many different things (see Figure 4.3). Even while being away at college, or after starting their own families, individuals report ongoing language brokering for their parents (DeMent et al., 2005).

It is evident that language brokering spans the developmental periods of childhood, adolescence, and even adulthood. To date, studies have investigated language brokering and its correlates within specific age groups, but not across age groups. Given the cognitive and social-emotional changes attendant with different developmental periods, language brokering may be more stressful for certain age groups. One possibility is that younger children, who are in the early stages of language and cognitive development, may experience more difficulties with language brokering. On the other hand, adolescents striving for greater autonomy while shouldering more competing responsibilities and demands from parents, peers, and school, may be more negatively affected by language brokering. The quality of the parent-child relationship at different developmental periods may also impact on how well children cope with their language-brokering activities.

The purpose of this chapter is to review the literature on language brokering among Latinos by first placing it within the context of immigration to the United States. The chapter then examines the relationship of language brokering to linguistic/cognitive factors, parent-child relationships, and psychological well-being. We also present new age related cross sectional data on the relationships between language brokering, parent-child bonding, and depression. In making these age related comparisons we hope to determine if these relationships vary for different age groups, and if any particular age group of Latino children is at greater risk due to their language-brokering activities.

HISTORICAL BACKGROUND ON LANGUAGE BROKERING AND LATINOS

Shouldering a Language Burden.
In Immigrant Families, Children's Role as Interpreters Full of Pressures, Peril.
—Ginsberg, *The Philadelphia Inquirer* headline, 2003

The first author of this chapter often gets phone calls from journalists wanting to interview him for newspaper articles that they are writing about language brokers. Usually, the journalists' first question is, "Why is language brokering bad for children?" The following 3 to 5 minutes of the interview are taken up explaining that language brokering is not inevitably harmful to children and that there are documented positive outcomes associated with language brokering. Nevertheless, upon reading the published article later, the first author's comments are usually buried beneath a heap of impressionistic views regarding the deleterious effects that language brokering has for children. These journalists' lack of an immigrant historical perspective often gives them, and in turn, their readers, the impression that language brokering is a developmental anomaly that imperils the psychological well-being of children.

Ever since English became the dominant institutional language in the United States, the children of non-English speaking immigrants have served as language brokers for their families. The millions of immigrants who came to this country from eastern and southern Europe between 1892 and 1915, undoubtedly relied on their U.S. schooled children to serve as language brokers. Unfortunately, research on immigrant adaptation to this country during this period focused almost exclusively on the acculturation experiences of adults (Child, 1943; Park, 1928; Stonequist, 1937). Although the schooling and institutional efforts to assimilate the children of immigrants did receive attention (Cubberley, 1909), the unique settlement and adaptation roles that these children played within their immigrant families and communities was overlooked. As a result, the stories of language brokers were never recorded, and any developmental advantages or liabilities connected with their experiences in that era were never documented.

Between 1910, when the Mexican Revolution erupted, and the present, there has been a constant stream of Latino immigrants to the United States, coming from many parts of Latin America. This influx of Latino immigrants peaked in the 1980s. The rise in immigration from Latin America since the mid 1980s has drawn attention to differences in language and culture between immigrants and the settled mainstream population (Portes & Rumbaut, 1990). Today, because the majority of Euro Americans are several generations removed from their immigrant past, they have no memory of when language brokering may have taken place in their own families. Therefore, from the perspective of the mainstream population, language brokering sometimes appears novel, and out of line with the normal role of children within the family. Language brokering is viewed as a uniquely Latino (and Asian) immigrant cultural practice, rather than as a common experience for all immigrants who have ever come to the United States from non-English speaking countries. It is this historically shortsighted view that tends to distort and problematize language brokering in the public's eye. Thus, when viewed from outside the immigrant experience, language brokering is so inconsistent with normal parenting practices that it is thought to be associated with parent-child role reversal, loss of parental authority, and parentification of the child (Athey & Ahearn, 1991; Diaz-Lazaro, 2002; Mercado, 2003; Umana-Taylor, 2003), all of which result in severe psychological stress and impairment for children (Baptise, 1987; Hardy-Fanta & Montana, 1982). In the case of Latino children, language brokering is perceived as a "risk" factor that can impair the normal development of children from immigrant families. Nevertheless, although much of the newspapers' coverage on language brokering is negative, the emerging behavioral science research on this topic is mixed, showing both positive and negative social, emotional, and cognitive outcomes for children who serve as interpreters and translators for their parents. The nature of some of these outcomes appear related to children's gender, and the affective quality of the relationship with their parents, for whom they language broker.

In concluding this brief historical section, we would like to quote the Latina historian, Antonia Castañeda (1996), who reminds us of the profound role that children's language brokering has played in the destiny of the Latino population in the Americas:

> It is by no means solely or even principally an immigrant experience, at least not historically. Beginning with Malintzin, or La Malinche, as she is also known—a fourteen-year-old girl who was given, with nineteen other young women, by the Chontal Maya of the Tabasco coast to the Spaniards in 1519 and became translator, lover, and tactical advisor to Hernan Cortes—the experience of translating cultures has been lived by native-born children and adolescents. . . . (p. 209)

THE SOCIOLINGUISTIC AND COGNITIVE NATURE OF LANGUAGE BROKERING

> I have always been the language broker for my parents and have thus developed a better skill at translating stuff from English to Spanish, and have also always been treated more like and adult. I've always been more mature, maybe because I had to act more mature in order for the other adults to take me seriously.
>
> —M.A., Latina junior high school teacher

Language brokering involves more than being bilingual due to the accelerated and sophisticated social and cognitive demands associated with this role. Balanced bilingualism usually assumes age appropriate fluency in two languages on the part of an individual (Padilla & Lindholm, 1984). However, there are several ways in which the role requirements of language brokers go beyond the definition of bilingualism. First, bilingualism assumes dual language fluency for the benefit of the individual. In contrast, bilingualism on the part of language brokers is primarily for the benefit of others, namely parents, and the English-speaking agents with whom they communicate. Second, language brokers cannot pick and choose the circumstances where they will use their bilingualism, as this is usually determined by their parents and other adults. Third, language brokers are also sometimes decision makers because their parents, in some situations, rely on their judgment and bicultural experience (De Ment et al., 2005). In order to better help them represent their parents' views, language brokers also develop social self-efficacy (Buriel et al., 1998; De Ment et al., 2005) in the form of adult-like interpersonal skills. Shannon (1990) found that Latino children who served as language brokers knew how to address and speak with professionals such as doctors, while at the same time maintaining the dignity of their parents. Because children language broker in many diverse settings having their own unique vocabularies, such as schools, banks, hospitals, social services offices, and government agencies, they develop words and concepts related to these places (Heath, 1986), in two languages. Thus, children who language broker in diverse places are likely to develop sophisticated language competencies that exceed the age-appropriate vocabularies of typical bilingual children who do not language broker.

In many situations, language brokering involves literacy in two languages. Language brokers are often called upon to translate documents written in English into oral Spanish messages (e.g., messages from school), or to convert oral Spanish messages into written English (e.g., filling out job applications) (De Ment et al., 2005). The biliteracy requirements associated with language brokering may explain why Latino high school students with more language-brokering experience have higher academic grade point averages (Buriel et al., 1998). An intriguing developmental question is whether language brokering contributes to accelerated cognitive development, or if children who demonstrate accelerated cognitive development are selected by parents to serve as language brokers. In the course of their language-brokering interactions, children come to realize that they must not only label and describe things, they must also explain them, ask for clarification, and recognize that what they and others say is not always understood as intended by the different parties. Because some Latino children begin language brokering as early as age five, their accelerated understanding of the needs and internal states of others, and their ability to take other people's perspectives, may contribute to a precocious theory of mind development. Love (2006) found that pre-adolescent Latino children who served as the primary language broker in their family out-performed non-primary language brokers on theory of mind ability, things brokered, GPA, and reading achievement test scores.

Using a longitudinal design, Dorner, Orellana, and Li-Grining (2007), compared the reading and math-achievement test scores of Latino children between grades one and five. Based on their measures, they categorized their participants in descending levels of language-brokering activity, ranging from active-, partial-, and non-language brokers. Active language brokers translated eight or more items at four or more places. Partial language brokers translated four to eight items at three places. Non-language brokers did not report extensive translating. At grades one and two, active language brokers tended to score lower in reading and math in comparison with partial brokers, while scoring either lower or about the same in comparison with non-language brokers. However, by the fifth-grade, after controlling for test scores in early elementary school, active language brokers scored higher in reading and math than non-language brokers. Based on these findings, the authors noted, "This suggests that it may be the more intense work of active language brokering, which occurs in varied and challenging circumstances, that matters for students' standardized test performances" (p. 467). When viewed through the lens of high parental and societal expectations for children who serve as language brokers, it appears that, with proper support, children rise to the occasion of meeting the role demands placed upon them. Parental support often takes the form of acknowledgement and appreciation for the contributions children make to the family (Villanueva & Buriel, 2010). In addition, as children are socialized into their role as language brokers, there are attendant social and cognitive benefits that accrue to them in the process. Valdez (2003) has argued that the definition of "giftedness" should be expanded to include young language brokers in recognition of their extraordinary ability to successfully handle the many adult-like cognitive and social demands associated with their role. Furthermore, she recommends that, like the special curriculum that gifted children receive, the curriculum for language brokers should be tailored to reflect the real-world activities in which these children participate. Thus, bank statements, real estate forms, and job applications could be used as the basis to teach math concepts and English vocabulary and writing (Valdez, 2003). The label of giftedness and special curriculum suggested by Valdez (2003), help to draw positive attention to the many special qualities of language brokers, and reduce the stigma that is sometimes associated with this role.

LANGUAGE BROKERING AND PARENT-CHILD RELATIONSHIPS

> When I was younger my parents did not speak English well, so any homework that my siblings and I brought home we helped each other because our parents could not help us with lack of English skills. Fortunately, my siblings and I were used to it and understood that our parents were our providers and caretakers, and we were their translators.
> —C. T., Vietnamese American elementary school teacher

A common assumption is that all Latinos have large families and extended kin networks that provide social and material support. This assumption overlooks the fact that many Latino adults are immigrants, who have left their extended families back home in their countries of origin (Suro, 2005). Over the span of two to three generations, Latinos do extend their family networks in this country through marriage and births. However, lacking large family networks, many adult immigrants and their children rely heavily on each other to adapt to this country and fulfill their reasons for immigrating. Consequently, family roles and expectations differ between immigrant families and their later generation counterparts (Buriel, 1993b), especially in ways that enable newcomer families to successfully adapt to this country. For example, Mexican immigrant parents expect greater individual self-reliance and productive use of time from their children relative to native-born Mexican American parents (Buriel, 1993b). Within a collectivist Latino culture, self-reliance means that one can fend for him/herself, and therefore not draw from and deplete the group's resources. Productive use of time means "time is money," and that as much time and energy as necessary should be spent to help one's family succeed financially in this country.

As is more typical in their Latin American countries of origin, children from immigrant families assume adult-like responsibilities earlier in life (Rogoff, 2003; Valenzuela, 1999), that contribute to the family's economic well-being. Older siblings, especially girls, have responsibility for younger siblings, which frees mothers to work outside the home. Not surprisingly, Latina adolescents report that responsibilities such as childcare represent more important contributions to their families than language brokering (Villanueva & Buriel, 2010). In addition, many immigrant Latinos are employed in the service industry, which makes it possible for them to have their children assist them in their work as gardeners, landscapers, house cleaners, janitors, seamstresses, masons, and restaurant and shop owners (Valenzuela, 1999; Villanueva & Buriel, 2010). Although it has not been researched, it seems likely that the children of Latino immigrants may spend more time with their parents as a result of assisting them with their work and serving as their language brokers. Moreover, 71 percent of Latino children from immigrant families live in two parent households, relative to 52 percent of Latino children of native-born parentage (Fry & Passel, 2009), which means there is more adult supervision and opportunity to interact with adult parents. According to Delgado-Gaitan (1992) and Zelizer (1994), this may contribute to positive parent-child interdependence or a greater sense of responsibility and concern for others, as well as feelings of belongingness to the family. Thus, in the context of the collectivist Latino immigrant family, children's assumption of greater responsibility represents more interdependence rather than independence.

Greater responsibility for parents and others represents an avenue for fulfilling the Latino cultural value of life-long obligation and duty to the family (Fuligni, Tseng, & Lam, 1999). Weisskirch (2005), found that Latino adolescents described translating for others as helping them to care more for their parents, and to feel more grown up. Chao (2006), also found that as language brokering increases among Latino adolescents, so does respect for parents. A qualitative study with an ethnically diverse sample of college students from immigrant families found that language brokering gave these students more insight and appreciation for the sacrifices their parents made in coming to this country (De Ment et al., 2005). As a result, many reported that language brokering gave them an opportunity to show their appreciation for their parents' sacrifices and in the process became more bonded with their parents than their other siblings.

Some research indicates that the positive association between language brokering and parent-child relationships may be mediated by the feelings connected with the language-brokering role, rather than the actual amount of language brokering. In a study of Latino high school students, Buriel et al. (2006), found no relationship between parent-child bonding and language brokering involving persons, places, and things. However, for both boys and girls, feelings about language brokering were positively related to parent-child bonding. In other words, the more children liked language brokering, the more they felt emotionally connected to their parents. Another study by Weisskirch (2007), with Latino middle school students, found that adolescents with more problematic family relations reported higher ratings of negative emotions connected to their language-brokering experiences.

In a sample of Latino college students, Anguiano (2007), found that feelings about language brokering mediated the relationship between the language-brokering experience and family self-efficacy.

When viewed from outside the familistic nature of Latino immigrant culture, language brokering may appear like a type of parent-child role reversal or parentification of the child. From the perspective of the adult English speaker in a language-brokering situation, meaningful communication is taking place with the child and not the Latino adult, who may therefore appear passive. Also, the prevailing public opinion that all immigrants should learn English, can give the impression that Latino parents are incapable of learning English, and therefore hand over parental authority to their children. Role reversal, parentification, and loss of parental authority represent maladaptive forms of parent-child relationships that have been associated with language brokering. Some of these negative associations are anecdotal in nature (Athey & Ahearn, 1991; Santiago, 2003; Umaña-Taylor, 2003), while others are based on isolated clinical case studies (Baptiste, 1993; Hardy-Fanta & Montana, 1982). The empirical evidence on this issue with Latinos is limited to three studies, two of which are unpublished doctoral dissertations. The two dissertations both used the persons, places, and things subscales of Buriel's multidimensional measure of language brokering (Buriel et al., 1998). The earliest study was by Diaz-Lazaro (2002), who investigated the effects of language brokering on perceptions of family authority structure, parental locus of control, and problem solving among Latino adolescents and their parents from New York, Massachusetts, and Texas. Perceptions of family authority assessed adolescents' perceptions of authority and decision making at home. An important aim of this study was to examine the possibility that children's language brokering is associated with a loss of parental control and authority. Parental locus of control assessed the parents' perceptions of their efficacy, responsibility, and control over their children's behavior. Results showed no relationship of language brokering to either adolescents' perceptions of family authority or their parents' locus of control for parenting. However, language brokering and family authority structure predicted adolescents' problem-solving abilities. That is, more language brokering and participation in family decision making contributed positively to adolescents' perceptions of having better problem-solving abilities. The results of Diaz-Lazaro's (2002) study challenge the view that language brokering is associated with maladaptive parent-child relations.

Another dissertation by Mercado (2003), examined the relationship of language brokering, stress, and parentification among Latino university students in New York City. The study tested the hypotheses that language brokering would be related to both parentification and stress. The Parentification Questionnaire (Jurkovic, Morell, & Thirkield, 1999) was used to measure parentification, which was defined the subjective experience of caretaking responsibility over time between the respondents and their parents. The Parentification Questionnaire is a 42 item, true-false, measure that is scored in the direction of higher parentification. Perceived stress was measured with a 14-item scale designed to tap the degree to which respondent found their lives unpredictable, uncontrollable, and overloading. Mercado found significant positive correlations between parentification and the three language-brokering subscales. In addition, stress was positively related to parentification. However, none of the language-brokering subscales was related to stress. These findings indicate that although the parentification and language-brokering scales share some aspects with each other, only the parentification scale is related to stress. It may be that the two scales are tapping into some aspect of family obligation because both measures involve different types of assistance to parents. However, in addition to mild forms of assistance, the parentification scale includes extreme forms, as well, which may account for its relationship with stress. Language brokering, on the other hand, may represent a normal range of parental assistance behaviors for Latinos, therefore yielding no relationship to stress.

Martinez, McClure, and Eddy (2009), conducted an interesting study based on the theory that an acculturation gap between children and their immigrant parents contributes to maladaptive family environments. According to these researchers, "Families in which children are bilingual with monolingual parents are likely to reflect a more substantial acculturation gap than families in which one or both parents are also bilingual" (Martinez et al., 2009, p. 77). The greater the parent-child acculturation gap in Latino families, the greater the risk for poor behavioral health outcomes for children and parents. Based on this model, Martinez et al. (2003) identified two family types that included those with a high and low need for language brokering, which mirrored the degree of language concordance between adolescent children serving as language brokers and their parents. Language-brokering context was derived from a single five-point Likert-type question administered to parents and children: "My child helps our family by interpreting in various situations (school, post office, with landlord, with service providers, etc.)." Both parents and children were surveyed regarding a number of behavioral variables. Based on between group comparisons, parents in low language-brokering families generally reported greater parenting effectiveness than those in high language-brokering contexts, as well as less perceived psychological maladjustment in their children who language brokered for them. From the adolescents' perspective, there were no differences in depression between the two language-brokering contexts. Alcohol and tobacco use was higher for children in high language-brokering contexts. While these results seem to support the acculturation-gap theory, an unfortunate shortcoming of this study is that it did not investigate the correlation between language brokering and the different behavioral health outcomes. Language brokering and certain behavioral outcomes may occur in the same contexts, but this does not necessarily mean that they are correlated with each other. Although correlation does not imply causation, correlations (writ large to include multiple regression and structural equation modeling) in the expected direction, with appropriate controls, do add to the support of a theoretical model. Between group differences without additional confirmatory analyses leave results open to wide-ranging interpretations. Moreover, the reliability and generalizability of the findings are limited by the study's reliance on only one question to assess language brokering.[1]

LANGUAGE BROKERING AND PSYCHOLOGICAL WELL-BEING

In Valdez' (2003) book, *Expanding the Definition of Giftedness*, a director of interpreter services in one area of a hospital comments that, "the use of young interpreters by families exploits young children and exposes them to particular kinds of psychological injury." I find this sort of statement untrue. I was once a child that told her dad that he did not get a job he was hoping for. I was the child that translated and filled out documents for court situations, applications for jobs, and information for doctors and dentists. I also had to tell my mother that she had a disease that was not curable, cancer. I am a normal person who has simply taken on a bit more responsibility than other people. I am still on the track that I wanted to be on before anything "traumatic" happened.

—L. G., Latina first grade dual immersion teacher

Latino language brokers, ranging from elementary school age (Weisskirch & Alva, 2002) through college age and beyond (De Ment et al., 2005), have reported some discomfort and annoyance with their translating and interpreting duties. At least among Latinos, language brokering begins in elementary school (Buriel et al., 1998; Tse, 1995) and often continues into adulthood (De Ment et al., 2005). This means there is the possibility that individuals experience discomfort and annoyance with their language-brokering responsibilities over the developmental periods spanning childhood, adolescence, and young adulthood. The stress connected to language brokering can be viewed as a form of acculturative stress because translating and interpreting are done on behalf of the family's efforts to adapt to this society. Prolonged exposure to acculturative stress may eventuate in more serious psychological conditions such as depression (Hovey & King, 1996).

Studies have examined the relationship of language brokering to depression among Latinos at the middle school, high school, and college age levels. In a study with middle school age Latinos, Love and Buriel (2007), found that language brokering for more people, other than one's own parents (e.g., relatives, neighbors, teachers, doctors, strangers, etc.), was positively related to depression for both boys and girls. These researchers concluded that language brokering for many people is stressful because the adolescent is less aware of the specific needs and expectations of the different persons for whom they are called upon to serve as interpreter. In this same study, Love and Buriel (2007) also examined the role of autonomy in mediating the relationship between language brokering and depression. Using a measure developed by Roer-Strier and Rivlis (1998), autonomy was measured in three areas: privileges, responsibilities, and psychological autonomy. Results showed that for girls only, those who language brokered in more *places*, and also received more responsibilities, reported less depression. The authors surmised that language brokering in more places, and receiving more responsibilities, boosts young girls' status within the family. This may be especially the case for junior high school age girls who are in the early stages of establishing their maturity by assuming greater responsibilities within their homes. Later, when they are in high school and involved in more activities outside the home, their household responsibilities may become a source of stress.

Among high school age Latinos, Buriel et al. (2006), found that depression scores were significantly higher for girls than boys. In addition, girls scored significantly higher than boys did on all dimensions of language brokering (persons, places, things, feelings). However, when language brokering was regressed on depression, there was no relationship for girls, and only one positive relationship for boys. Language brokering in more places was associated with higher depression for boys. These researchers concluded that language brokering may be more consistent with the gender role socialization of girls because they are expected to be emotionally closer and spend more time with parents than boys. As a result, they are more available, and perhaps willing to language broker than boys, who separate more from the family than girls. Over time, therefore, language brokering becomes a more gendered activity among Latinos, with girls assuming greater responsibility for translating and interpreting. Also, because language brokering is more consistent with the gender role socialization of girls, it may become less stressful for them than boys. Nevertheless, high school age Latinas may be more stressed than boys due to the multitude of responsibilities they have at home (childcare, cleaning, cooking, etc.), which compete with time for other activities such as school work, socializing, and employment outside the home (Villanueva & Buriel, 2010).

In a high school sample that included Chinese, Korean, and Mexican American students Chao (2006), found no relationship of language brokering to depression anxiety for either boys or girls of Mexican descent. The inconsistency in the findings between Chao's (2006) study and Buriel et al's. (2006) may be due to differences in language-brokering measures. Chao (2006) used a nine-item language-brokering measure, yielding a single score that did not differentiate between persons, places, things, and feelings. Chao's (2006) did find that more language brokering among Chinese and Korean descent students was related to depression anxiety. Chao's (2006) findings indicate that the stress associated with language brokering may not operate in the same manner in different ethnic and cultural contexts. One reason for this may be the greater dissimilarity between English and different Asian languages, which makes language brokering more difficult for children. Also, parental self-disclosure may be more sensitive in some Asian cultures, thus arousing more stress in language-brokering situations for parents and children (Chao, 2006). Conclusions about language brokering, and the nature of its relationship to other variables, therefore need to be ethnically and culturally specific in order to avoid overgeneralizations.

Sy (2006) modified Chao's (2006) language-brokering scale to make it specific to translating/interpreting for school-related issues. Using a sample of Latina college students, she found that trust in mothers' wisdom and advice was positively related to language brokering. However, Latinas who language brokered more had higher levels of school related stress. The school-centered nature of how language brokering was measured in this study may explain its relationship to school related stress. A qualitative study with Latina middle school students also found that school-related issues represent the most stressful language-brokering situations for these young women (Villanueva & Buriel, 2010). It seems obvious that having to serve as interpreter/translator between one's parents and teachers, regarding one's own academic performance, represents an especially stressful form of language brokering.

AGE RELATED DIFFERENCES IN LANGUAGE-BROKERING ACTIVITIES AND THEIR RELATIONSHIP TO PARENT-CHILD BONDING AND DEPRESSION

> Translating has always been part of my life. Not only have I translated for my parents as a young child, but for strangers who were Spanish speaking. To me, translating for my parents was a customary practice that I thought most children did.
>
> —L. G., Latina elementary school teacher

To date, the relationship between language brokers' age and developmental outcomes has not been investigated. Maturational factors associated with childhood and adolescent development may have implications for the kinds of language-brokering activities Latino children perform, and their relationship to outcome variables. The following section of this chapter presents cross-sectional data for Latino children at three age groups: elementary, middle, and high school. We performed analyses intended to reveal any developmental trends that may exist between the three age groups involving language-brokering activities and their relationship to parent-child bonding and depression. The analytic plan involved two steps. First, chi square analyses were used to investigate age related differences in the frequency with which children performed language-brokering activities involving different people, places, and things. Second, for each age group, Pearson correlations were computed between the four language-brokering dimensions (person, places, things, and feelings), and parent-child bonding and depression.

The participants in this age-related analysis were first and second generation Latino students attending public school in Southern California. Only students who reported language brokering for their parents or another party were included in the study. Data were collected from three age groups: 59 elementary school students in the fourth and fifth grades (26 boys/33 girls); 192 middle school students in the seventh and eighth grades (78 boys/114 girls); and 146 high school students in the ninth and tenth grades (58 boys/88 girls). All the children were administered the same language-brokering scale and parent-child bonding scale used by Buriel and colleagues in previous research.

The language-brokering measure consisted of four subscales. The *people* subscale measured the different people for which the students brokered. The *places* subscale measured the different places where the students brokered. The *things* subscale measured the different types of things that students brokered. The *feelings* subscale measured how students felt about brokering. In addition, an age-appropriate measure of depression was administered. Elementary school students received the Reynolds Child Depression Scale (Reynolds, 1989); middle school students received the Children's Depression Inventory (Kovacs, 1985); high school students received the Wareheit Depression Scale (Warheit, Hozer, & Arey, 1974; Warheit, Holzer, & Schwab, 1973).

Chi-square analyses were used to investigate age-related differences in the frequency with which children language brokered for different people, places, and things. Figures 4.1, 4.2, and 4.3 present graphic representations of the findings.

A summary of the results for the People translated for is as follows:

1. Elementary school age children: Translate/interpret more for friends, people at the door, and store employees. They interpret/translate less for parents and strangers.
2. Middle school age children: Translate/interpret more for parents and strangers.
3. High school age children: Translate/interpret more for parents and strangers than elementary school age children, but less than middle school age children.

More elementary school age children language broker for parties other than their parents and strangers. Furthermore, these young children language broker for teachers and school personnel at the same rate as middle and high school students. Thus, at a young age, many Latino children have experience language brokering for a diversity of people.

Language brokering for parents and strangers increases significantly between elementary and middle school age children. Except for parents and strangers, there is no difference between middle and high school age children in their rates of language brokering for different parties. The findings suggest that, in general, the rates of language brokering for different parties does not increase after middle school age for Latino children. A glance at Figure 4.1 shows that for children of all three age groups, language brokering is highest for non-parent relatives. This suggests that from an early age children are expected to use their language-brokering skills for the benefit of their extended *familia*. Moreover, it is likely that some of this extended *familia* includes fictive kin, as described in the following quote concerning a Latina college graduate: "Erandi willingly helped her mother, but in addition, she translated for

Figure 4.1
Developmental Trends for *People* Translated

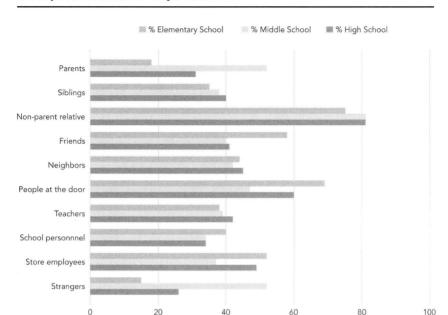

other adults in her community who were adopted 'uncles' " (Cabrera & Padilla, 2004, p. 107).

Figure 4.2 presents the findings for the different places where children language broker. It is evident that in the present sample, 50 percent or more children of all three age groups language broker at home, at school, and at the doctor's office. There are slight, non-significant trends for more children translating/interpreting at hospitals and government offices as they get older. There were three significant differences between the different age groups. More high school age students reported language brokering at school, at stores, and on the street than members of the other two age groups. The overall picture that emerges is that more children language broker at the two places where they spend most of their time, namely home and school. Another observation is that approximately forty percent or more of Latino children of all three age groups language broker in medical settings.

Figure 4.3 presents the findings for things translated. When examining the frequency with which the three age groups translated various things, notes from school and things over the phone were reported most often. Over 60 percent of students of all three age groups reported translating these two things. Chi-square analyses revealed that elementary school

Figure 4.2
Developmental Trends for *Places* Translated

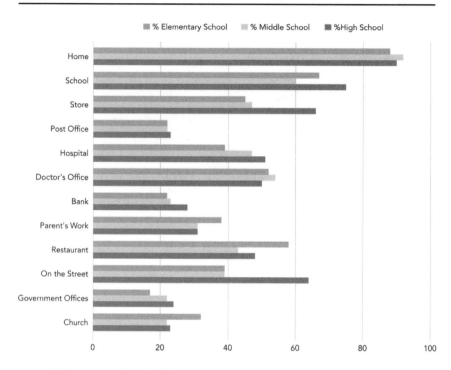

age children translated things at the door (e.g., informational or sales flyers and messages from solicitors) significantly more often than middle and high school age children. High school age children translated telephone bills significantly more often than both elementary and middle school age children. Both middle and high school age children translated credit card bills, insurance forms, bank statements, immigration forms, and job applications more often than elementary school age children.

The findings for things translated present the most evident age-related trends for language brokering. Unlike people and places, the things one translates can more reliably be placed on a continuum of activities requiring increasing literacy and cognitive complexity. Translating credit card bills, bank statements, immigration forms, and job applications usually involves more sophisticated vocabulary and cognitive understanding than what is typically required for notes from school and things over the phone. Because vocabulary and cognitive development increase with age it is to be expected that parents more often involve older children in the translation of complex documents. Our findings strongly suggest that Latino

Figure 4.3
Developmental Trends for *Things* Translated

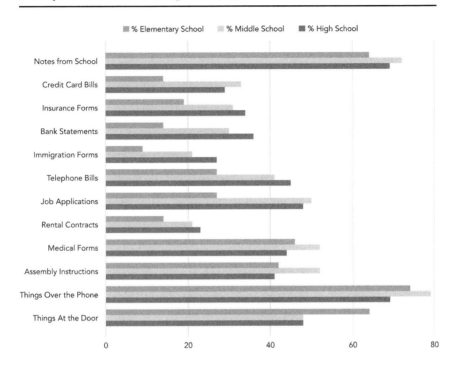

parents understand their children's age-related cognitive abilities, and take them into account when assigning language-brokering activities. This awareness may represent a parental folk theory of child development that is culturally based, and which has been transmitted over many generations of child rearing.

Scores for parent-child bonding and depression were correlated with the four language-brokering dimensions for each age group. These results are presented in Table 4.1. For elementary school age children, parent-child bonding was positively related to the language-brokering dimensions of people, places, and feelings. There was no association between any of the language-brokering dimensions and depression. Among middle school age children, parent-child bonding was positively related to the language-brokering dimensions of places and feelings. In addition, the language-brokering dimension of people was positively related to depression. Among high school age children, parent-child bonding was positively correlated with the language-brokering dimensions of places and feelings. In addition, the language-brokering dimension of things was positively associated with depression.

Table 4.1
Correlations of Parent-Child Bonding and Depression to Language Brokering by Age Group

Age Group	Variable	People	Places	Things	Feelings
Elementary	Bonding	.30**	.27*	.02	.45***
	Depression	.07	.11	.06	−.03
Middle School	Bonding	.06	.13*	.04	.26***
	Depression	.17**	.06	.10	.05
High School	Bonding	.10	.21*	.12	.37**
	Depression	.16	.16	.22**	−.03

$**p < .05$,
$**p < .01$,
$***p < .001$.

Overall, there is a strong positive association between language-brokering feelings and parent-child bonding among the Latino children of all three age groups. It is interesting to note that the language-brokering dimension of things is unrelated to parent-child bonding for any of the three age groups. Perhaps the more impersonal nature of things that are translated adds nothing to the emotional bond between parent and child that is formed in the language-brokering relationship. It is notable, that the language-brokering dimension of places is positively related to parent-child bonding for all three age groups. If parents take children with them to more places for the purposes of language brokering, the added time spent with each other may strengthen the bond between them. Moreover, it is through language brokering in diverse settings that children learn more personal information about the sacrifices their parents have made to in order to make a life for their families in this country. Being privy to this information has repeatedly been reported as a reason for the gratitude language brokers feel for their parents (De Ment et al., 2005).

There was no relation of any of the language-brokering dimensions to depression for elementary school age children. For middle school age children, the language-brokering dimension of people was positively correlated with depression. Among high school age children, the language-brokering dimension of things was positively associated with depression. Perhaps elementary school age children consider language brokering a privilege for someone of their age, which lessens any stress connected with this activity. In addition, parents' folk theory of child development may restrict these children's language-brokering activities to less stressful activities. Middle school age is a time when children seek greater independence from parents. Yet it is at this age group that more Latino children language broker more for their parents (see Figure 4.1). This conflict between the desire for greater independence and more parentally related language brokering may lead to more stress among members of this age group. As already noted, middle and high school age children translate more difficult things than elementary school age children. Translating these documents requires more intense concentration and time. For high school age children, translating documents may be a greater source of stress because it competes with other time intensive activities associated with this age group such as more rigorous homework, extra curricular school activities, and after school jobs. Routine language brokering for parents and others is much less time consuming and difficult than working on mortgage loan documents and immigration papers, which can take weeks and months to complete (De Ment et al., 2005).

CONCLUSION AND FUTURE DIRECTIONS

Language brokering is very common among children of Latino immigrants. On average, children begin language brokering by age 10, and in some cases earlier, and often continue in this role into adulthood. Many children see language brokering as an ordinary part of family life, much like caring for younger siblings or helping parents at their work. Language brokering appears to strengthen the parent-child bond, which may lessen the stress associated with this role. Under age-appropriate circumstances, language brokering may contribute to children's linguistic and cognitive development, and in turn, to their academic performance. Although many children report feeling uncomfortable at times while language brokering, most report that is a satisfying and personally rewarding experience.

To the present, the research by Dorner, Orellana, and Li-Grining (2007), is the only longitudinal work on language brokering. There is a pressing need for comprehensive longitudinal research on language brokering that can address and clarify important developmental issues. Among these issues are the cumulative effects of language brokering on children's cognitive and social-emotional development, and its impact on their overall adjustment and well-being. Longitudinal research could also help explain the role of gender in how children are selected as language brokers, and why some individuals continue in this role through adulthood.

With rare exception (Martinez et al., 2009; Love, 2006), research on language brokering with Latinos has taken place in traditional immigrant gateway cities and communities of the southwest. Such gateway areas have long-standing Latino communities with extensive social networks for newcomers, and cultural resources such as Spanish speaking personnel in businesses, government offices, and medical settings. The presence of such networks and resources may reduce the range of people, places, and things requiring children's language brokering, and thus mitigate some of the stress connected with their role. Today, however, there are areas in the southeast part of the country that, for the first time in their history, are experiencing large numbers of Latino immigrants. For example, between 1990 and 2000, the Latino school age population (ages 5–17) grew by 322 percent across five southern states, due primarily to the arrival of new immigrants (Kochhar, Suro, & Tafoya, 2005). Because these new Latino settlements lack the extensive social networks and cultural resources of long-standing immigrant gateway communities, there may be a greater need for children to serve as language brokers. Moreover, southern Americans' unfamiliarity with Latinos, and competition for jobs, may create a prejudicial social climate that intensifies any stress connecting to language brokering. There is a need for research in the new Latino south to better understand how children cope with language brokering, and other settlement activities they perform for their families (Perreira, Chapman, & Stein, 2006). This research should aim to promote social policies that help language brokers overcome the challenges they face, and to identify cultural strengths in immigrant Latino families that contribute to their children's healthy development.

NOTE

1. Despite the fact that language brokering is multidimensional and complex, some of the emerging research in this area uses only a single question or a small number of general questions to assess the level of language-brokering activity. Language brokering involves a variety of people, in different places, and many things. Moreover, there are feelings connected directly to language brokering for people, places, and things. In general, someone may feel good about language brokering for parents, but uncomfortable with doing so in certain settings. The multidimensional nature of language brokering needs to be measured in order to prevent overgeneralizations based on only one or a few undifferentiated questions assessing this behavior. A growing body of literature is also revealing that the different dimensions of language brokering are selectively related to theoretically important outcome variables. Thus, among Latino high school students, the places where one language brokers is related to academic grade point average (Buriel et al., 1998), whereas feelings about language brokering is related to parent-child bonding (Buriel et al., 2006). The distinct dimensions of language brokering involve different social, emotional, and cognitive mechanisms that have implications for how language brokering is described, and the nature of its relationship to other variables of interest.

REFERENCES

Anguiano, R. M. (2007, April). The effects of language brokering on academic self-efficacy, familial self-efficacy, and peer social self-efficacy. In J. A. Love (Chair), *Socio emotional and cognitive aspect of Language brokering among Latino adolescents.* Paper presented at the meeting of the Society for Research in Child Development, Boston, MA.

Athey, J. L., & Ahearn, F. L. (1991). The mental health of refugee children: An overview. In J. L. Athey & F. L. Ahearn (Eds.), *Refugee children: Theory, research and services* (pp. 1–19). Baltimore: The John Hopkins University Press.

Baptiste, D. A. (1993). Immigrant families, adolescents and acculturation: Insights for therapists. *Marriage & Family Review 19,* 341–346.

Buriel, R. (1993a). Acculturation, respect for cultural differences, and biculturalism among three generations of Mexican American and Euro American school children. *The Journal of Genetic Psychology 154,* 531–543.

Buriel, R. (1993b). Childrearing orientations in Mexican American families: The Influence of generation and sociocultural factors. *The Journal of Marriage and the Family 55,* 987–1000.

Buriel, R., Love, J. A., & De Ment, T. L. (2006). The relationship of language brokering to depression and parent-child bonding among Latino adolescents. In M. H. Bornstein & L. R. Cote (Eds.), *Acculturation and parent-child relationships* (pp. 249–270). Mahwah, NJ: Lawrence Erlbaum.

Buriel, R., DeMent, T., Perez, W., Chavez, D. V., & Moran, V. R. (1998). The relationship of language brokering to academic performance, biculturalism and self-efficacy among Latino adolescents. *Hispanic Journal of Behavioral Sciences 20,* 283–297.

Cabrera, N. L., & Padilla, A. M. (2004). Entering and succeeding in the "Culture of College": The story of two Mexican heritage students. *Hispanic Journal of Behavioral Sciences 26,* 152–170.

Castañeda, A. I. (1996). Language and other lethal weapons: Cultural politics and the rites of children as translators of culture. In A. V. Gordon & C. Newfield (Eds.), *Mapping multiculturalism* (pp. 201–214). Minneapolis, MN: University of Minnesota Press.

Chao, R. K. (2006). The prevalence and consequences of adolescents' language brokering for their immigrant parents. In M. H. Bornstein & L. R. Cote (Eds.), *Acculturation and parent-child relationships* (pp. 271–296). Mahwah, NJ: Lawrence Erlbaum.

Child, I. (1943). *Italian or American? The second generation in conflict.* New Haven, CT: Yale University Press.

Cubberley, E. P. (1909). *The changing conceptions of education.* Boston, MA: Houghton.

Delgado-Gaitan, C. (1992). Socializing young children in Mexican American families: An intergenerational perspective. In P. M. Greenfield & R. R.

Cocking (Eds.), *Cross-cultural roots of minority child development* (pp. 55–86). Mahwah, NJ: Lawrence Erlbaum.

DeMent, T., Buriel, R., & Villanueva, C. (2005). Children as language brokers: A narrative of the recollections of college students. In R. Hoosain & F. Salili (Eds.). *Language in multicultural education* (pp. 255–272). Greenwich, CT: Information Age.

Diaz-Lazaro, C. M. (2002). *The effects of language brokering on perceptions of family authority structures, problem solving abilities, and parental locus of control in Latino adolescents and their parents.* Unpublished doctoral dissertation, Graduate School of the State University of New York at Buffalo.

Dorner, L. M., Orellana, M. F., & Li-Grining, C. P. (2007). I helped my mom and it helped me: Translating the skills of language brokers into improved standardized test scores. *American Journal of Education 113*, 451–478.

Fry, R., & Passel, J. S. (2009). *Latino children: A majority are U.S.-born offspring of immigrants.* Report: Pew Hispanic Center. Washington, DC: Pew Research Center.

Fuligni, A. J., Tseng, V., & Lam, M. (1999). Attitudes toward family obligations among American adolescents with Asian, Latin American, and European backgrounds. *Child Development 70*, 1031–1044.

Ginsberg, T. (2003). Shouldering a language burden in immigrant families: Children's roles as interpreters full of pressures, peril. *Philadelphia Inquirer*, pp. A1–A11.

Hardy-Fanta, C., & Montana, P. (1982). The Hispanic female adolescent: A group therapy model. *Journal of Group Psychotherapy 32*, 351–366.

Heath, S. B. (1986). Sociocultural contexts of language development. *Beyond language: Social and cultural factors in schooling language minority students* (pp. 143–186). Los Angeles: California State University, Los Angeles, Evaluation Dissemination and Assessment Center.

Hernandez, D. J., Denton, N. A., & Macartney, S. E. (2008). *Children in immigrant families: Looking to America's future.* Social Policy Report, Society for research in Child Development. Ann Arbor, MI.

Hovey, J. D., & King, C. A. (1996). Acculturative stress, depression, and suicidal ideation among immigrant and second-generation Latino adolescents. *Journal of the American Academy of Child and Adolescent Psychiatry 35*, 1183–1192.

Jurkovic, G. J., Morell, R., & Thirkield, A. (1999). Assessing childhood parentification. In N. D. Chase (Ed.), *Burdened children: Theory, research, and treatment of parentification* (pp. 92–109). London, England: Sage Publications.

Kochhar, R., Suro, R., & Tafoya, S. (2005). *The New Latino South: The context and consequences of rapid population growth.* Report. Pew Hispanic Center. Washington, DC: Pew Research Center.

Kovacs, M. (1985). The Children's Depression Inventory (CDI). *Psychopharmacology Bulletin 21*, 995–998.

Love, J. A. (2006). *Theory of mind ability in the preadolescent language broker: Connections between language brokering, social cognition, and academic achievement.* Unpublished doctoral dissertation, Claremont Graduate University, Claremont CA.

Love, J. A., & Buriel, R. (2007). Language brokering, autonomy, parent-child bonding, biculturalism, and depression: A study of Mexican American adolescents from immigrant families. *Hispanic Journal of Behavioral Sciences 29*, 472–491.

Martinez, C. R., Jr., McClure, H. H., & Eddy, J. M. (2009). Language brokering contexts and behavioral and emotional adjustment among Latino parents and adolescents. *Journal of Early Adolescence 29*, 71–98.

McQuillan, J., & Tse, L. (1995). Child language brokering in linguistic minority communities: Effect of cultural interaction, cognition and literacy. *Language and Education 9*, 195–215.

Mercado, V. (2003). *Effects of language brokering on children of Latino immigrants.* Unpublished doctoral dissertation, pace University, New York.

Morales, A., & Hanson, W. E. (2005). Language brokering: An integrative review of the literature. *Hispanic Journal of Behavioral Sciences 27*, 471–503.

Padilla, A. M., & Lindholm, K. J. (1984). Child bilingualism: The same old issues revisited. In J. L. Martinez, & R. H. Mendoza (Eds.), *Chicano psychology, 2nd edition* (pp. 369–408). Orlando, FL: Academic Press.

Park, R. E. (1928). Human migration and the marginal man. *American Journal of Sociology 33*, 881–893.

Perreira, K. M., Chapman, M. V., & Stein. G. L. (2006). Becoming an American parent: Overcoming challenges and finding strength in a new immigrant Latino community. *Journal of family Issues 27*, 1383–1414.

Portes, A., & Rumbaut, R. G. (1990). *Immigrant America.* Berkeley, CA: University of California Press.

Reynolds, W. M. (1989). *Reynolds child depression scale (about me).* Psychological Assessment Resources, Inc., Odessa, FL.

Roer-Strier, D., & Rivlis, M. (1998). Timetable of psychological and behavioral autonomy expectations among parents from Israel and the former Soviet Union. *International Journal of Psychology 33*, 123–135.

Rogoff, B. (2003). *The cultural nature of human development.* New York: Oxford University Press.

Santiago, S. (2003). Language brokering: A personal experience. In M. Coleman & L. H. Ganong (Eds.), *Points and counterpoints: Controversial relationship and family issues in the 21st century: An anthology* (pp. 160–161). Los Angeles: Roxbury.

Shannon, S. M. (1990). English in the barrio: The quality of contact among immigrant children. *Hispanic Journal of Behavioral Sciences 12*, 256–276.

Stonequist, E. V. (1937). *The marginal man: A study in personality and culture conflict.* New York: Russell & Russell, 1961.

Suro, R. (2005). *Attitudes about immigration and major demographic characteristics.* Survey of Mexican Immigrants: Part one. Pew Hispanic Center. Washington, DC: Pew Research Center.

Sy, S. R. (2006). Family and work influences on the transition to college among Latina adolescents. *Hispanic Journal of Behavioral Sciences 28*, 368–386.

Tse, L. (1995). Language brokering among Latino adolescents: Prevalence, attitudes, and school performance. *Hispanic Journal of Behavioral Sciences 17*, 180–193.

Umana-Taylor, A. (2003). Language brokering as a stressor for immigrant children and their families. In M. Coleman & L. Ganong (Eds.), *Points and counterpoints: Controversial relationship and family issues in the 21st century: An anthology* (pp. 157–159). Los Angeles, Roxbury.

Valdez, G. (2003). *Expanding definitions of giftedness: The case of young interpreters from immigrant communities*. New Jersey: Lawrence Erlbaum Associates.

Valenzuela, A., Jr. (1999). Gender roles and settlement activities among children and their immigrant families. *American Behavioral Scientist 42*, 720–742.

Villanueva, C. M., & Buriel, R. (2010). Speaking on behalf of others: A qualitative study of the perceptions and feelings of Latina language brokers. *The Journal of Social Issues 66*, 197–210.

Warheit, G. J., Holzer, C. E., & Arey, S. A. (1974). Race and mental illness: An epidemiologic update. *Journal of Health and Social Behavior 16*, 243–256.

Warheit, G. J., Holzer, C. E., & Schwab, J. (1973). An analysis of social class and racial difference in depressive symptomatology: A community study. *Journal of Health and Social Behavior 4*, 291–299.

Weisskirch, R. S. (2005). The relationship of language brokering to ethnic identity for Latino early adolescents. *Hispanic Journal of Behavioral Sciences 27*, 286–299.

Weisskirch, R. S. (2007). Feelings about language brokering and family relationships among Mexican American early adolescents. *Hispanic Journal of Behavioral Sciences 27*, 545–561.

Weisskirch, R. S., & Alva, S. A. (2002). Language brokering and the acculturation of Latino children. *Hispanic Journal of Behavioral Sciences 24*, 369–378.

Zelizer, V. A. (1985). *Pricing the priceless: The changing social value of children*. New York: Basic Books.

Chapter 5

PEER RELATIONS OF LATINA/O CHILDREN IN MIDWEST U.S. ELEMENTARY SCHOOLS

Travis Wilson and Philip C. Rodkin*

The peer relations field has lagged far behind others in studying Latino children despite frequent calls to increase attention to diversity. Research has primarily studied White, middle class samples and—at a distant second—African American children (Graham, Taylor, & Ho, 2009). There are compelling reasons to increase scholarship on Latino children. First, there is wide variation in the peer relations of Latino children themselves. Latino sub-populations have varied histories of immigration, colonization, and acculturation that manifest different patterns of socialization in the United States. Likewise, Latino students attend a variety of schools—public, parochial, ethnically diverse, and homogeneous—that offer different social environments and different pedagogical approaches to address racial and ethnic diversity. Nuanced understandings of Latino children's social experiences will better inform policy and practice regarding the betterment of Latino children's adjustment at school. Second, as Latino children form an increasing presence in American society, they are reshaping the social landscapes of schools and neighborhoods. In many locales, the Black-White dichotomy of the integrated school has been replaced by a multi-cultural dynamic that features complex intergroup relations.

*This research was supported by grants to the second author from the *Eunice Kennedy Shriver* National Institute of Child Health and Human Development (R03 HD48491-01) and the Spencer Foundation (Small Grant #20050079).

Knowledge of how Latino children feel about and engage in their peer relationships is necessary to develop a deeper understanding of today's diverse schools. In short, gaining knowledge about Latino children's peer relations is a critical goal in its own right, but advances in this area also promise to reshape thinking about child development more broadly.

The purposes of this chapter are twofold: (1) to provide a review of the peer relations literature on Latino children, with a focus on friendships, social status, aggressive behavior, and peer victimization at school; and (2) to identity new directions for future research—for Latino children in particular and, by extension, the peer relations field in general. Part one reviews the contemporary literature on Latino children vis-à-vis the mainstream corpus of peer relations research. Where relevant, discussion elaborates (or postulates) how country of origin, generation of immigration, socioeconomic status, and geographical location—though often overlooked—are key sources of variability (Azmitia, Ittel, & Brenk, 2006). Part two presents an empirical analysis of a modest sample of Latino children in a small city in the Midwest. Because most research on Latino children is conducted in places where Latino families represent a substantial portion of the population, it is hoped that a portrayal of Latino children in this predominantly bicultural (i.e., European American and African American) setting will stimulate new thinking about Latino children's development.

PART ONE: A REVIEW OF CONTEMPORARY
RESEARCH ON LATINO CHILDREN

Friendships within and across Ethnic Groups in School Settings

Perhaps in no other period of the lifespan are friendships more central to development than during childhood. Marked by responsivity, similarity, and coordination of behavior, friendships shape and give meaning to children's social experiences (Bukowski, Motzoi, & Meyer, 2009). How might the friendships of Latino children serve their unique developmental needs for social cooperation and academic engagement? How are Latino children's friendship patterns responsive to cross-ethnic contact? The answers to these questions offer a view into how Latino children navigate their social worlds at home and school in today's diversifying landscapes.

Friendships and Social Adjustment

Friends offer positive regard, companionship, and intimacy—in short, they give each other a sense of validation (Sullivan, 1953). Children who have close friendships (versus those who do not) are more self-confident

(Hartup, 1996), perform better academically (Berndt, Hawkins, & Hoyle, 1986), and have greater access to other social resources (Lempers & Clark-Lempers, 1992). Friendships also protect children against negative outcomes, including depression and loneliness (Parker & Asher, 1993), peer victimization (Hodges, Malone, & Perry, 1997), and externalizing difficulties (Criss, Pettit, Bates, Dodge, & Lapp, 2002).

Latino children's friendships afford additional benefits. For recent Latino immigrants, friendships ease the stresses of acculturation that challenge family dynamics (Suarez-Orozco & Todorova, 2003). For low-income urban Latino youth, friendships often materialize into "fictive kinships" that blend peer and family ties; this integration of networks at times helps children transcend low levels of social trust in their communities brought on by ecological stressors (Way, 2006; Way, Gingold, Rotenberg, & Kuriakose, 2005). Indeed, the Latino adolescents in Way and colleagues' (2005) qualitative study valued qualities in their friendships akin to family interdependence, or *familism*: sharing money and secrets, protection from physical and emotional harm, and reciprocal aid in matters from homework to babysitting. Latinos' peer relationships also serve important roles in bridging the worlds of family and school—perhaps another effect of a *familism* orientation toward friendships (Cooper, Cooper, Azmitia, Chavira, & Gullat, 2002).

But do the qualities of Latino children's friendships depend on who is available in the social setting? Given that Latino children attend an array of schools with different ethnic compositions, an important new direction for research will be to study how the quality and patterns of Latino children's friendships vary across school contexts. Recent work in political science (Putnam, 2007) offers the provocative claim that despite the many potential benefits of social diversity, living in more diverse settings actually leads to less interpersonal connection. Aptly termed "hunkering down," this phenomenon signals that both "bonding" social capital (i.e., ties to the in-group) and "bridging" social capital (i.e., ties to out-groups) can suffer for years in the face of increasing diversity as society matures (Putnam, 2007, p. 144). Yet to be explored is whether Latino children "hunker down" in the presence of more cross-ethnicity peers in the classroom or school. If so, reductions in social capital would likely be accompanied by other social and academic costs, perhaps more so for children who live in families with low human capital.

Friendship and Academic Adjustment

Children's friendships impact multiple dimensions of academic functioning, including motivation, cognitive development, and achievement. At a basic level, friendship provides a contextual affordance for academic success (Wentzel, 2009): Simply having friends at school is associated with positive classroom engagement (Ladd, 1990) and academic achievement (Wentzel, Barry, & Caldwell, 2004). Friendships serve as direct agents of socialization, too. Students select friends and peer groups with similar motivational orientations (Kindermann, 1993), who, in turn, provide models for academic self-efficacy (Crockett, Losoff, & Petersen, 1984). It is not just having friends—but also *who* your friends are—that matters.

Scholarship has provided mixed evidence as to how friendships and other peer affiliations affect school outcomes for Latino students. Some research has found that peer support and peer belonging contribute positively to Latinos' academic resilience and valuing school (Gonzalez & Padilla, 1997), school engagement (Garcia-Reid, Reid, & Peterson, 2005), and school connectedness (Loukas, Suzuki, & Horton, 2006). Other research, however, has detected no links between peer affiliations and school outcomes (Alfaro, Umana-Taylor, & Bamaca, 2006; DeGarmo & Martinez, 2006). Greater clarity is needed, particularly regarding how peers influence Latinos differentially by SES, generational status, and gender. Developmental models that incorporate culturally relevant factors (i.e., "place culture at the center") are critical to addressing these questions (Raffaelli, Carlo, Carranza, & Gonzalez-Kruger, 2005).

One recent study implemented a culturally relevant model to assess the direct and indirect influences of teachers, family, and friends on Latino middle school students' academic success (Woolley, Kohl, & Bowen, 2009). Drawing upon an ecological framework (Bronfenbrenner, 1979) and social capital theory (Coleman, 1988), the authors postulated a model that considered how Latino family values (i.e., *familism*, *respeto*, and *educación*) conjoin with peer associations to impact students' behavior and academic outcomes. Parent support and parent education monitoring were positively correlated with friend support, consistent with the view that Latino students appropriate *familism* values (emphases on loyalty, interconnectedness, and mutual responsibility) into their peer relationships. In turn, friendship support, via pathways through teacher support and school behavior, was positively associated with higher grades and more time spent on homework. The authors concluded that "the support students receive from teachers engages and enhances the support they receive from parents and friends" (Woolley et al., 2009, pp. 64–65). This study underscores the importance of considering how relevant cultural factors, such as emphases on respect for adults and interpersonal skills, act concomitantly via parents, teachers, and peers to impact academic outcomes for Latino students.

Cultural factors may affect Latino boys and girls in different ways. Latino boys, in particular, may face unique challenges for sustaining academic motivation. A recent study of Latino and African American students' achievement values indicated that Latino (as well as African American) boys are less likely than their female counterparts to value achievement as they move from elementary school into middle school (Taylor & Graham, 2007). Taylor and Graham (2007) surveyed 615 Latino and African American boys and girls in second, fourth, and seventh grades. Second- and fourth-grade boys and girls of both ethnic groups disproportionately nominated high- or average-achieving same-gender peers as the classmates they most admired. However, whereas seventh-grade girls of both ethnic groups disproportionately valued high- and average-achieving same-gender peers, Latino and African American boys valued low-achievers more. The authors concluded that it is not until middle school that minority boys begin "to look more admiringly on less academically inclined peers" (Taylor & Graham, 2007, p. 60). All of this suggests that for Latino boys on the cusp of adolescence, wise selections for friendships and peer groups may be a critical factor for establishing positive, resilient academic trajectories.

Cross-Ethnic Relations

Since the U.S. Civil Rights era and the desegregation of schools, scholars have generated a wealth of knowledge about children's cross-ethnic relations. Most of this research has focused exclusively on African American and White youth, although recent attention has included Latino samples as well (e.g., Hamm, Brown, Heck, 2005; Mouw & Entwisle, 2006; Quillian & Campbell, 2003). Three salient patterns have endured: (1) children generally prefer same-ethnicity to cross-ethnicity friendships, although rates vary by the ethnic compositions of classrooms and schools (Hallinan & Teixeira, 1987; Moody, 2001; Rodkin, Wilson, & Ahn, 2007; Wilson & Rodkin, in press); (2) same-ethnicity friendships tend to be of higher quality than cross-ethnicity friendships (Aboud, Mendelson, & Purdy, 2003; Kao & Joyner, 2004); and (3) friendship choices that cross ethnic boundaries come with psychological benefits and costs (Bellmore, Nishina, Witkow, Graham, & Juvonen, 2007; Kawabata & Crick, 2008; Lease & Blake, 2005).

Less than 50 percent of United States children have a friend of another racial group (DuBois & Hirsch, 1990), and the frequency of cross-race friendship typically declines as children get older (Hallinan & Teixeira, 1987; Shrum, Cheek, & Hunter, 1988). Some evidence indicates that Latino and African American children have more segregated relationships than do White children (Kawabata & Crick, 2008), supporting the view that ethnic minority children's same-ethnicity friendships satisfy needs for an emerging ethnic identity (Tatum, 2003). Moreover, Latino and African American students form cross-ethnicity relationships with each other more than with their White or Asian peers (Hamm, Brown, & Heck, 2005), suggesting that the common experience of being a marginalized ethnic group is a source of bonding. To be sure, research on Latino children's cross-ethnicity friendship is limited in scope and largely bound to traditional (i.e., Black-White) conceptual frameworks; as a consequence, potential sub-group differences and other culturally relevant effects are too often masked or ignored.

In contrast, recent work on adolescents has incorporated culturally relevant constructs to study the integration patterns of older students (Mouw & Entwisle, 2006; Quillian & Campbell, 2003). Drawing from the Longitudinal Study of Adolescent Health, a representative sample of all students in the United States in grades seven to 12, Quillian and Campbell (2003) examined how three factors influence Latino (the authors use the term "Hispanic") adolescents' friendship segregation: generational status, racial categorization (i.e., do "White" and "Black" Hispanics differ?), and school racial composition. Results confirmed ethnic segregation was the norm for Hispanics, but no difference between first-, second-, and third-generation immigrants emerged. Second, White and Black Hispanics evidenced diverging integration patterns. As the authors concluded, "[W]hite Hispanics and Black Hispanics are being incorporated into White and Black friendship circles, respectively, with Hispanic origin as an important secondary influence" (Quillian & Campbell, 2003, p. 554). Last, Hispanics' segregation was strongest in schools where they were small racial minorities. These results held true after controlling for parental socioeconomic status. Considering the whole of their findings, the authors promote policies that maintain more racially balanced schools where the intensification of homophily is less likely to occur. An important new direction for research will be to apply Quillian and Campbell's (2003) questions to Latino students in middle childhood, when social competencies burgeon.

Another question yet to be explored is whether peer ecologies reinforce segregation behavior among Latino children: Do Latino children value peers who have many positive cross-ethnicity relationships and few negative cross-ethnicity relationships? Studies with predominantly African American and European samples reveal mixed evidence. In some cases, Black and White children who have integrated social relationships are particularly well adjusted, and have reputations as influential class leaders

(Kawabata & Crick, 2008; Lease & Blake, 2005). Other studies have found positive associations between children's preference for same-ethnicity peers and their own acceptance by same-ethnicity peers—in other words, that children with more segregated relationships enjoy higher social status within their ethnic group (Bellmore et al., 2007; Castelli, De Amicis, & Sherman, 2007). But do elementary school peer ecologies support or challenge segregation behavior among Latino children? The answers to this question will stimulate new thinking about how Latino children learn to navigate an increasingly heterogeneous society.

Social Status

Two Types of Social Status

If middle childhood engenders a tension between the needs for social connectedness and social status, then researchers have been equally challenged to describe what social status means and how children attain it. Traditional measures of children's social status have focused on sociometric popularity, or social preference—that is, the extent to which children are nominated by peers as "someone I like the most" as opposed to "someone I like the least" (e.g., Coie, Dodge, & Coppotelli, 1982). More recent empirical studies have identified a second type of social status, perceived popularity, a measure of social power and influence (e.g., LaFontana & Cillessen, 1998; Parkhurst & Hopmeyer, 1998). The two types of social status are conceptually distinct and have different behavioral profiles. A child can like another without perceiving him or her to be generally popular, just as a child can perceive another to be popular without feelings of personal affection, and possibly even with feelings of personal dislike (Adler & Adler, 1998). Whereas social preference expresses a personal sentiment (i.e., who do *you* like?), perceived popularity represents a judgment about what others value and the consensual norms of the peer ecology (Hartup & Abecassis, 2002). And whereas social preference is positively associated with prosocial characteristics and negatively associated with aggressive characteristics, perceived popularity has only modest (in some cases positive, in other cases negative) correlations with aggression (Cillessen & Rose, 2005; Parkhurst & Hopmeyer, 1998).

The development of this strand of the peer relations literature—social status and its behavioral correlates—has emerged from studies with predominantly European American and, to a lesser extent, African American children (e.g., Rodkin et al., 2000; Rodkin et al., 2006). Are the peer ecologies of Latino children also characterized by such clear distinctions between social preference and perceived popularity? If so, do some highly popular Latino children also exhibit aggressive behavior, as evidenced in other samples? Answers to these questions will offer a glimpse into the values promoted by the peer culture of Latino children as they interface with other ethnic groups in today's schools.

One important question that has received attention is how ethnic context moderates social status for Latino children. Bellmore and colleagues (2007) surveyed Latino, Asian, White, and African American students in sixth grade. The authors examined the degree to which students of different ethnic groups nominated same-ethnicity (versus cross-ethnicity) peers for acceptance (i.e., "like to hang around with"), rejection (i.e., "do not like to hang around with"), and perceived coolness (i.e., "the coolest kids"). Whereas African American students demonstrated a global bias to nominate same-ethnicity peers for all three items, Latino children (as well as White and Asian children) disproportionately nominated same-ethnicity peers for the acceptance and cool items but not for the rejected item. Additionally, students of all four ethnic groups were more accepted by same-ethnicity peers when they gave more acceptance nominations to same-ethnicity peers. This finding may simply be a residual of homophily—that children affiliate with children they like and, in turn, are more accepting of children with whom they affiliate. However, for the Latino students—and for this ethnic group only—in Bellmore and colleagues' (2007) study, the link between acceptance *of* and acceptance *by* same-ethnicity peers was stronger when they had fewer same-ethnicity peers in the classroom. This finding extends beyond homophily; rather, it signals that Latino children may value peers who demonstrate loyalty to the ingroup, particularly when they are numerically marginalized (see also Castelli, De Amicis, & Sherman, 2007). This study opens the door to other questions. Will these findings generalize from heterogeneous urban schools to less diverse settings where Latino children represent a much smaller minority? If so, what social costs (to Latino children and their cross-ethnicity peers alike) might accompany Latino children's rewarding of "loyal" same-ethnicity peers?

The prevailing use of sociometric methods has reflected an emphasis on children's *attainment* of social status. There is cause to look within the motivational system of the child as well—that is, to one's *striving* for social status. Research has identified distinct motivation orientations towards social competence among adolescents (Ryan & Shim, 2008) and children (Ryan, Rodkin, Jamison, & Wilson, 2009). Social development goals privilege the growth and improvement of one's social relationships. Social demonstration-approach goals focus on gaining positive evaluations from others. Social demonstration-avoid goals focus on avoiding negative evaluations from others. To date, not a single study has explicitly investigated the social goal orientations of Latino children, much less their associations with attained social status. An examination of Latino children's social goal orientations would offer a glimpse into the extent to which Latino children internalize cultural values such as familism into their strivings for social connectedness and social status among peers.

Peer Victimization and Aggression

A long history of scholarship on children's peer relations has painted a rich, intricate picture of many facets of children's social adjustment at school, including peer acceptance, academic engagement with peers, social withdrawal, and externalizing behavior, to name a few. To better complement other sections of this chapter, this section narrows the scope to (1) *peer victimization;* and (2) *antisocial behavior*, with a focus on aggression.

Peer Victimization

Peer victimization is characterized by the infliction of overt forms of aggression (e.g., hitting, threatening, taunting) and/or indirect forms of aggression (e.g., gossiping, social exclusion, spreading rumors) that cause psychological, relational, or physical harm. Peer victimization is a common experience during childhood: As many as one in five children suffer moderate to severe levels of peer abuse upon entering kindergarten, and victimization increases in frequency and stability throughout the elementary years before subsiding in adolescence (Kochenderfer & Ladd, 1996; Kochenderfer-Ladd, & Wardrop, 2001). The negative psychological effects of peer victimization have been extensively documented. Children who have been victimized by peers are significantly more likely to feel depressed and lonely (e.g., Boivin, Hymel, & Bukowski, 1995), to evidence suicidal ideation (Rigby, 1998), and to suffer school adjustment difficulties (e.g., Kochenderfer & Ladd, 1996).

Only a fraction of the abundance of studies on peer victimization has examined large numbers of Latino children (e.g., Baumann & Summers, 2009; Bellmore, Witkow, Graham, & Juvonen, 2004; Buhs, McGinley, & Toland, 2010; Graham, Bellmore, Nishina, & Juvonen, 2009; Hanish & Guerra, 2000; Hanish & Guerra, 2002; Juvonen, Nishina, & Graham, 2006), and scarcely few have directly measured the prevalence of victimization among Latino children (e.g., Baumann & Summers, 2009; Buhs,

McGinley, & Toland, 2010; Hanish & Guerra, 2000; Bellmore et al., 2004). Extant data indicates that compared to White children, Latino children evidence lower rates of victimization (Hanish & Guerra, 2000) and less severe symptoms of loneliness, anxiety, and depression when they are victimized (Baumann & Summers, 2009; Bellmore et al., 2004). Some scholars attribute the less severe patterns for victimization among Latino children to their having a more collectivistic and less competitive worldview (Baumann & Summers, 2009).

However, much depends on social context. Research indicates that the *levels* of victimization among Latino children vary by the ethnic composition of a classroom or school. With a sample of primarily Latino (46%) and African American (29%) middle school students, Juvonen and colleagues (2006) examined perceptions of school safety and peer victimization, loneliness, and self-worth as functions of school and classroom ethnic diversity. The authors found that students felt safer and less lonely, experienced less peer harassment, and exhibited higher self-worth the more ethnically diverse their classrooms and schools were. As this study indicates, having a shared numerical balance of power among ethnic groups clearly has benefits.

Recent studies have investigated the role of ethnic context in Latino children's *adjustment* to victimization as well (Bellmore et al., 2004; Graham, 2006; Graham et al., 2009; Hanish & Guerra, 2000). Bellmore and colleagues (2004) investigated 1630 sixth-grade students—including 751 Latinos—across 77 classrooms. In addition to the main effects that peer-reported victimization predicted stronger feelings of loneliness and social anxiety, the authors reported a critical individual x context interaction: Victims felt more lonely and anxious when there were more same-ethnicity peers in the classroom. Bellmore and colleagues (2004, p. 1170) surmised that having dual status as both a victim and a member of the group in numerical power promotes attributions for failure to the self ("It must be me") and discourages esteem-protecting attributions to external factors ("It must be them"); however, the authors did not measure attributions directly. In a follow-up study with mostly Latino (45%) and African American (26%) students, Graham and colleagues (2009) directly examined whether self-blaming attributions do in fact mediate victimization-maladjustment associations. Results were confirmatory: In more ethnically homogeneous settings, victimization predicted characterological self-blame for students of the ethnic majority, but not for students of the ethnic minority; characterological self-blame, in turn, predicted higher levels of maladjustment.

In sum, a limited number of studies indicates that Latino youth suffer from peer victimization at slightly lower rates than their White counterparts, but the experience of peer victimization is better depicted within an ethnicity-by-context framework: Whereas students who are in the ethnic *minority* may be at greater risk for being victimized, victimized students who are members of the ethnic *majority* may be particularly vulnerable to self-blaming attributions (see Graham, 2006, for an extensive analysis of the ethnic context of peer victimization). More research is needed to discern developmental patterns in how context moderates victimization. A positive step toward this end, one recent study offers measurements of overt and relational victimization that have equivalence across ethnic groups (Latinos and European Americans), gender, and grade level during early adolescence (Buhs, McGinley, & Toland, 2010).

Aggression and Antisocial Behavior

The study of childhood aggression notoriously defies simplification. Although aggressive children are typically disliked, they nonetheless form friendships and enter peer groups at similar rates as non-aggressive children (Bagwell, Coie, Terry, & Lochman, 2000; Cairns, Cairns, Neckerman, Gest, & Gariepy, 1988). The *quality* of aggressive children's relationships, however, tends to suffer; lower levels of positive qualities (e.g., closeness and intimacy; Grotpeter & Crick, 1996) and higher levels of conflict (Coie et al., 1999) are the norm. Aggressive children typically form liaisons with similarly aggressive peers who reinforce each other's behavior over time (Cairns et al., 1988); this pattern precipitates a dilemma: Acts of aggression can secure greater prominence within a network of peers (Xie et al., 2002), but persistent aggression is associated with a host of maladjustments, including poor academic performance (e.g., Ladd & Burgess, 2001) and later delinquent behavior (Moffitt, 1993).

For Latino children, family conditions play an integral—albeit complex—role in their social development. Given that a disproportionate number of Latino children live in economically disadvantaged communities—a reliable predictor for family stress and aggression in children (e.g., Conger & Conger, 1994)—it is not surprising that much research has focused on the destabilizing effects of economic hardship on Latino children's social behavior. Stated simply, as the number of environmental risk factors increases, levels of externalizing (and internalizing) problems in Latino children also increase (Loukas & Prelow, 2004). Having associations with other aggressive and deviant peers—a common experience for aggressive children—puts Latino youth at further risk for antisocial behavior and substance use (Barrera, Biglan, Ary, & Li, 2001).

Other dimensions of family life apart from socioeconomic status are also critical to Latino children's behavior, yet they remain understudied. Better parent-child relationship quality (Murray, 2009), maintenance of family routines (Loukas & Prelow, 2004), and higher levels of parent involvement (Davidson & Cardemil, 2009) all are associated with lower levels of externalizing behavior among Latino youth. A family characteristic especially relevant to Latino culture also has impact on Latino children's social behavior: *familism* values (e.g., Germán, Gonzales, & Dumka, 2009), a topic that deserves closer attention.

With a sample of 598 early adolescents of Mexican origin, Germán and colleagues (2009) investigated how students' and parents' endorsement of familism values moderate the association between students' having affiliations with deviant peers and their own levels of externalizing behavior. Results indicated that students' endorsement of familism values served as a buffer against exposure to deviant peers: Analyses evidenced a significant interaction between students' familism values and deviant peer affiliations on teacher reports of externalizing behavior. Additional effects were found for parents' endorsement of familism values. When parents endorsed familism values more, their children exhibited lower levels of externalizing behaviors and evidenced a weaker relation between deviant peer affiliations and externalizing problems. The findings by Germán and colleagues (2009) are consistent with other studies that have shown that familism values positively affect Latino students' academic achievement as well (Valenzuela & Dornbusch, 1994).

Summary

The mainstream corpus of peer relations research has accumulated a wealth of knowledge regarding children's friendships, social status, racial integration, school adjustment, peer victimization, and aggression. Latino children, by comparison, remain understudied. Extant studies suggest that friendships provide unique affordances to Latino children, such as easing processes of acculturation and mitigating ecological stressors. The social context of the classroom—particularly ethnic composition—moderates Latino children's integration patterns, social status, and experiences of victimization. Multiple dimensions of family life, including parent-child relationship quality, socioeconomic status, and familism values, impinge on Latino children's social behavior and academic adjustment. Several gaps in the literature deserve closer attention, especially those regarding developmental processes and the disentangling of SES, ethnicity, and culture. Another area of need is knowledge regarding how Latino children's peer relations vary across geographic regions and types of setting (i.e., rural, urban, suburban). Part two of this chapter attempts to contribute to the literature by investigating multiple dimensions of the peer relations of Latino children in a small urban community.

PART TWO

The present study examines the peer relations of Latino children in a small city in the Midwest United States. Hardly boasting a robust Latino population, such a setting may seem an odd choice. Much of the extant empirical knowledge on Latino children stems from samples in which Latinos compose a substantial presence in the community under study. Even in large cities where Latinos compose just 20–40 percent of the population, Latino children are able to attend schools where they form a majority. In contrast, Latino children in smaller towns are necessarily minorities at school as well as in the community at large. Studying a smaller community provides an uncommon glimpse into what school experiences are like for Latino children who are "double minorities," that is, in institutional and community life.

Four sets of questions frame this study. First, to what extent do Latino children prefer friendships with same-ethnicity peers? Is ethnic segregation reinforced by the status structures of the peer ecology? Second, how are Latino children generally perceived by their peers in terms of social status and behavior? Does their perceived social status and/or behavior depend on the ethnic context of their schools? Third, do Latino children evidence social goal orientations similar to children of other ethnic groups? Last, as minorities in their respective schools and in the community at large, are Latino children especially vulnerable to peer victimization? Or, inversely, are Latino children more prone to bullying other children?

METHOD

Setting

The urban hub of a large agricultural region in the Midwest, Prairie City (pop. 71,000) was the seat of our study. European Americans (71%) and African Americans (16%) composed the bulk of this ethnically segregated community. Latinos (5%) were an increasing presence, however—the only ethnic group to increase in size over the previous 10 years. Of note: Whereas European Americans' and African Americans' residential patterns were palpably segregated, the percentage of Latinos was similar across the city's census tracts (i.e., 2.3–6.4%).

Charged with failing to adequately serve its minority and low-income students, the Prairie City School District (PCSD) was under federal court scrutiny. The court imposed a number of measures to rectify educational disparities, including a busing policy that enabled children to attend schools beyond neighborhood boundaries. We targeted 5 out of the 11 elementary schools in PCSD to capture different ethnic enclaves. Table 5.1 presents demographic information for the five schools and their encompassing neighborhoods (census tracts). Two patterns are evident: (a) neighborhood ethnic compositions and average income levels vary widely, and (b) assymetries between neighborhood ethnic composition and the corresponding school ethnic composition reflect the district's busing policy to integrate children.

On the west end of town, PCSD 1 Elementary School was located in a mostly African American (87% AA, 5% EA, 4% Lat) and poor (per capita income = $11,100; 37% poverty rate) census tract. Across town, literally on the other side of the train tracks, PCSD 5 Elementary School was located in a more affluent (per capita income = $36,600; 16% poverty rate), mostly European American (4% AA, 90% EA, 2% Lat) census tract. The two neighborhoods surrounding PCSD 2 and PCSD 3 were similar to the census tract encompassing PCSD 5: mostly White and relatively affluent. Distinct from the other schools, PCSD 4 was located in the one racially balanced census tract in our study (51% EA, 44% AA, 4% Lat); situated near a food-processing plant, this tract was the second poorest locale (per capita income = $15,000; 22% poverty rate).

A brief comparison of school demographic data with the corresponding census tract information illustrates the district's busing policy. The ethnic distributions of children were more balanced across schools (i.e., 30–42% AA, 14–63% EA) than across neighborhoods (i.e. 4–87% AA, 5–90% EA). Latinos comprised 2–8 percent of the enrolments in four out of five schools, a range not far astray from the census tract range of 2–4 percent.

Standing in bold relief was PCSD 1 Elementary School. Whereas Latino families were dispersed relatively evenly throughout the city's census tracts, 40 percent of all elementary-aged Latino children in the district attended PCSD 1 Elementary School on the south side of town, where they comprised 41 percent of this school's enrollment. PCSD 1 housed the district's elementary bilingual program. Thus, there were two vastly different types of school environments for Latino children in Prairie City: one in

Table 5.1
Demographic Information for Prairie City Elementary Schools and Their Encompassing Census Tracts

		Prairie City Elementary Schools				Encompassing Census Tract					
School	Enrollment	% Low Income	% EA	%AA	%Lat	% Below Poverty	Per capita Income	% > 25 Bachelor's +	% EA	%AA	%Lat
PCSD 1	240	80	14	40	41	37	11,100	14	5	87	4
PCSD 2	268	33	63	30	3	18	22,000	61	82	9	4
PCSD 3	386	56	54	38	2	6	18,100	29	73	16	3
PCSD 4	327	62	35	42	6	22	15,000	19	51	44	4
PCSD 5	380	49	45	35	8	16	36,600	57	90	4	2
District/City	8,897	41	50	36	5	22	18,700	44	73	16	4

Note: Students of Asian descent comprised 8% of the Prairie City School District; because this ethnic group was underrepresented in the five schools selected, we have omitted these children from our descriptive analyses. "% > 25 Bachelor's +" indicates the percentage of adults 25 years or older in the census tract who had attained a bachelor's degree or higher. PCSD, Prairie City School District; EA, European American; AA, African American; Lat, Latino.

which Latinos were an extreme minority (as in PCSD 2, 3, 4, 5) and one in which they had a substantial group presence (PCSD 1).

Throughout the district, younger Latino elementary school children performed more similarly to European Americans than to African Americans on state achievement exams, though this pattern changed by fifth grade. Among third and fourth graders, 81 percent of Latinos, 86 percent of European Americans, and 56 percent of African Americans met or exceeded the state learning standards for reading; similarly, 94 percent of Latinos, 95 percent of European Americans, and 75 percent of African Americans met or exceeded the state learning standards for mathematics. However, by fifth grade, 63 percent of Latinos, 88 percent of European Americans, and 55 percent of African Americans met or exceeded the state learning standards for reading; 72 percent of Latinos, 94 percent of European Americans, and 66 percent of African Americans met or exceeded the state learning standards for Mathematics.

Participants

We surveyed 235 children in 16 classrooms (6 fourth-grade, 10 fifth-grade) in which there was at least one Latina/o student. The participation rate was 81 percent. Participants did not differ from non-participants in any discernable ways. The ethnic distribution within each classroom varied considerably: from 0 percent to 75 percent African American (median = 47%), 0 percent to 52 percent European American (median = 32%), and 4 percent to 100 percent Latino (median = 7.5%). There were 100 African American (55 female), 65 European American (29 female), 42 Latino (21 female), 16 Asian (10 female), and 14 other ethnicity (1 female) participants in these classrooms. Analyses are restricted to African American, European American, and Latino students.

There were clear differences between the classrooms at PCSD 1 and the classrooms at other schools regarding the prevalence of Latino children. In the seven classrooms at PCSD 1, the percentage of Latinos ranged from 9–100 percent (median = 26%). In the remaining nine classrooms distributed across four schools, the percentage of Latinos ranged from 4 to 10 percent (median = 5%). Where relevant, descriptive analyses compare Latino boys and girls, as well as the 34 Latino participants in PCSD 1 (where Latinos had a substantial presence) to the eight Latino participants in other schools (where Latinos were an extreme minority). Comparisons between subgroups of Latinos in this sample are exploratory at best. Nevertheless, they may point to important questions for future investigation.

Procedure

Study participation required parental/guardian active consent and individual assent. There were two waves of data collection, one in the Fall semester and one in the Spring semester. Surveys, consent letters, and assent forms were translated into Spanish and back translated. The order of administration of measures was randomized for each classroom.

Measures

Friendship (Fall and Spring)

Children were asked to circle yes or no to the question, "Some kids have a number of close friends, but others have just one best friend, and still others don't have a best friend. What about you? Do you have a best friend?" Children responding affirmatively were prompted to write an unlimited number of names of children whom they considered to be their best friends.

Calculating Friendship Segregation and Cross-Ethnicity Dislike (Fall and Spring)

Ethnic biases for friendship and like least nominations were calculated from the patterns of a child's nominations of his/her peers. Calculating an index of segregation was similar for both constructs, so we first describe the process for friendships and then explain how it differed slightly for like least nominations.

To index friendship segregation, the logarithm of the compositionally invariant odds ratio was used; this index controls for opportunities present for same- and cross-ethnic contact in classrooms of varying ethnic composition (Gorard & Taylor, 2002). The formula for friendship segregation is $\log \alpha = \log(AD/BC)$, where A is the number of same-ethnicity ties, B is the number of cross-ethnicity ties, C is the number of same-ethnicity peers with whom the child did not have ties, and D is the number of cross-ethnicity peers with whom the child did not have ties. Wherever there was a zero value in one or more cells of the cross-tabulation, .5 was added to each cell. On this scale, positive values denote biases favoring same-ethnicity friendships, negative values denote biases favoring cross-ethnicity friendships, and a value of zero denotes complete neutrality. The larger the absolute value of the index, the stronger is the same- or cross-ethnicity bias. The scale was reversed for like least nominations (i.e., $\log \alpha = \log(BC/AD)$; positive values reflect a disproportionate number of like least nominations to cross-ethnicity peers (i.e., cross-ethnicity dislike), whereas negative values reflect a disproportionate number of nominations to same-ethnicity peers (i.e., same-ethnicity dislike).

Peer Nomination Items (Fall)

All social status and behavior measures used an unlimited peer nominations method. Proportions were calculated for each child from the quotient of nominations received over the number of nominators in a classroom, with self-nominations excluded. Two items were used to assess *social preference*: "These are the kids whom I would LIKE MOST to play with"; and "These are the kids whom I would LIKE LEAST to play with." Consistent with prior research (Coie, Dodge, & Coppotelli, 1982; Prinstein & Cillessen, 2003), social preference scores were calculated by subtracting LIKE LEAST nominations from LIKE MOST nominations ($\alpha = .73$). Two items were used to assess *perceived popularity*: "These are the most POPULAR kids in my class"; and "These are the most UNPOPULAR kids in my class" ($\alpha = .74$; cf., LaFontana & Cillessen, 2002). To assess peer perceived *coolness*, children were asked, "These kids are the COOLEST kids in my class." For *prosociality*, the two measures were, "These kids cooperate. Here are kids who really cooperate—they pitch in, share, and give everyone a turn"; and "These kids are always willing to do something NICE for somebody else, and are really nice people" ($\alpha = .88$). *Relational aggression* was the average of makes fun (i.e., "These kids MAKE FUN of people. They like to make fun of other kids and embarrass them in front of other people.") and says mean things (i.e., "These kids SAY MEAN THINGS to other kids, and they spread nasty rumors about other kids.") ($\alpha = .91$). *Overt aggression* was the average of fights (i.e., "These kids start FIGHTS. These kids push other kids around, or hit them or kick them.") and trouble (i.e., "These kids get into TROUBLE. These kids don't follow the rules, don't pay attention, and talk back to the teacher.") ($\alpha = .89$).

Self-Reports of Social Goals (Fall)

The social goals instrument was adapted from a survey developed for adolescents (Ryan & Shim, 2006) as appropriate for elementary school children. The 15 items were used as indicators of *Social Development* goals (e.g., "I like it when I learn new ways to make friends"; $\alpha = .77$), *Social Demonstration-Approach* goals (e.g., "It is important to me that other kids think I am popular"; $\alpha = .82$), or *Social Demonstration-Avoid* goals (e.g., "It is important to me that I don't embarrass myself around my friends"; $\alpha = .60$). All items were on a 5-point scale (1 = not at all true to 5 = very true).

Self-Reports of Bullying and Victimization (Fall)

Self-report items were adopted from the revised bully/victim questionnaire (Olweus, 1994). The *bullying* composite was the average of three items: "How often have you taken part in bullying another student at school in the past couple of months?"; "I called another student mean names, made fun of or teased him or her in a hurtful way"; and "I hit, kicked, pushed, or shoved another student around" ($\alpha = .81$). The *victimization* composite was the average of three items: "How often have you been bullied at school in the past couple of months?"; "I was called mean names, was made fun of, or teased in a hurtful way"; and "I was hit, kicked, pushed, or shoved around" ($\alpha = .79$). All items were on a 5-point scale (1 = Never to 5 = Several times a week).

RESULTS

Table 5.2 presents the means and standard deviations of the ethnic segregation variables (Fall and Spring) for Latino children, overall and disaggregated by gender. Table 5.3 presents the means and standard deviations for all other variables for the entire sample, disaggregated by ethnic group. Findings on Latino children are highlighted below.

Ethnic Segregation and Cross-Ethnicity Dislike

Of the 42 Latino participants in our sample, 10 had no cross-ethnicity classmates and seven had no other Latina/o peer classmate; segregation

Table 5.2

Means and Standard Deviations for Latino Children's Ethnic Segregation Variables (Fall and Spring)

	Overall		Boys		Girls	
	M	*SD*	*M*	*SD*	*M*	*SD*
Friendship Segregation						
Fall semester	.64	.68	.40	.72	.90	.55
Spring semester	.67	.72	.50	.70	.88	.72
Peer Dislike						
Fall semester	−.20	.51	−.36	.47	−.07	.52
Spring semester	.41	.69	.47	.99	.37	.41

Note: Ethnic segregation scores are log α values: for friendship segregation, positive values connote disproportionate same-ethnicity favoritism and negative values connote cross-ethnicity favoritism; for dislike, positive values represent disproportionate cross-ethnicity dislike and negative values connote disproportionate same-ethnicity dislike.

Table 5.3

Means and Standard Deviations for Individual-Level Variables by Ethnicity (Fall Semester)

	Latino		African American		European American	
	M	SD	M	SD	M	SD
Peer Nominations						
Social preference	.05	.26	.01	.29	−.02	.35
Perceived popularity	.00	.37	.25	.42	−.03	.43
Cool	.41	.21	.47	.26	.35	.23
Prosocial	.61	.17	.34	.21	.46	.27
Relational aggression	.13	.14	.36	.23	.15	.18
Overt aggression	.15	.19	.35	.27	.15	.21
Social Goals (self-report)						
Development	.26	.84	−.33	.98	−.06	1.02
Demonstration approach	−.15	.92	−.17	1.16	−.37	.89
Demonstration avoid	.02	.93	−.28	.93	−.05	.82
Olweus (self-report)						
Bullying	1.30	.47	1.69	.98	1.31	.45
Victimization	1.81	.99	1.78	1.07	2.06	1.07

Note: All variables were measured in Fall only. Social goals variables are factor scores derived from an exploratory factor analysis.

indices for these children were not calculated. The remaining 25 students (13 boys) were dispersed across five classrooms; 24 were in PCSD 1.

In the Fall semester, the Latino students in our sample, on average, disproportionately preferred same- versus other-ethnicity peers as friends. The mean friendship segregation index (log α) was .64 (t = 4.73, $p < .01$), indicating that Latino children preferred same-ethnicity peers as friends. The sample mean for girls (log α = .90) was higher than that for boys (log α = .40); though a statistical trend (t = 1.93, $p = .07$), this gender difference may not reflect real differences in the population. To interpret the segregation indices: For the Latina girls in this sample, on average, the odds that a same-ethnicity classmate was a friend was 7.9 times the odds that a cross-ethnicity classmate was a friend; for Latino boys, the corresponding odds ratio was 2.5. Preferences for same-ethnicity friendships persisted into the Spring semester (log α = .67). The sample mean for girls (log α = .88) was higher than that for boys (log α = .50); this difference was not significant (t = 1.25, $p > .10$). The correlation between friendship segregation in the Fall and Spring was .62; there was no substantial change in friendship segregation over time (t = .23, $p = .82$).

Regarding peer dislike, in the Fall semester, the Latino children in our sample disproportionately disliked *same*-ethnicity versus cross-ethnicity classmates (log $\alpha = -.20$; t $= 1.83$, $p = .08$); there was no difference by gender. The ingroup tendencies for dislike were more moderate than friendship patterns: The odds of nominating a Latino classmate as liked least was 1.58 times the odds of nominating a cross-ethnicity classmate. However, by the Spring semester, the trend for disliking flipped. At this point, Latinos disproportionately nominated *cross*-ethnicity rather than same-ethnicity peers as liked least (log $\alpha = .41$; t $= 2.62$, $p < .02$); there was no difference by gender. The change in dislike patterns over time was statistically significant (t $= 2.70$, $p < .02$).

In sum: The Fall data, rather than painting a picture of "same-ethnicity preference coupled with cross-ethnicity dislike," suggest that Latino children simply interacted with each other disproportionately more than with cross-ethnicity peers, befriending some and disliking others. By the Spring semester, however, Latino children disproportionately preferred same-ethnicity peers as friends *and* disproportionately disliked cross-ethnicity peers.

Peer Nominations of Social Status and Behavior

A multiple analysis of variance was performed with gender and ethnicity as independent variables; peer nominations of social status and behavior were the dependent variables. Gender was significant for prosocial behavior only ($p < .01$); no gender x ethnicity interaction was significant. Ethnicity was significant for prosocial, perceived popularity, relational aggression, and overt aggression (all ps $< .01$). Post hoc results confirmed four significant differences between Latino and African American children and one significant difference between Latino and European American children. Compared to African American children, Latino children were viewed by classmates as less popular (mean difference $= -.25$, $p < .02$), more prosocial (mean difference $= .27$, $p < .01$), less relationally aggressive (mean difference $= -.23$, $p < .01$), and less overtly aggressive (mean difference $= -.20$, $p < .01$). Compared to European American children, Latino children were viewed as more prosocial (mean difference $= .15$, $p < .01$). Compared to Latino boys, Latina girls were viewed by classmates as more popular (mean difference $= .32$, $p < .01$) and more prosocial (mean difference $= .15$, $p < .01$). Latino children at PCSD1 were viewed as more relationally aggressive (mean difference $= .09$, $p < .01$) and more overtly aggressive (mean difference $= .15$, $p < .01$) than Latino children at other schools.

Social Goals

In a factor analysis of the social goals questionnaire, a three-factor solution fit the data well ($R^2 = .52$), with Demonstration Approach (eigenvalue = 5.15), Social Development (eigenvalue = 2.86), and Demonstration Avoid (eigenvalue = 1.29) factors. A multiple analysis of variance was performed with gender and ethnicity as independent variables to test for group differences in factor scores. There was no significant effect for gender or the gender x ethnicity interaction. Ethnicity was significant for Social Development ($p < .01$) and marginally significant for Demonstration Avoid ($p < .06$). Post hoc analyses indicated that Latinos differed from at least one other ethnic group only in the Social Development factor: Latinos scored higher than African Americans but not European Americans (mean difference = .59, $p < .05$).

Bullying and Victimization

A multiple analysis of variance was performed with gender and ethnicity as independent variables. There was no significant effect for gender or the gender x ethnicity interaction. Self-reported levels of bullying varied significantly by ethnicity ($p < .01$). Post hoc analyses detected only one statistical trend involving Latino children: Latino children reported themselves to bully at lower rates than African Americans (mean difference = −.39, $p = .08$) but not European Americans. There were no gender differences among Latino children. Self-reported bullying also did not differ between Latino children at PCSD 1 (where Latinos were a substantial presence) and Latino children at other schools (where Latinos were an extreme minority) (M = 1.32 and 1.21, respectively; t = .62, $p > .10$).

Self-reported levels of peer victimization did not differ significantly across ethnic groups ($p > .10$). Self-reported victimization also did not differ between Latino children at PCSD 1 and Latino children at other schools (Ms = 1.75 and 2.04, respectively; t = .73, $p > .10$).

Bivariate Correlations

Ethnic Segregation, Social Status, and Social Goals

Among Latino children, there was a marginal, positive correlation between Fall (not Spring) friendship segregation and perceived coolness ($r = .33, p < .07$). No other segregation-status link approached significance. The Demonstration-Approach factor was negatively correlated with Spring (not Fall) cross-ethnicity dislike ($r = −.42, p < .05$). Friendship segregation was not correlated with any social goal factor in either semester.

The Developmental social goal factor was negatively correlated with perceived popularity for Latinos ($r = −.28, p < .09$) and African Americans ($r = −.34, p < .01$), but not for European Americans; no other status-goal association approached significance for Latinos or African Americans. European Americans evidenced one significant status-goal association: The Demonstration Approach goal orientation was negatively correlated with social preference ($r = -.28$, $p < .03$); this correlation was non-significant for Latino and African American children.

Perceived Status and Behavior

For all three ethnic groups, prosocial behavior was positively associated with social preference ($.43 \leq r \leq .50$, all $ps < .01$) and perceived popularity ($.16 \leq r \leq .28$, all $ps < .08$). Conversely, the sample correlations between social preference and overt aggression were negative for all three ethnic groups ($-.41 \leq r \leq -10$), although this correlation was non-significant for Latinos. There was a significant positive correlation between perceived popularity and relational aggression for African Americans ($r = .20, p < .03$), but not for Latinos ($r = .14, p > .10$) or European Americans ($r = .02, p > .10$).

Summary

There was modest evidence (i.e., a positive status-segregation association) that the peer ecology supports Latinos' friendship segregation but not their cross-ethnicity dislike. Latino children who were oriented to gain positive evaluations from others (i.e., demonstration-approach social goals) were less likely to disproportionately dislike cross-ethnicity peers. Regarding links between social goals and social status, Latino children were more similar to African Americans than to European Americans. The peer ecology rewards prosocial behavior and dislikes overt aggression in all three ethnic groups, whereas relational aggression was significantly associated with perceived status only for African American children.

DISCUSSION

Ethnic Segregation

On average, Latino children had moderately segregated friendships in the Fall and Spring semesters, a pattern consistent with research on European American and African American children in elementary classrooms (e.g., Hallinan & Teixeira, 1987; Rodkin, Wilson, & Ahn, 2007; Shrum, Cheek, & Hunter, 1988; Wilson & Rodkin, in press). Moreover, there was modest evidence that Latino children who had more segregated friendships were perceived by classmates as more cool. In other words, the classroom peer ecology may reinforce Latino children's segregation.

Patterns for cross-ethnicity dislike were more complex. Latino children initially demonstrated modest dislike for same-ethnicity peers versus cross-ethnicity peers, but then exhibited disproportionate dislike for cross-ethnicity peers by the Spring semester. However, the increasing levels of cross-ethnicity dislike were tempered by a link with social goals: Latino students who had strivings to gain positive evaluations from peers (i.e., demonstration-approach goal orientations) were *less* likely to dislike cross-ethnicity peers. Although Latino children may increasingly dislike cross-ethnicity peers over time, they perceive disliking outgroups to undermine their efforts to attain high peer regard—a positive sign for integrated elementary classrooms. The increase over time in Latinos' negative sentiments towards outgroups invites further longitudinal study. One intriguing direction will be to employ microgenetic studies advocated by Cillessen and Mayeaux (2007, p. 141) to isolate how small events might influence long-term trajectories of interpersonal sentiments.

Comparisons between Ethnic Groups

On balance, Latino children evidenced patterns of behavior, social status, and social goal orientations that were different from both African American and European American children. Latino children were viewed by peers as more prosocial than African Americans and European Americans alike. Compared to African Americans, Latinos were viewed as less aggressive and less popular, and self-reported lower levels of bullying behavior. Though exploratory, to be sure, these findings are consistent with the view that Latino children's interactions and relationships with peers are influenced by the cultural values of familism and respeto, whereby interpersonal conflict is tempered for the sake of group cohesiveness and interpersonal harmony.

Of course, there is wide variability among Latino children, even in the small sample featured in this study. For example, Latino students at PCSD 1 elementary school (where Latinos were a large minority presence) were viewed as more relationally and overtly aggressive than their Latino counterparts at other schools. This finding should be interpreted with caution, however, as it may be an artifact of the peer nomination procedure (at PCSD 1 there were more Latino peers to nominate). Unfortunately, there were an insufficient number of students in PCSD 2–5 to calculate meaningful segregation indices for children in these schools. An important follow-up to this study will be to investigate whether Latino children's friendships are more segregated when they are extreme minorities, as Quillian and Campbell (2003) found to be the case among Latino adolescents. Beyond sample size, this study was limited by not having critical information on other culturally relevant variables such as generational status, SES, and country of origin.

CONCLUSION

There is cause to augment traditional methodological paradigms in the study of peer relations. Even when using conventional survey measures that have withstood the test of time, there is a need to incorporate other covariates to capture the heterogeneity in social experiences—not just of Latino children, but of other ethnic groups as well. Ethnic context and busing are two critical factors, as the present study exemplifies: Whereas Latinos composed 5 percent of the community's population; roughly 40 percent of all elementary-aged Latino children in the district attended one elementary school. Finer-grained analyses are needed to better capture how children's intergroup relations and the broader landscape of the school take on different social meaning when the school ethnic composition differs from those of children's home neighborhoods.

At a more fundamental level, there is a need to frame culturally relevant developmental models (Raffaelli, Carlo, Carranza, & Gonzalez-Kruger, 2005). This can mean different things for different lines of study. Regarding research on Latino children, Raffaelli and colleagues (2005) urge scholars to pay explicit attention to cultural diversity between and within subgroups, to the positive and normative development of Latino children, and to factors such as geographic concentration patterns and bilingualism. Azmitia and colleagues (2006) argue for more qualitative, open-ended approaches to allow for children's own conceptualizations of peer relationships to emerge.

Another corollary of framing culturally relevant models is to move beyond studying ethnicity in isolation in favor of considering the intersectionality of multiple social identities such as ethnicity, gender, and class (Azmitia et al., 2006). Social network analysis, now enjoying a resurgence in developmental psychology, offers an analytically powerful and conceptually flexible approach towards this end (see Rodkin & Hanish, 2007). The challenge for researchers will be to creatively leverage developmental theory and innovative methodologies to better inform public policies in service of the developmental needs of Latino children.

REFERENCES

Aboud, F. E., Mendelson, M. J., & Purdy, K. T. (2003). Cross-race peer relations and friendship quality, *International Journal of Behavioral Development 27*, 165–173.

Adler, P. A., & Adler, P. (1998). *Peer power: Preadolescent culture and identity.* New Brunswick, NJ: Rutgers University Press.

Alfaro, E. A., Umaña-Taylor, A. J., & Bámaca, M.Y. (2006). Interpersonal support and Latino adolescents' academic motivation. *Family Relations 55,* 279–291.

Azmitia, M., Ittel, A., & Brenk, C. (2006). Latino-heritage adolescents' friendships. In X. Chen, D. C. French, & B. H. Schneider (Eds.), *Peer relationships in cultural context,* (pp. 426–452). New York: Cambridge University Press.

Bagwell, C. L., Coie, J. D., Terry, R. A., & Lochman, J. E. (2000). Peer clique participation and social status in preadolescence. *Merrill-Palmer Quarterly 46,* 280–305.

Barrera, M., Biglan, A., Ary, D., & Li, F. (2001). Replication of a problem behavior model with American Indian, Hispanic, and Caucasian youth. *Journal of Early Adolescence 21,* 133–157.

Bauman, S., & Summers, J. J. (2009). Peer victimization and depressive symptoms in Mexican American middle school students: Including acculturation as a variable of interest. *Hispanic Journal of Behavioral Sciences 31,* 515–535.

Bellmore, A. D., Nishina, A., Witkow, M. R., Graham, S., & Juvonen, J. (2007). The influence of classroom ethnic composition on same- and other-ethnicity peer nominations in middle school. *Social Development 16,* 720–740.

Bellmore, A. D., Witkow, M. R., Graham, S., & Juvonen, J. (2004). Beyond the individual: The impact of ethnic context and classroom behavioral norms on victims' adjustment. *Developmental Psychology 40,* 1159–1172.

Berndt, T. J., Hawkins, J. A., & Hoyle, S. G. (1986). Changes in friendship during a school year: Effects on children's and adolescents' impressions of friendship and sharing with friends. *Child Development 57,* 1284–1297.

Boivin, M., Hymel, S., & Bukowski, W. M. (1995). The roles of social withdrawal, peer rejection, and victimization by peers in predicting loneliness and depressed mood in childhood. *Development and Psychopathology 7,* 765–785.

Bronfenbrenner, U. (1979). *The ecology of human development: Experiments by nature and design.* Cambridge, MA: Harvard University Press.

Buhs, E. S., McGinley, M., & Toland, M. D. (2010). Overt and relational victimization in Latinos and European Americans: Measurement equivalence across ethnicity, gender, and grade level in early adolescent groups. *Journal of Early Adolescence 30,* 171–197.

Bukowski, W. M., Motzoi, C., & Meyer, F. (2009). Friendship as a process, function, and outcome. In K. H. Rubin, W. M. Bukowski, & B. Laursen (Eds.), *Handbook of peer interactions, relationships, and groups* (pp. 217–231). New York: The Guilford Press.

Cairns, R. B., Cairns, B. D., Neckerman, H. J., Gest, S. D., & Gariepy, J. L. (1988). Social networks and aggressive behavior: Peer support or peer rejection? *Developmental Psychology 24,* 815–823.

Castelli, L., De Amicis, L., & Sherman, S. J. (2007). The loyal member effect: On the preference for ingroup members who engage in exclusive relations with the ingroup. *Developmental Psychology 43*, 1347–1359.

Cillessen, A. H. N., & Mayeux. (2007). Variations in the association between aggression and social status: Theoretical and empirical perspectives. In P. H. Hawley, T. D. Little, & P. C. Rodkin (Eds.), *Aggression and adaptation: The bright side to bad behavior* (pp. 135–156). Mahwah, N. J.: Erlbaum.

Cillessen, A. H. N. , & Rose, A. J. (2005). Understanding popularity in the peer system. *Current Directions in Psychological Science 14*, 102–105.

Coie, J. D., Dodge, K. A., & Coppotelli, H. (1982). Dimensions and types of social status: A cross-age perspective. *Developmental Psychology 18*, 557–570.

Coie, J. D., Cillessen, A. H. N., Dodge, K. A., Hubbard, J. A., Schwartz, D., Lemerise, E. A., & Bateman, H. (1999). It takes two to fight: A test of relational factors and a method for assessing aggressive dyads. *Developmental Psychology 35*, 1179–1188.

Coleman, J. S. (1988). Social capital in the creation of human capital. *American Journal of Sociology 94*, 95–120.

Conger, K. J., & Conger, R. D. (1994). Differential parenting and change in sibling differences in delinquency. *Journal of Family Psychology 8*, 287–302.

Cooper, C. R., Cooper, R. G., Azmitia, M. Chavira, G., & Gullat, Y. (2002). Bridging multiple worlds: How African American and Latino youth in academic outreach programs navigate math pathways to college. *Applied Developmental Science 6*, 73–87.

Criss, M. M., Pettit, G. S., Bates, J. E., Dodge, K. A., & Lapp, A. L. (2002). Family adversity, positive peer relationships and children's externalizing behavior: A longitudinal perspective on risk and resilience. *Child Development 73*, 1220–1237.

Crockett, L., Losoff, M., & Petersen, A. C. (1984). Perceptions of the peer group and friendship in early adolescence. *Journal of Early Adolescence 4*, 155–181.

Davidson T. M., & Cardemil, E. V. (2009). Parent-child communication and parental involvement in Latino adolescents. *The Journal of Early Adolescence 29*, 99–121.

DeGarmo, D. S., & Martinez, C. R., Jr. (2006). A culturally informed model of academic well-being for Latino youth: The importance of discriminatory experiences and social support. *Family Relations 55*, 267–278.

Dubois, D. L., & Hirsch, B. J. (1990). School and neighborhood friendship patterns of Blacks and Whites in early adolescence. *Child Development 61*, 524–536.

Garcia-Reid, P., Reid, R. J., & Peterson, N. A. (2005). School engagement among Latino youth in an urban middle school context. *Education and Urban Society 37*, 257–275.

Germán, M., Gonzales, N. A., & Dumka, L. (2009). Familism values as a protective factor for Mexican-origin adolescents exposed to deviant peers. *The Journal of Early Adolescence 29*, 16–42.

Gonzalez, R., & Padilla, A. M. (1997). The academic resilience of Mexican American high school students. *Hispanic Journal of Behavioral Sciences 19*, 301–317.

Gorard, S., & Taylor, C. (2002). What is segregation? A comparison of measures in terms of 'strong' and 'weak' compositional invariance. *Sociology 36*, 875–895.

Graham, S. (2006). Peer victimization in school: Exploring the ethnic context. *Current Directions in Psychological Science 15*, 317–320.

Graham, S., Bellmore, A. D., Nishina, A., & Juvonen, J. (2009). It must be me: Ethnic diversity and attributions for peer victimization in middle school. *Journal of Youth and Adolescence 38*, 487–499.

Graham, S., & Juvonen, J. (2002). Ethnicity, peer harassment, and adjustment in middle school: An exploratory study. *The Journal of Early Adolescence 22* 173–199.

Graham, S., Taylor, A. Z., & Ho, A. Y. (2009). Race and ethnicity in peer relations research. In K. H. Rubin, W. M. Bukowski, & B. Laursen (Eds.), *Handbook of peer interactions, relationships, and groups* (pp. 531–547). New York: The Guilford Press.

Grotpeter, J. K., & Crick, N. R. (1996). Relational aggression, overt aggression, and friendship. *Child Development 67*, 2328–2338.

Hallinan, M. T., & Teixeira, R. A. (1987). Students' interracial friendships: Individual characteristics, structural effects and racial differences. *American Journal of Education 95*, 563–583.

Hamm, J. V., Brown, B. B., & Heck, D. J. (2005). Bridging the ethnic divide: Student and school characteristics in African American, Asian-descent, Latino, and White adolescents' cross-ethnic friend nominations. *Journal of Research on Adolescence 15*, 21–46.

Hanish, L., & Guerra, N. (2000). The roles of ethnicity and school context in predicting children's victimization by peers. *American Journal of Community Psychology 28*, 201–223.

Hanish, L., & Guerra, N. (2002). A longitudinal analysis of patterns of adjustment following peer victimization. *Development and Psychopathology 14*, 69–89.

Hartup, W. W. (1996). The company they keep: Friendships and their developmental significance. *Child Development 67*, 1–13.

Hartup, W. W., & Abecassis, M. (2002). Friends and enemies. In P. K. Smith & C. H. Hart (Eds.), *Blackwell handbook of social development* (pp. 285–306). Oxford, UK: Blackwell.

Hodges, E. V. E., Malone, M. J., & Perry, D. G. (1997). Individual risk and social risk as interacting determinants of victimization in the peer group. *Developmental Psychology 33*, 1032–1039.

Juvonen, J., Nishina, A., & Graham, S. (2006). Ethnic diversity and perceptions of safety in urban middle schools. *Psychological Science 17*, 393–400.

Kao, G., & Joyner, K. (2004). Do race and ethnicity matter among friends? Activities among interracial, interethnic, and intraethnic adolescent friends. *The Sociological Quarterly 45*, 557–573.

Kawabata, Y., & Crick, N. R. (2008). The role of cross-racial/ethnic friendships in social adjustment. *Developmental Psychology 44*, 1177–1183.

Kindermann, T. A. (1993). Natural peer groups as contexts for individual development: The case of children's motivation in school. *Developmental Psychology 29*, 970–977.

Kochenderfer, B. J., & Ladd, G. W. (1996). Peer victimization: Cause or consequence of school maladjustment? *Child Development 67*, 1305–1317.

Kochenderfer-Ladd, B., & Wardrup, J. (2001). Chronicity and instability in children's peer victimization experiences as predictors of loneliness and social satisfaction trajectories. *Child Development 72*, 134–151.

Ladd, G. W. (1990). Having friends, keeping friends, making friends, and being liked by peers in the classroom: Predictors of children's early school adjustment? *Child Development 61*, 1081–1100.

Ladd, G. W., & Burgess, K. B. (2001). Do relational risks and protective factors moderate the linkages between childhood aggression and early psychological and school adjustment? *Child Development 72*, 1579–1601.

LaFontana, K., & Cillessen, A. H. N. (2002). Children's perceptions of popular and unpopular peers: A multimethod assessment. *Developmental Psychology 38*, 635–647.

Lease, A. M., & Blake, J. J. (2005). A comparison of majority-race children with and without a minority-race friend. *Social Development 14*, 20–41.

Lempers, J. D., & Clark-Lempers, D. S. (1992). Young, middle, and late adolescents' comparisons of the functional importance of five significant relationships. *Journal of Youth and Adolescence 21*, 53–96.

Loukas, A., & Prelow, H. M. (2004). Externalizing and internalizing problems in low-income Latino early adolescents. *The Journal of Early Adolescence 24*, 250–273.

Loukas, A., Suzuki, R., & Horton, K.D. (2006). Examining school connectedness as a mediator of school climate effects. *Journal of Research on Adolescence 16*, 491–502.

Moffitt, T. E. (1993). Adolescence-limited and life-course-persistent antisocial behavior: A developmental taxonomy. *Psychological Review 100*, 674–701.

Moody, J. (2001). Race, school integration, and friendship segregation in America. *American Journal of Sociology 107*, 679–716.

Mouw, T., & Entwisle, B. (2006). Residential segregation and interracial friendships in schools. *American Journal of Sociology 112*, 394–441.

Murray, C. (2009). Parent and teacher relationships as predictors of school engagement and functioning among low-income urban youth. *The Journal of Early Adolescence 29*, 376–404.

Olweus, D. (1994). Bullying at school: Long-term outcomes for the victims and an effective school-based intervention program. In L. Huesmann (Ed.), *Aggressive behavior: Current perspectives* (pp. 97–130). New York: Springer.

Parker, J. G., & Asher, S. R. (1993). Friendship and friendship quality in middle childhood: Links with peer group acceptance and feelings of loneliness and social dissatisfaction. *Developmental Psychology 29*, 611–621.

Parkhurst, J., & Hopmeyer, A. (1998). Sociometric popularity and peer-perceived popularity: Two distinct dimensions of peer status. *Journal of Early Adolescence 18*, 135–144.

Prinstein, M. J., & Cillessen, A. H. N. (2003). Forms and functions of adolescent peer aggression associated with high levels of peer status. *Merrill-Palmer Quarterly 49*, 310–342.

Putnam, R. D. (2007). E pluribus unum: Diversity and community in the twenty-first century: The 2006 Johan Skytte Prize lecture. *Scandinavian Political Studies 30*, 137–174.

Quillian, L., & Campbell, M. E. (2003). Beyond Black and White: The present and future or multiracial friendship segregation. *American Sociological Review 68*, 540–566.

Raffaelli, M., Carlo, G., Carranza, M. A., & Gonzalez-Kruger, G. E. (2005). Understanding Latino children and adolescents in the mainstream: Placing culture at the center of developmental models. In R. Larson & L. Jensen (Eds.), *New horizons in developmental research: New directions for child and adolescent development* (pp. 23–32). San Francisco: Jossey-Bass.

Rigby, K. (1998). Suicidal ideation and bullying among Australian secondary school children. *Australian Educational and Developmental Psychologist 15*, 45–61.

Rodkin, P. C., & Hanish, L. (Eds.). (2007). *Social network analysis and children's peer relations*. San Francisco: Wiley.

Rodkin, P. C., Farmer, T. W., Pearl, R., & Van Acker, R. (2000). Heterogeneity of popular boys: Antisocial and prosocial configurations. *Developmental Psychology 36*, 14–24.

Rodkin, P. C., Farmer, T. W., Pearl, R., & Van Acker, R. (2006). They're cool: Social status and peer group supports for aggressive boys and girls. *Social Development 15*, 175–204.

Rodkin, P. C., Wilson, T., & Ahn, H. J. (2007). Social integration among African- and European- American children in majority White, majority Black, and multicultural elementary classrooms. In P. C. Rodkin & L. Hanish (Eds.), *Social network analysis and children's peer relations* (pp. 25–42). San Francisco: Wiley.

Ryan, A. M., Rodkin, P. C., Jamison, J., & Wilson, T. (2009, April). *Social goals in middle childhood: Relations to social behavior and social status*. Paper presented at the biennial meeting of the Society for Research on Child Development, Denver, CO.

Ryan, A. M., & Shim, S. S. (2008). An exploration of young adolescents' social achievement goals and social adjustment in middle school. *Journal of Educational Psychology 100*, 672–687.

Shrum, W., Cheek, N. H., & Hunter, S. M. (1988). Friendship in school: Gender and racial homophily. *Sociology of Education 61*, 227–239.

Suárez-Orozco, C., & Todorova, I. (2003). The social world of immigrant youth. In C. Suárez-Orozco & I. Todorova (Eds.), *Understanding the social world of immigrant youth* (pp. 15–24). San Francisco: Jossey-Bass.

Sullivan, H. S. (1953). *The interpersonal theory of psychiatry.* New York: Norton.

Tatum, B. D. (2003). *Why are all the Black kids sitting together in the cafeteria? A psychologist explains the development of racial identity.* New York: Basic Books.

Taylor, A. Z., & Graham, S. (2007). An examination of the relationship between achievement values and perceptions of barriers among low-SES African American and Latino students. *Journal of Educational Psychology 99*, 52–64.

Valenzuela, A., & Dornbusch, S. M. (1994). Familism and social capital in the academic achievement of Mexican origin and Anglo adolescents. *Social Science Quarterly 75*, 18–36.

Way, N. (2006). The cultural practice of close friendships among urban adolescents in the United States. In X. Chen, D.C. French, & B. H. Schneider (Eds.), *Peer relationships in cultural context* (pp. 403–425). New York: Cambridge University Press.

Way, N., & Chen, L. (2000). Close and general friendships among African American, Latino, and Asian American adolescents from low-income families. *Journal of Adolescent Research 15*, 274–301.

Way, N., Gingold, R., Rotenberg, M., & Kuriakose, G. (2005). The development of friendships among African American, Latino, and Chinese American youth: A qualitative account. In N. Way & J. Hamm (Eds.), *Close friendships among adolescents.* (pp. 41–59). San Francisco: Jossey Bass.

Wentzel, K. R. (2009). Peers and academic functioning at school. In K. H. Rubin, W. M. Bukowski, & B. Laursen (Eds.), *Handbook of peer interactions, relationships, and groups* (pp. 531–547). New York: The Guilford Press.

Wentzel, K. R., Barry, K. R., & Caldwell, K. A. (2004). Friendships in middle school: Influences on motivation and school adjustment. *Journal of Educational Psychology 96*, 195–203.

Wilson, T., & Rodkin, P. C. (in press). African American and European American children in diverse elementary classrooms: Social integration, social status, and social behavior. *Child Development.*

Woolley, M. E., Kol, K. L., & Bowen, G. L. (2009). The social context of school success for Latino middle school students: Direct and indirect influences of teachers, family, and friends. *The Journal of Early Adolescence 29*, 43–70.

Xie, H., Cairns, R. D., & Cairns, B. D. (2002). The development of social aggression and physical aggression: A narrative analysis of interpersonal conflicts. *Aggressive Behavior 28*, 341–355.

Chapter 6

LATINOS' EDUCATIONAL PATHWAYS: RESEARCH AND PROGRAM PERSPECTIVES

Jill Denner and Gwendelyn Rivera

In April 2009, President Barak Obama made a speech at the National Academies where he described the national imperative to increase the number of people in science, technology, engineering, and mathematics (STEM). He stated that, "Science is more essential for our prosperity, our security, our health, our environment, and our quality of life than it has ever been before" (The White House, 2009). This speech was followed by a series of proposals designed to stimulate innovation starting in kindergarten. In particular, he called for strategies to enable young people "to create and build and invent—to be makers of things, not just consumers of things" (The White House, 2009). These strategies are to be aimed at all students, but are particularly relevant to efforts that aim to include groups that have had fewer opportunities to contribute to innovation in STEM.

In 2007, the National Academies hosted a workshop focused on undergraduate education in STEM called "Understanding interventions that encourage minorities to pursue research careers" (Olson & Fagen, 2007). The participants concluded that more research is needed to determine whether existing interventions are effective, and how to strengthen them. Similarly, Newcombe et al. (2009) recently called for psychologists to use their knowledge of theory and related research studies to study and to strengthen interventions to increase student involvement and achievement in mathematics and science. To this end, this chapter will summarize what we can learn from psychological frameworks and existing interventions in order to identify key factors that must be addressed to increase the number of Latinos in STEM.

Latinos are vastly underrepresented in the fields of science, technology, engineering, and mathematics (STEM). This is due, in part, to their low rates of college graduation. A college degree has become the minimum standard for quality of life in the United States, but only 10 percent of Latinos attain one (Gándara & Contreras, 2009). Indeed, 41 percent of U.S. Latinos over the age of 25 have earned less than a high school diploma (Frehill, Di Fabio, & Hill, 2008). In the fields of science, technology, engineering, and mathematics, where there is growing concern about America's competitiveness (National Academy of Sciences, 2005), Latinos, particularly females, are largely absent (Dowd, Malcom, & Bensimon, 2009).

A large body of research suggests that education is correlated with mental health (Newport, 2007). In this chapter, we describe the psychological and ecological factors that influence the educational outcomes of Latino children living in the United States. We begin the chapter by using statistics to describe the current state of educational achievement by Latinos, and highlight gender differences, particularly in the STEM fields. We then describe several psychological frameworks that have proven useful for explaining barriers and opportunities for Latinos to enroll in college and pursue a STEM degree. In the next part of the chapter, we describe recent efforts to increase the representation of Latinos in STEM fields, and the factors that seem particularly promising for reaching students in middle and high school. Finally, we provide suggestions for implementation for practitioners and policy makers.

ACADEMIC PATHWAYS OF LATINO YOUTH

Latinos are the fastest growing ethnic minority population in the United States (U.S. Census, 2001, 2008). Therefore, it is not surprising that Latino children are rapidly becoming the majority in various school districts across the country. Whereas other immigrant groups have made social, economic, and political gains by attaining advanced degrees, Latinos have stalled in their educational advancement at the high school level as the number of Latinos who have completed high school has not surpassed 39 percent (its highest) in over 30 years (National Center for Education Statistics, 2008). The high school dropout rate for Latinos is currently twice the standard national average, and three times greater than their European American peers (National Center for Education Statistics, 2009). While there have been gains in the enrollment of Latinos in college, especially by Latinas who enroll at higher rates than their male counterparts, they do so at much lower rates than their European American, African American, and Asian peers (National Center for Education Statistics, 2008).

Once in college, Latinos are vastly underrepresented in most STEM majors. In 2005, Latinos earned 6.5 percent of physical science bachelor's degrees, 7.5 percent of Engineering bachelor's degrees, 6.8 percent of computer science bachelor's degrees, and 5.8 percent of mathematics bachelor's degrees (Frehill, Di Fabio, & Hill, 2008). Latinos were less likely than non-Hispanic Whites to earn degrees in natural and physical sciences, and account for 13 percent of this labor force, but just 5.8 percent of the engineering workforce (Frehill et al., 2008). Although Latinas enrolled in college at higher rates than their male counterparts, they earned less than 2 percent of computer science or engineering bachelors degrees (National Science Board, 2008). It follows that, in the 2006 workforce, Latinos were only 4–5 percent of mathematical and computer scientists, engineers, and postsecondary teachers (National Science Foundation, 2009). Thus, one reason that Latinos are not participating in the STEM workforce is that few graduate from college, and even fewer earn advanced degrees in STEM fields.

BARRIERS TO COLLEGE ENROLLMENT AND STEM CAREERS

Academic achievement and social-emotional functioning are intertwined (Weissberg, Kumpfer, & Seligman, 2003), so efforts to address underrepresentation in college and STEM fields are a critical part of promoting mental health throughout the life course. However, the statistics on degree attainment do not tell the whole story about where and why to target efforts to increase the number of U.S.-based Latina/o students in STEM fields. The barriers are both institutional and relational in nature, with consequences for psychological processes that undermine motivation.

Studies show that a college education is highly valued by most Latinos, but this does not necessarily translate into enrolling or attaining a degree. Although 89 percent of Latinos ages 16–25 said a college education plays an important role in a successful life, only 48 percent said that they planned to attain one (Lopez, 2009). Studies have identified a host of factors to explain the disconnect between values and expectations and institutional factors appear to play an important role. For example, a survey of Latina/o high school seniors found that barriers to college enrollment and completion include a lack of information about requirements and aid, and a lack of instrumental support from knowledgeable adults or teachers, as well as the need or desire to make money right away (Immerwahr, 2003). Other institutional factors include a lack of role models, limiting gender role expectations, low parent education, and a disparity across ethnicities in the digital divide (Cleary, Pierce & Trauth, 2006; Gándara & Contreras, 2009; May & Chubin 2003).

College enrollment and completion are also strongly influenced by relational factors. The Bridging Multiple Worlds model has been used to describe how expectations of family members, peers, and school personnel influence racial and ethnic minority students in the United States (Cooper, 1999; Cooper & Denner, 1998; Phalen, Davidson, & Yu, 1991). In contrast to a social capital model in which parent support and resources are positively correlated with academic achievement, Cooper et al (2002) described how relationships can be both resources and challenges for students' educational pathways. This view of the family is different from the long-held assumption that more support leads to greater achievement, and is consistent with research on barriers to women pursuing information and communications technology careers (Burger, Creamer, & Meszaros, 2007).

Studies of underrepresented minorities in STEM are few, but suggest that both institutional and relational factors are also influential. Similar to the disconnect between the values and plans related to college enrollment, Latino students enter computing, engineering, and mathematics majors at relatively similar rates to White students, but they are much less likely to complete their degree (Anderson & Kim, 2006). Little is known about the reasons for such high rates of attrition from the STEM major among Latino students, but Hispanic leaders suggest that institutional barriers that include a lack of role models or preparation in science and math during K–8 education play a critical role in whether or not students persist in STEM majors (Gasbarra & Johnson, 2008). In fact, a recent study of urban high schools found that Latino students have limited access to high school computer classes that go beyond typing skills, which results in fewer Latina/o students who are prepared to pursue computing (Margolis, 2008). The lack of opportunities to take high-level STEM courses is problematic, as many immigrant families view educational institutions as a primary source of information and resources and may not seek out other opportunities to prepare their children for these fields (Gasbarra & Johnson, 2008).

In addition to institutional factors, in order to understand and promote the education of Latino, and particularly immigrant students, we need to understand their experiences in the context of sociohistorical factors (Gutiérrez, 2006). Policy changes that affect Affirmative Action, bilingual education, and access to public schooling for undocumented immigrants, have a measurable impact on student pathways. For example, undocumented students are discouraged from pursuing college because they are not eligible for federal financial aid for higher education, cannot obtain a drivers license, or legally get a job even if they graduate from college (Thorpe, 2009). When these factors are not considered, individual students are categorized based on group performance, resulting in lower expectations and opportunities to pursue non-traditional careers, such as computing (Margolis, 2008).

Studies provide some information about how relational factors play a role in academic pathways. Interviews with college students majoring in computer and information sciences suggest that Latinos are more likely to describe the importance of overcoming family challenges (e.g., expectations that family obligations come before studying) in order to persist in that major (Varma, Prasad, & Kapur, 2006). This finding is consistent with Cooper et al.'s (2002) research with Latina/o high school students on the pathway to college. While family needs (especially financial needs) serve as motivators to pursue higher education and contribute to their families and communities (Cooper et al., 2005), those who are lower income and have a stronger sense of family obligation are less likely to pursue a college degree (Fuligni & Pedersen, 2002). Traditional gender role expectations may also be a barrier for Latinas. For example, some Latino parents encourage gender-specific jobs (Ginorio, 2007), and low expectations by key adults can undermine females' motivation to persist when faced with challenges (Margolis & Fisher, 2002; Meszaros, Lee & Laughlin, 2007). The presence of an adult who strongly believes in the students' ability plays a crucial role in students' perceived self-competence and their academic achievement in math and science classes (Bouchey & Harter, 2005).

These institutional and relational factors influence academic decisions and performance through the mechanism of psychological processes. Research shows that students who succeed academically and major in STEM fields have positive self-perceptions. Gándara and Contreras (2009) review several studies that describe the critical role that student self-perceptions of ability play in shaping their academic performance and aspirations. A positive self-perception has also been demonstrated to buffer familial risks (e.g., stressful events), which could have a direct affect on academic achievement. Data on self-perceptions provides some explanation for gender differences in STEM fields. In one study with college freshman, girls (both White and Latina) rated themselves lower than White or Latino boys on academic ability and intellectual self-confidence, despite reporting higher GPAs in high school (Hurtado, Sáenz, Santos, & Cabrera, 2008).

Self-perceptions of ability are strongly linked to interests and aspirations, and as early as middle school, Latina students express limited interest in STEM careers. In a survey of middle school girls attending a STEM event, only 7 percent of the Latinas stated an interest in a science, engineering, or math career, compared with 15 percent of the White and 9 percent of the Black students (Barker, Snow, Garvin-Doxas, & Weston, 2006). In our study of Latina middle school girls who chose to participate in a computing-intensive after school program, only 29 percent stated an interest in a STEM career upon completion of the program (Denner, Werner, Bean, & Martinez, under review). However, attitudes may be more positive among males and among female students already on the pathway to college. A recent survey of college-bound youth found that while Latino boys held positive views of careers in computing—78 percent said that being a computer scientist/software designer would very good or good profession for them or someone like them—only 32 percent of Latina girls said the same thing (New Image for Computing, 2009). These early attitudes have long-term implications for aspirations and academic achievement, as well as occupational opportunities and mental health (Portes & Fernández-Kelly, 2008).

Two other psychological processes involve the development of a social identity and a response to stereotypes about the kinds of people who participate in STEM. Suárez-Orozco & Suárez-Orozco (2001) describe how the academic experiences of children of immigrants involve discrimination and negative stereotyping of Latinos. Research on "stereotype threat" shows how negative beliefs about the group to which they belong can limit a student's performance, and has been found to partially explain lower math scores by females and some minority students (Good, Aronson, & Harder, 2008). Group identity can undermine school engagement for some students, who view succeeding in school as a departure from their family and ethnic group. Others build bicultural or transcultural identities that allow them to succeed and stay connected in both worlds, in an effort to give back to their families for their sacrifices (Bettie, 2003). The achievement of a "dual identity" may be easier for female than for male students (Wortham, 2002).

In summary, there are a host of social and institutional factors that play a role in why Latino students' interest in college and STEM does not transfer into the attainment of degrees and participation in the STEM workforce. Valenzuela's (1999) concept of "subtractive schooling," incorporates these factors when she shows how schools are often organized in ways that "fracture students' cultural and ethnic identities, creating linguistic and cultural divisions among the students and the staff" (p. 5). At the institutional level, subtractive schooling environments do not value the cultural assets and practices that Latino youth bring with them to the school. At the social level, expectations at the peer and adult level serve to reinforce social cliques that are based on race/ethnicity and social class, and membership often determines students' educational trajectory (Bettie, 2003). In this section, we have focused on barriers, and in the next section, we describe the supports that lead some Latino students to pursue college and STEM.

SUPPORTS FOR COLLEGE ENROLLMENT AND STEM CAREERS

As discussed above, relationships play a key role in whether Latinos obtain the information and resources required to attend and graduate from college. The theoretical construct of social capital has been used to describe the ways that social networks provide key resources for academic achievement by promoting norms and values (Coleman, 1990). Social capital consists of the mediating role of relationships with people and institutions that help students achieve goals that would not otherwise be possible (Coleman, 1989).

Social capital is a useful explanatory framework because while Latinos aspire for careers that require higher education, many lack the knowledge of educational requirements, and the specific steps needed to achieve their goals (DeLeon 1996; Reyes, Kobus & Gillock 1999; Rivera & Gallimore, 2006). Valenzuela (1999) found that students' concepts of *educación* meant that they must have a caring relationship with an adult at school in order to be engaged. Along with establishing caring relationships with school personnel, they must also build instrumental relationships that provide valuable information and assistance. In order for the relationships to have academic benefits, they must be with people that can facilitate the transference of key resources that will be helpful in the pursuit of college (Conchas, 2006; Stanton-Salazar, 2001). Students who are on college pathways are less likely to rely solely on mentors in their communities or peers and classmates that may not be able to provide the guidance needed to pursue their educational or career objectives (Pérez & McDonough, 2008; Rivera & Gallimore, 2006). For example, Latinas who enrolled in college were more likely to have sought out college counselors for direct guidance and request for college track courses than those who did not enroll in college (Zarate & Gallimore, 2005). In some communities, cultural brokers—members of the community who have successfully negotiated educational and familial demands—play a pivotal role when they can familiarize parents with their children's educational demands, and help youth strategize how to best assist their families while pursuing their education (Cooper, Denner & Lopez, 1999).

Family support is most often described as emotional, rather than instrumental. Many parents immigrated to the United States in order to provide better schooling options for their children, suggesting a high value placed on education (Gándara & Contreras, 2009). Immigrant parents who arrive with limited formal education and few institutional connections can still contribute to their child's education through other means, such as emotional support (Cooper et al., 2005; Denner, 2009). Although Perez and Padilla (2000) have found no differences in perceived family support among first-, second-, and third-generation adolescents, the nature of that support is dependent on the economic resources available. Parent involvement plays a critical role in whether students enroll in advanced mathematics classes, but this involvement may be more beneficial among higher-income Latinos because of their familiarity with the school system (Valdez, 2002). In addition, parental involvement may be more beneficial for male than female students: In a longitudinal study, high parental aspirations and expectations were positively correlated with college enrollment for Latinos but not Latinas (Zarate & Gallimore, 2005). These same parents also stated that getting a college education is a more important step toward improving one's economic status for males than for females. However, they encouraged girls to pursue their education in order to stay out of trouble (i.e., not get pregnant) and as a backup in case they became divorced (Zarate & Gallimore, 2005). These expectations can be conveyed through implicit or explicit messages and have important implications for whether students pursue college and their choice of major.

Students recognize that their families play a critical role in their educational and career pathways. In a study of Latina middle school girls in a computing-intensive after-school program, students reported that their family was the main influence on their career goals and interests: Most said parents, but one quarter mentioned a female relative specifically (Denner, 2009). Thus, it is families, not just parents, who play an important role in students' career goals and interests. Further, the majority believed that their parents would be supportive of them choosing a career in computer science, but very few described a computer- or information technology-specific goal (Denner, 2009). Most described a goal within the "helping" professions, such as doctor, teacher, or veterinarian.

In summary, key supports for college enrollment and the pursuit of a STEM major include instrumental relationships with highly resourced adults outside the family, as well as people who believe in the students' ability to succeed in these fields. The instrumental and emotional support provided by families appears to be tied to economic resources as well as gender role expectations. In the next section, we describe several interventions designed to build social capital for Latinos to pursue college and STEM majors.

INTERVENTIONS

There have been a multitude of efforts to increase the number of college-bound Latino students, and several have focused on STEM. Research on the effectiveness of these approaches is limited; few have been rigorously evaluated, and most do not provide clear evidence due in part to methodological limitations, such as a lack of a comparison group, or lack of clarity about the selection criteria. For example, a recent overview of research on girl-focused STEM programs finds limited evidence of their effectiveness, and most of the programs lacked a research design that allowed for strong evaluation (Halpern et al., 2007). Below we provide examples of interventions that have evidence that they prepare Latino students for college and several that focus specifically on STEM pathways.

The Puente program aims to increase the enrollment of Latinos in higher education by providing information and resources to high school students. Puente has three components: 1) a two-year English course that incorporates and emphasizes critical thinking, Latino literature, and sociopolitical topics, 2) college and personal counseling, and 3) mentoring (Gándara & Contreras, 2009). The program serves a range of students, including high achievers, and those with low grades but a demonstrated interest in college. Studies of Puente show that the program not only provides information on college requirements, but also provides other types of instrumental and emotional support. For example, students built a support network of peers who have similar aspirations and connections to institutional agents (Gándara, 2002; Moreno, 2002). In addition, Puente students reported similar educational aspirations as their White and Asian peers, and were more likely to be aware of the college entrance requirements and take the SAT before the twelfth grade than non-Puente students (Gándara, 2002, 2005).

STEM-focused interventions are fewer, but there are some promising, research-based approaches. Mathematics, Engineering, Science Achievement (MESA), is an in-school program that aims to increase the numbers of economically disadvantaged Latinos that pursue degrees in STEM. The MESA Schools program builds a network of support and prepares students for STEM classes at competitive colleges and universities by partnering with school districts and industry representatives. Activities include academic planning, SAT preparation, career and college exploration, and hands-on math and science competitions. By working closely with a teacher and a group of fellow students, there are opportunities to build both content knowledge and positive self-perceptions. MESA graduates attend college in significantly higher rates than students who did not participate in MESA, and in 2006–7 of the MESA high school graduates, 54 percent went on to postsecondary education as math, science, or engineering majors.

The Girl Game Company (GGC) is an after-school and summer program for Latina girls that challenges traditional gender role expectations and builds a STEM identity that is both positive and consist with cultural values. Three research-based strategies have proven effective for engaging Latina girls and promoting positive self-perceptions related to computing: building cultural connections, leveraging existing interests in IT, and encouraging collaborative learning (Denner, Bean, & Martinez, 2009). The strategy of building cultural connections includes being responsive to students with a range of English language proficiency, fostering parent involvement, and offering access to virtual mentors, such as students or professionals in IT. The strategy of leveraging existing interests in IT includes teaching students to design and program original computer games, an approach that engages girls with both graphics and programming interests while teaching some fundamental computing concepts and skills. Finally, collaborative learning is a fundamental part of the program, as students work with a partner to design and build their computer game, and interact with peers in an online tween community. An evaluation of 59 students who participated for 50 or more hours show significant increases in students' expectations for success with computing, the extent to which they value computing and computing-related jobs, and perceived parent support.

Some intervention programs are designed to leverage the important role played by parents and families in students' academic pathways. These efforts aim to build students' academic achievement and interest in STEM in ways that do not undermine students' connections to family and community. Using a "funds of knowledge" perspective, these educational approaches involve families and communities by building on their cultural resources (Moll & Ruiz, 2005). Efforts to involve Latino parents as learners, facilitators, and leaders in their children's mathematics education, have been used successfully in low-income Latino communities (Civil & Bernier, 2006). A new project, called Animando Estudiantes con Tecnología (Supporting students in the field of information technology) funded by the National Science Foundation, will create a parent leadership committee that will work within their rural community to promote parent knowledge and interest in their children's STEM pathways (Bean, Denner, & Martinez, 2009).

Gateway to Higher Education is a four-year high school program in New York City that prepares students from underrepresented minority groups to pursue majors in science, technology, engineering, and medicine. Students take additional coursework in math or science, participate in small-group study and after-school tutoring, and attend academic summer programs. There are also opportunities for internships, social outings, campus visits, college fairs, and research experiences. An evaluation of the impact of the Gateway to Higher Education program involved a retrospective matched comparison group of non-participants (Campbell et al., 1998). The results suggest that Gateway students were more likely to graduate from high school, take the SAT at least once, and earn a higher combined SAT score than their matched comparison students. (Schultz & Mueller, 2006). Four years after participating, 52 percent were majoring in STEM.

In summary, several approaches are common across these promising or proven approaches to increasing the number of Latina/o students that pursue STEM. All the interventions involve a mixture of individual, relational, and institutional efforts that build social capital related to college enrollment and STEM. To varying degrees, these approaches incorporate several factors that play a key role in sustaining participation rates and impact: long duration, attention to factors outside the individual student, and financial assistance (US Department of Education, National Center for Education Statistics, 2001). They also incorporate certain teaching practices that are found to result in more positive experiences in STEM. For example, Colbeck, Cabrera, and Terenzini (2001) found that among women and minorities in STEM majors, hands-on, collaborative learning experiences promote positive self- perceptions and achievement. Finally, these interventions are designed to help students negotiate multiple identities across various contexts and demands by incorporating three key components described by Oyserman, Brickman & Rhodes (2007): equating academic achievement with a positive ethnic identity, feeling connected to their ethnic group, and awareness of racism.

DISCUSSION

Most of the research on Latinos and STEM focuses on enrollment and persistence in college; much less is understood about what leads Latinos on to STEM educational pathways and keeps them there. The literature review above describes research that sheds some light on the barriers and supports to college enrollment and the pursuit of STEM careers among Latina/o students. The research and theoretical perspectives highlight the individual, relational, and institutional factors that play a role in these pathways. And the interventions described above provide examples of how the research has been put into practice in an effort to ensure that the next generation of STEM innovators will include a representative number of Latina/o students.

The literature review leads to key lessons for practitioners and policymakers. Specifically, we describe five promising strategies that can be implemented in K–12 to increase the number of Latinos who earn college degrees in STEM. Although these strategies focus on STEM, there is significant overlap with the key features of effective programs for preparing underserved students for college (Gandara & Bial, 2001; Schultz & Mueller, 2006; Zalaquett, 2005). All of these are examples of what De Jesús (2005) calls "additive schooling" that "seeks to disrupt the social and cultural reproductive processes associated with subtractive schooling" (p. 368). The strategies are: build social capital, help students bridge multiple worlds, build students' expectations for success, focus on identity, and reform institutions.

> Strategy #1: Build social capital. Families and communities play a critical role in whether or not students will pursue STEM fields. Interventions must go beyond the individual student to provide support to families with limited education or familiarity with STEM areas, including information about pre-college preparation. It is also important to strengthen the student's and families' connections to key non-family resources that can provide instrumental support in the form of links to financial aid, navigating the college application system, and sharing what it is like to be a minority in STEM classes and careers. Virtual role models and mentors are a particularly good option in resource-poor or isolated communities.
>
> Strategy #2: Help students bridge multiple worlds. To minimize the disconnect that some students feel when they move between home and school, educators must have a greater understanding of their students' cultural practices, and incorporate activities that build on cultural capital. This will require creating mechanisms to facilitate communication between college outreach programs and K–12 focused interventions. In addition, more community-based strategies are needed to involve parents and families in shaping the STEM pathways of their children, and to educate parents as to how the goals of the STEM workforce are consistent with their cultural values and goals for their community.

Strategy #3: Build students' expectations for success. Rather than trying to increase the number of Latinos that are interested in STEM, a first step is to minimize the disconnect between values, interests, and the pursuit of those interests. To have the most immediate impact, efforts can target students with a stated interest in STEM and give them opportunities for mastery experiences to build positive self-perceptions. One approach is to increase students' beliefs that achievement in STEM fields is a result of hard work rather than membership in a particular group.

Strategy #4: Focus on identity. Interventions that build strong communities of support help students see that success in college and STEM fields is NOT inconsistent with having a strong ethnic identity. Strategies include connecting students with peers and mentors that share their background and have a strong interest in STEM, and fostering long-term relationships where developmentally normative questions of identity can be explored and discussed. Other effective strategies are those that help students connect STEM content to their non-academic interests (e.g., engaging students in computer programming by teaching them to program a computer game).

Strategy #5: Reform institutions. Improving the quality and availability of STEM classes for Latino students in middle and high schools can increase the likelihood that students will be prepared for college. It is also important to provide clear and equitable access to financial aid, and to reduce institutionalized discrimination.

CONCLUSION

The literature review suggests that all five strategies are essential for reversing the economic and psychological impact of Latino underrepresentation in STEM. Not surprisingly, our conclusion is that in order to increase the number of Latinos that become future innovators, it is necessary to understand not only the psychological factors that influence day-to-day decisions about schooling and future goals, but also the institutional and relational factors that shape how students think about their future. However, to our knowledge, these strategies, when applied, exist in isolation from each other. There is a need for funding and incentives that can develop well-run collaboratives that cut across research and practice, academic disciplines, and institutions.

There is also a need for stronger research on best practice for engaging Latinos in STEM. The knowledge base is small, lacks a theoretical framework that allows us to look across studies or disciplines, and has little longitudinal data to help us understand what approaches work in the long term. There is also a need for better documentation and more rigorous research on existing interventions that can lead to a research-based list of best practices, rather than the broad guidelines for strategies that we present here.

REFERENCES

Anderson, E., & Kim, D. (2006). *Increasing the success of minority students in science and technology.* Washington, DC: American Council on Education.

Barker, L. J., Snow, E., Garvin-Doxas, K., & Weston, T. (2006). Recruiting middle school girls into IT: Data on girls' perceptions and experiences from a mixed-demographic group. In J.M. Cohoon & W. Aspray (Eds.), *Women and information technology: Research on underrepresentation*, (pp.115–136). Cambridge, MA: The MIT Press.

Bean, S., Denner, J., & Martinez, J. (2009). *Animando estudiantes con tecnología.* Retrieved September 9, 2009 from http://itestlrc.edc.org/animando-estudiantes-con-technologia-aet-encouraging-students-field-information-technology.

Bettie, J. (2003). *Women without class: Girls, race, and identity.* Berkeley: University of California Press.

Bouchey, H. A., & Harter, S. (2005). Reflected appraisals, academic self perceptions, and math/science performance during early adolescence. *Journal of Educational Psychology 97*, 673–686.

Burger, C. J., Creamer, E. G., & Meszaros, P. S. (2007) *Reconfiguring the firewall: Recruiting women to information technology across cultures and continents*, Wellesley, MA: AK Peters, Ltd.

Campbell, P. B., Wahl, E., Slater, M., Iler, I., Moeller, B., Ba, H., & Light, D. (1998). Paths to success: An evaluation of the Gateway to Higher Education program. *Journal of Women and Minorities in Science and Engineering 4*, 297–308.

Civil, M., & Bernier, E. (2006). Exploring images of parental participation in mathematics education: Challenges and possibilities. *Mathematical Thinking and Learning 8*(3), 309–330.

Cleary, P. F., Pierce, G., & Trauth, E. M. (2006). Closing the digital divide: understanding racial, ethnic, social class, gender and geographic disparities in Internet use among school age children in the United States. *Universal Access in the Information Society 4*(4): 354–373.

Colbeck, C. L., Cabrera, A. F., & Terenzini, P. T. (2001). Learning professional confidence: Linking teaching practices, students' self-perceptions, and gender. *The Review of Higher Education 24*, 173–191.

Coleman, J. (1988). Social capital in the creation of human capital. *American Journal of Sociology 94*, 95–120.

Coleman, J. (1990). *Foundations of social theory.* Cambridge, Harvard University Press.

Conchas, G. Q. (2006). *The color of success: Race and high-achieving urban youth.* New York: Teachers College Press.

Cooper, C., Cooper, R., Azmitia, M., Chavira, G., & Gullatt, Y. (2002). Bridging multiple worlds: How African American and Latino youth in academic outreach programs navigate math pathways to college. *Applied Developmental Science 6*, 73–87.

Cooper, C., García Coll, C. T., Thorne, B., & Orellana, M. F. (2005). Beyond demographic categories: How immigration, ethnicity and "race" matter for children's identities and pathways through school. In C. R. Cooper, C. T. García-Coll, W. T. Bartko, H. Davis, & C. Chatman (Eds.), *Developmental pathways through middle childhood: Rethinking contexts and diversity as resources.* (pp. 181-206). Mahwah, NJ: Lawrence Erlbaum.

Cooper, C. R., & Denner, J. (1998). Theories linking culture and psychology: Universal and community-specific processes. *Annual Review of Psychology 49*, 559–584.

Cooper, C. R., Denner, J., & Lopez, E. M. (1999). Cultural brokers: Helping Latino children on pathways toward success. *The Future of Children 9*, 51–57.

De Jesús, A. (2005). Theoretical perspectives on the underachievement of Latino/a students in U.S. schools: Toward a framework for culturally additive schooling. In P. Pedraza & M. Rivera (Eds.), *Latino education: An agenda for community action research*, pp. 343–371. Mahwah, NJ: Erlbaum.

De Leon, B. (1996). Career development of Hispanic adolescent girls. In B. Leadbeater & N. Way (Eds.), *Urban girls: Resisting stereotypes, creating identities* (pp. 380–398). New York: New York University Press.

Denner, J. (2009). The role of the family in the IT career goals of middle school Latinas. *AMCIS 2009 Proceedings.* Paper 334. Retrieved September 9, 2009 from http://aisel.aisnet.org/amcis2009/334

Denner, J., Bean, S., & Martinez, J. (2009). The girl game company: Engaging Latina girls in information technology. *Afterschool Matters 8*, 26–35.

Denner, J., Werner, L., Bean, S., & Martinez, J. (under review). Computing goals, values, and expectations: Results from an IT-intensive after school program for girls.

Dowd, A. C., Malcom, L. E., & Bensimon, E. M. (2009). *Benchmarking the success of Latina and Latino students in STEM to achieve national graduation goals.* Los Angeles, CA: Center for Urban Education, University of Southern California.

Espinosa, L. L. (2008). The academic self-concept of African American and Latina(o) men and women in STEM majors. *Journal of Women in Science and Engineering 14*, 177–203.

Frehill, L. M., DiFabio, S. M., & Hill, T. (2008). Confronting the "new" American dilemma—underrepresented minorities in engineering: A data-based look at diversity. *National Action Council for Minorities in Engineering.* Retrieved on August 12, 2009 from http://hub.mspnet.org/index.cfm/17110

Fuligni, A., & Pedersen, S. (2002). Family obligation and the transition to young adulthood. *Developmental Psychology 38*, 856–868.

Gándara, P. (2002). A study of high school puente: What we have learned about preparing Latino youth for postsecondary education. *Educational Policy 16*(4), 474–495.

Gándara, P. (2005). Addressing educational inequities for Latino students: The politics of "forgetting". *Journal of Hispanic Higher Education 4*(3), 295–313.

Gándara, P., & Contreras, F. (2009). *The Latino education crisis: The consequences of failed social policies.* Cambridge, MA: Harvard University Press.

Gasbarra, P., & Johnson, J. (2008). *Out before the game begins: Hispanic leaders talk about what's needed to bring more Hispanic youngsters into science, technology, and math professions.* A Public Agenda Report prepared for America's Competitiveness: Hispanic Participation in Technology Careers Summit, Palisades, New York.

Ginorio, A. (2007). Gender equity for Latina/os. In S. Klein (Ed.), *Handbook for achieving gender equity through education*, pp. 485–488. Mahwah, NJ: Erlbaum.

Good, C., Aronson, J., & Harder, J. (2008). Problems in the pipeline: Women's achievement in high-level math courses. *Journal of Applied Developmental Psychology 29, 17–28.*

Gutiérrez, K. (2002). Studying cultural practices in urban communities. *Human Development 45,* 312.

Gutiérrez, K. (2006) *Culture matters: Rethinking educational equity.* New York: Carnegie Foundation.

Halpern, D., Aronson, J., Reimer, N., Simpkins, S., Star, J., & Wentzel, K. (2007). *Encouraging girls in math and science* (NCER 2007-2003). Washington, DC: National Center for Education Research, Institute of Education Sciences, U.S. Department of Education. Retrieved August 14, 2009 from http://ncer.ed.gov.

Hurtado, S., Sáenz, V. B., Santos, J. L., & Cabrera, N. L. (2008). *Advancing in higher education: A portrait of Latina/o college freshman at four-year institutions: 1975–2006.* Los Angeles: Higher Education Research Institute, UCLA.

Immerwahr J. (2003). With diploma in hand: Hispanic high school seniors talk about their future. National Center Report #03-2. Retrieved October 4, 2009, from http://www.highereducation.org/reports/hispanic/hispanic.shtml.

Lopez, M. H. (2009). *Latinos and education: Explaining the attainment gap.* Pew Hispanic Center. Washington, DC: Pew Research Center.

Margolis, J. (2008). *Stuck in the shallow end: Education, race, and computing.* Cambridge, MA: MIT Press.

Margolis, J., & Fisher, A. (2003). *Unlocking the clubhouse.* Cambridge, MA: MIT Press.

May, G. S., & D. E. Chubin, (2003). A retrospective on undergraduate engineering success for underrepresented minority students. *Journal of Engineering Education 92*(1) 27–38.

Meszaros, P. S., Lee, S., & Laughlin, A. (2007). Information processing and information technology career interest and choice among high school students. In C. J. Burger, E. G. Creamer, & P. S. Meszaros (Eds.), *Reconfiguring the firewall: Recruiting women to information technology across cultures and continents*, pp. 77–95. Wellesley, MA: AK Peters, Ltd.

Moll, L. C., & Ruiz, R. (2005). The educational sovereignty of Latino/a students in the United States. In P. Pedraza & M. Rivera (Eds.) *Latino Education: An agenda for community action research.* (pp. 295–230). Mahwah, NJ: Erlbaum.

Moreno, J. F. (2002). The long-term outcomes of Puente. *Educational Policy 15*, 572–587.

National Academy of Sciences, National Academy of Engineering, and Institute of Medicine (2005). *Rising above the gathering storm: Energizing and employing America for a brighter future.* Washington, DC: National Academies Press.

National Center for Education Statistics (2008). Table. 204. Enrollment rates of 18- to 24-year-olds in degree-granting institutions, by type of institution and sex and race/ethnicity of student: 1967 through 2007. Retrieved October 10, 2009 from http://nces.ed.gov/programs/digest/d08/tables/dt08_204.asp.

National Center for Education Statistics (2009). The Condition of Education 2009. Retrieved October 10, 2009 from http://nces.ed.gov/fastfacts/display .asp?id=16.

National Science Board (2008). http://www.nsf.gov/statistics/seind08/

National Science Foundation, Division of Science Resources Statistics, *Women, minorities, and persons with disabilities in science and engineering: 2009*, NSF 09-305, (Arlington, VA; January 2009). Retrieved September 9, 2009 from http://www.nsf.gov/statistics/wmpd/.

Newcombe, N. S. (2009, April). *APA-SRCD joint task force addresses psychology's role in math and science education.* Developments: Newsletter of the Society for Research in Child Development, 1, 7.

New Image for Computing (2009). http://www.acm.org/membership/NIC.pdf. WGBH Educational Foundation and the Association for Computing Machinery.

Newport, F. (2007). Strong relationship between income and mental health. Retrieved January 26, 2010 from http://www.gallup.com/poll/102883/strong-relationship-between-income-mental-health.aspx.

Olson, S., & Fagen, A. P. (2007). *Understanding interventions that encourage minorities to pursue research careers: Summary of a workshop.* Washington DC: The National Academies Press.

Oyserman, D., Brickman, D., & Rhodes, M. (2007). Racial-ethnic identity: Content and consequences for African American, Latino, and Latina youths. In A. Fuligni (Ed.), *Contesting stereotypes and creating identities: Social categories, social identities, and educational participation*, pp. 91–114. New York: Russell Sage.

Pérez, P. A., & McDonough, P. M. (2008). Understanding Latina and Latino college choice: A social capital and chain migration analysis. *Journal of Hispanic Higher Education 7*(3), 249–265.

Perez, W., & Padilla, A. M. (2000). Cultural orientation across three generations of Hispanic adolescents. *Hispanic Journal of Behavioral Sciences 22*, 390–398.

Portes, A., & Fernández-Kelly, P. (2008). No margin for error: Educational and occupational achievement among disadvantaged children of immigrants. *Annals of the American Academy of Political and Social Science 620*(1), 12–36.

Reyes, O., Kobus, K., & Gillock K. (1999). Career aspirations of urban, Mexican American adolescent females. *Hispanic Journal of Behavioral Sciences 21*, 366–382.

Rivera, W., & Gallimore, R. (2006). Latina adolescents career goals: Resources for overcoming obstacles. In Denner, J., & Guzman, B. (Eds.) *Latina Girls: Voices of Adolescent Strength in the U.S.* (pp. 109–122). New York, NY: New York University Press.

Schultz, J.L., & Mueller, D. (2006). *Effectiveness of programs to improve post-secondary education enrollment and success of underrepresented youth.* Retrieved September 9, 2009 from http://www.wilder.org/reportsummary.0.html?tx_ttnews[tt_news]=1948.

Spencer, S., Steele, C. M., & Quinn, D. M. (1999). Stereotype threat and women's math performance. *Journal of Experimental Social Psychology 35*, 4–28.

Stanton-Salazar, R. (Ed.). (2001). *Manufacturing hope and despair: The school and kin support networks of U.S.-Mexican youth.* New York, US: Teachers College Press.

Suárez-Orozco, C., & Suárez-Orozco, M. (2001). *Children of immigration.* Cambridge, MA: Harvard University Press.

Thorpe, H. (2009). *Just like us: The true story of four Mexican girls coming of age in America.* New York: Simon and Schuster.

U.S. Census (2001). *Total Population by age, race, and Hispanic or Latino origin for the United States: 2000* (Table 1). Retrieved October 18, 2009 from http://www.census.gov/population/www/cen2000/briefs/phc-t9/index.html.

U.S. Census (2008). Press release: U.S. Hispanic population surpasses 45 million, now 15 percent total. Retrieved October 18, 2009 from http://www.census.gov/Press-Release/www/releases/archives/population/011910.html.

U.S. Department of Education, National Center for Education Statistics. (2001). *Paving the way to postsecondary education: K–12 intervention programs for underrepresented youth, NCES 2001-205,* prepared by Patricia Gándara with the assistance of Deborah Bial for the National Postsecondary Education Cooperative Access Working Group. Washington DC. Retrieved September 10, 2009 from http://nces.ed.gov/pubSearch/pubsinfo.asp?pubid=2001205.

Valdez, J. R. (2002). The influence of social capital on mathematics course selection by Latino high school students. *Hispanic Journal of Behavioral Sciences 24*(3), 319–339.

Valenzuela, A. (Ed.). (1999). *Subtractive schooling: U.S.-Mexican youth and the politics of caring.* Albany, NY: State University of New York Press.

Varma, R., Prasad, A., & Kapur, D. (2006). Confronting the "socialization" barrier: Cross-ethnic differences in undergraduate women's preference for IT education. In J. M. Cohoon & W. Aspray (Eds.), *Women and information technology: Research on underrepresentation*, pp. 301–322. Cambridge, MA: MIT Press.

Weissberg, R. P., Kumpfer, K. L., & Seligman, M. E. P. (2003). Prevention that works for children and youth. *American Psychologist 58*(6–7), 425–432.

The White House. (2009). *Remarks by the President at the National Academy of Sciences Annual Meeting.* press release, April 27, 2009. Retrieved September 9, 2009 from http://www.whitehouse.gov/the_press_office/Remarks-by -the-President-at-the-National-Academy-of-Sciences-Annual-Meeting.

Wortham, S. (2002). Gender and school success in the Latino diaspora. In S. Wortham, E. G. Murillo Jr., & E. T. Hamann (Eds.) *Education in the new Latino diaspora: Policy and the politics of identity.* Westport, CT: Ablex Publishing.

Zalaquett, C. P. (2005). Study of successful Latina/o students. *Journal of Hispanic Higher Education 5*, 35–47.

Zarate, M. E., & Gallimore, R. (2005). Gender differences in factors leading to college enrollment: A longitudinal analysis of Latina and Latino students. *Harvard Educational Review 75*, 383–408.

Chapter 7

"SOMETIMES YOU NEED TO SPILL YOUR HEART OUT TO SOMEBODY": CLOSE FRIENDSHIPS AMONG LATINO ADOLESCENT BOYS[1]

Niobe Way, Carlos E. Santos, and Alexandra Cordero

It is the middle of June and the New York City heat is on full blast making it even hotter in the empty high school classroom where 15-year-old Justin and his interviewer José sit in the late afternoon. Justin, whose mother is Puerto Rican and whose father is Irish and Italian American, is being interviewed for our school-based research project on boys' social and emotional development. There is neither an air conditioner nor a fan in the classroom so Justin, in his baggy jeans and tee-shirt, pulls out a notebook from his backpack and begins to fan himself as he listens to Jose begin the interview protocol. This meeting is the second of four annual interviews. The first set of questions on the protocol is about Justin's friends in general and he responds by discussing his network of peers in school. Turning to the topic of close friendships, he says,

> [My best friend and I] love each other . . . that's it . . . you have this thing that is deep, so deep, it's within you, you can't explain it. It's just a thing that you know that that person is that person . . . and that is all that should be important in our friendship . . . I guess in life, sometimes two people can really, really understand each other and really have a trust, respect, and love for each other. It just happens, it's human nature. . . .

Listening to boys, particularly during early and middle adolescence, speak about their male friendships is like reading an old-fashioned romance novel in which the female protagonist is describing her passionate feelings for her man. At the edge of manhood when pressures to conform to gender expectations intensify (Hill & Lynch, 1983), boys talk with tremendous affect about their best friends with whom they share their deepest secrets and without whom they would "feel lost."

While this theme of emotional intimacy in friendships has been heard among most of the White, Black, Latino, and Asian American boys in our studies over the past two decades, it has been particularly evident among the Latinos. Set against an American culture that perceives males in general to be emotionally stoic, autonomous, and physically tough (Kimmel, 2008) and Latino males, in particular, to be "macho" or "hypermasculine" (Guttman, 1996), these stories are surprising. Puerto Rican, Dominican American, and boys from other Latin American countries valued their male friendships greatly and saw them as critical components to their psychological well-being, not because their friends were worthy opponents in the competition for manhood but because they were able to share their thoughts and feelings—their deepest secrets—with these friends.

Yet when one looks at the research literature on boys or on Latino youth more specifically, discussions of close friendships are almost entirely absent. Long considered the most important relationships during adolescence and crucial for social, emotional, and academic adjustment throughout the lifespan (Erdly, Nangle, Newman, & Carpenter, 2001; Nangle & Erdley, 2001; Sullivan, 1953; Vitaro, Boivin, & Bukowski, 2009), friendships among adolescent boys are remarkably underexplored. This pattern is particularly evident in the research on ethnic minority youth. While we have known for over a century about the association between close friendships and feelings of self worth and adjustment (Ladd & Troop-Gordon, 2003; Nangle & Erdley, 2001; Pelkonen, Martunnen, & Aro, 2003; Vitaro et al., 2009) the focus of research on ethnic minority youth has been on high-risk behavior and, more recently, immigration experience and identity development (Decker and Van Winkle, 1996; Padilla, 1992; Ureño, 2003).

The lack of attention to friendships among ethnic minority youth has implicitly suggested that such relationships are not important for such youth. Yet the few studies on this topic with ethnic minority youth underscore the critical role of friendships for the well-being of Latino, Black, Asian American, and White youth (Azmitia et al., 2006; Falicov, 1998; Santos et al., 2009; Way, in press). Falicov (1998), a family therapist for Latino families, writes: "Relationships with same-sex peers, whether relatives or friends, are so important for Latinos that it's not unusual for them to be implicated in the presenting problem of an individual or family" (p. 167). In this chapter, we present findings from our Latino subsample of boys and explore the development of their friendships throughout adolescence, the ways in which the micro and macro context shapes their friendships, and the critical role that these relationships play in their mental health.

THEORY AND RESEARCH ON FRIENDSHIPS

Harry Stack Sullivan maintained that during preadolescence (9–12 years of age) a need for intimacy arises which he defines as "that type of situation involving two people which permits validation of all components of personal worth" (Sullivan, 1953, p. 246). In response to this intimacy need, preadolescent boys begin to have extremely close relationships, with a male peer. This relationship "represents the beginning of very much like full-blown, psychiatrically defined, love . . ." (p. 245). It is during this period in which "a child begins to develop a real sensitivity to what matters to another person" (p. 245) and represents a significant developmental milestone. These "love" relationships are considered essential, according to Sullivan, for a development of self worth and the acquisition of the social skills necessary for engagement in future romantic relationships.

Drawing from Sullivan's theory, research has indicated that the sharing of intimate thoughts and feelings in friendships do, in fact, increase from childhood to adolescence (Azmitia, Ittel, & Brent, 2006; Berndt, 1981; Bigelow & LaGaipa, 1980; Furman & Bierman, 1984) and that such relationships provide a wide array of social, emotional, academic, and cognitive benefits for children and adolescents (see Rubin, Bukowski, & Laursen, 2009 for a review). Intimate (e.g., self-disclosing) and supportive friendships have been found, for example, to be associated with lower levels of depressive symptoms (Oldenburg & Kerns, 1997; Pelkonen et al., 2003; Vernberg, 1990), higher levels of self esteem (Bishop & Inderbitzen, 1995; Nangle & Erdley, 2001) and high levels of academic engagement (Santos, Way, & Hughes, in progress). A lack of close friendships has also been found to be associated with high levels of depressive symptoms, internalizing problems, and peer victimization (Ladd & Troop-Gordon, 2003). In one study, researchers found that a lack of close friends at age 16 predicted depressive symptoms at age 22, over and above previous levels of depressed mood (Pelkonen et al., 2003). Gender differences, however, have been reported in the association between mental health and friendship quality with the quality of best friendships being more strongly related to loneliness and depression for boys than for girls (Erdley et al., 2001).

A major limitation of the body of research on friendships has been that most studies focus primarily on American, White, middle class adolescents or young adults implicitly suggesting that such "normative processes" are only relevant to a particular group of young people. The studies that are the exceptions to this pattern, however, reveal few ethnic/racial differences in the quality (e.g., emotional or social support) or importance of friendships or in the association between psychological adjustment and friendship quality (Azmitia & Cooper, 2001; Azmitia, Ittel & Brent, 2006; Levitt et al., 1993; Santos, 2010; Way, 2011; Way & Chen, 2000; Way & Robinson, 2003). Emotionally supportive friendships appear to be beneficial for the well-being of all youth regardless of their cultural or ethnic background. Studies have found, however, ethnic variation in the extent to which friendships are valued over family relationships with more recent Latino immigrants being less likely to value their friendships over family relationships than later generation immigrants (Azmitia & Cooper, 2001). Yet European American and African American adolescents appear to be equally likely to value friendships over family relationships (Levitt, Guacci-Franco, Levitt, 1993).

Another limitation in the research on friendships is the almost exclusive reliance on survey methodology to assess the quality of friendships. While examining the frequency of a predetermined set of dimensions of friendship quality is important, especially if one wants to make group comparisons in the frequency of such responses, an over-reliance on survey methodology has resulted in the field knowing more about the "quantity" of friendships than the quality. While it may be true that boys, for example, are less likely than girls to endorse survey items related to intimacy in their friendships, it is not clear how boys' experience their male friendships. A survey study that detects sex differences in the frequency of endorsement of intimate dimensions tells us little about the experience or quality of friendships of either boys or girls. The importance of drawing from qualitative research in the study of friendships is underscored when one examines the findings from such research. Qualitative or interview-based research has typically found that adolescent boys have emotionally intimate male friendships and that they tend to speak about their friendships in similar ways as girls (Azmitia, Kamprath & Linnet, 1998; Radmacher & Azmitia, 2006; Way, 2004; Way, 2011). These latter findings do not contradict the survey-based studies that have detected gender differences in friendship quality, they simply point to the limited nature of survey-based research in understanding the experience of friendships during adolescence.

A third limitation in the study of friendships is the acontextual nature of much of the research. Even with the heavy ecological emphasis evident in most psychological research, the ways in which both micro and macro environments influence friendship is almost entirely absent from the scholarly literature. Developmental theory and research has suggested for decades that adolescent development is shaped by parents, peers, schools, neighborhoods, and macro political, social, and economic forces (Bowlby, 1969/1982; Bronfenbrenner, 1979; Eccles & Roeser, 1999; Spencer, 2006; Vitaro et al., 2009). Adolescent friendships are also influenced by relationships with mothers, fathers, siblings, peers, aunts, uncles as well as by teachers and mentors, by family characteristics (SES, family structure), schools, neighborhood resources, and by cultural norms, beliefs, and practices that stem from the political, economic, and social contexts (Bowlby, 1969/1982; Bronfenbrenner, 1979; Chen, French, & Schneider, 2006; Way, 2011). Boys are shaped by the beliefs and practices of their parents and peers but also by the larger American context or culture that includes the stereotypes and expectations maintained within that context (Hurtado & Sinha, 2008; Kimmel, 2008). Examining friendships in the micro contexts of families, peers, and schools as well as in the macro context of, for example, gender stereotypes is essential if we are to advance our understanding of the development of friendships.

Responding to these gaps in the literature, we have been exploring the experience of friendships among boys from early to late adolescence for nearly two decades. We have been interested specifically in the ways in which boys from different ethnic and racial groups experience friendships, and how these experiences change from early to late adolescence. We have also been interested in the ways in which families, schools, as well as gender and racial and ethnic stereotypes and expectations about "manhood" found within an American context infiltrate boys' narratives about friendships. (For more a more detailed discussion of these studies, see Way, 2011). This chapter focuses on our findings with respect to the Latino boys in our studies.

METHODS

Participants

This paper presents findings from the 48 (average age 14.1 at time one) Latino adolescents boys (26 Puerto Rican, 15 Dominican, and 7 boys from other Latin American countries or mixed culturally) who participated in one of three of our mixed method, longitudinal studies of social and emotional development of Blacks, Latinos, Whites, and Asian Americans from early to late adolescence (see Way, 2011 for more details). The Puerto Rican students were almost exclusively born in the United States while five of the

Dominican students were born in the Dominican Republic. The majority of the remaining seven students were born in the United States. All of the Latino boys in our studies who participated in at least two years of qualitative data collection (85 percent of our original sample of Latino students) were included in the analysis. The students attending the schools in which we conducted our studies were primarily from poor or working class families with 80–90% eligible for the free or reduced lunch program.

Procedure

Students were recruited in their freshman or sophomore year in public high schools and participated in surveys and semi-structured interviews annually (during the winter or spring each year) for a period of two to five years. We recruited students from mainstream English classes to ensure that the study participants were fluent in English since the interviews were conducted in English. The interviews asked the participants to discuss a range of topics (e.g., family, school, peers) including their friendships. The interview protocol included questions such as: "How would you describe your relationship with your best friend?" and "What kinds of things do you talk about with your best friend? Give an example?" Although each interview included a standard set of questions, follow-up questions varied across interviews to capture the adolescents' own ways of describing their friendships. The interviews were held during the school day, lasted approximately 90 minutes, and took place in an office or classroom in which confidentiality could be assured. The interviews were conducted by an ethnically diverse group of graduate students in psychology who had been extensively trained in interviewing techniques. All interviews were audiotaped and transcribed for analysis.

Data Analysis

We used a process of open coding (see Strauss & Corbin, 1990) to generate themes from the interview data. The research team first read through the transcripts and created narrative summaries that condensed the interview material while retaining the essence of the stories told by the adolescents (see Miller, 1991). Following that step, team members read each narrative summary independently, looking for themes in the summaries. In any one year of the study, a theme retained for further analysis had to be identified as a theme independently by at least two of the team members. Once themes were generated and agreed on, each team member returned to the original interviews and noted the year in the project and the specific place in the interview where these themes emerged. They also took note of if and how the themes changed during other years of the study (for more details, see Way, 2011).

FRIENDSHIPS DURING ADOLESCENCE

Our qualitative data analysis has consistently indicated 5 themes:1) Boys, particularly Latino boys, have emotionally intimate male friendships that entail shared secrets and much emotional vulnerability; 2) Emotionally intimate friendships are considered by the boys themselves to be essential to their mental health; 3)Boys begin to lose these friendships and/or become wary and distrustful of their male peers as they enter late adolescence; 4) Boys continue to desire intimate male friendships throughout adolescence; 5) Gender stereotypes and expectations about "manhood" was a primary reason for the loss of friendships and the increased levels of distrust during late adolescence.

Having Emotionally Intimate Friendships/Not Going "Wacko"

At the edge of adolescence, boys—the same boys the media claims are obsessed with girls, gangs, and pumped up cars—spoke about "circles of love," "spilling your heart out to somebody," "sharing deep depth secrets," and "feeling lost" without their male best friends. While this theme was evident among all of the boys in our studies (see Way, 2011), it was particularly true among the Latino boys. Ninety percent of the Latino boys suggested such themes especially during early and middle adolescence while only seventy-five percent of the non-Latino boys suggested such themes during their interviews. Benny, a 15-year-old Puerto Rican boy said, "I trust my friends. Like if I have a deep secret I don't want to tell anybody, I tell one of my friends that I know won't tell anybody else unless I give them permission to tell somebody else." When asked what he *likes* about his friend, Marcus, a Puerto Rican freshman, replied: "We share secrets that we don't talk about it in the open." When asked to explain why he felt close to his male friends, he stated: "If I'm having problems at home, they'll like counsel me, I just trust them with anything, like deep secrets, anything." Eddie, a Puerto Rican sophomore said, "It's like a bond, we keep secrets, like if there is something that's important to me like I could tell him and he won't go and make fun of it. Like if my family is having problems or something." He knows he can trust his best friend because "when we were like younger it's like a lot of thing that I told him that he didn't tell anybody, like it's like a lot of things he told me that I didn't tell anybody."

The boys even indicated that the intimacy or sharing of secrets in their friendships is what they *liked most* about their friendships. Junot, a Dominican American sophomore, said, "We always tell each other everything. And um like, if something happens and I save it for [my best friend]." In his junior year, he said, "[What I like most about my best friendship] is the connection. It's like, you know how you know somebody for so long you could talk about anything and you won't even think, I mean you won't even think about how 'oh what are they thinking?' You just talk."

The content of boys' secrets varied considerably and the term "secrets" was often used interchangeably with "problems." "Problems" were always "secrets" but "secrets" weren't necessarily problems. Marcelo, a Puerto Rican student, made distinctions between secrets when talking about the friends whom he does not trust in his sophomore year:

> I mean I can like joke around with them and like if I'm like having trouble in my classes, like if somebody knows the subject better than me, like I'll ask them. Like yeah, it's pretty much like that, not too deep though.... I wouldn't tell them like my two secretest things, not too secretive.. Yeah. Like maybe I would tell them about a girl or something. I mean that's the deepest, nothing deeper than that though.

The content of "regular" or "not too deep" secrets ranged from crushes on girls or girl related topics. "Really, really big secrets" or "secretest things" were almost always related to conflicts in the home or, on rare occasions, coping with disabilities or drug abuse of a family member. Paul, a Dominican American, revealed that he shares secrets with his best friends "all the time" and admitted that it is good to have a best friend because "sometimes, like you don't want to tell your family members 'cause it's probably about them and you just tell your friend and they'll keep a secret and help you." Family related "problems" or "secrets" were often considered the "deepest" secrets of all.

Such open discussion of thoughts and feelings, however, were not simply what boys did. They believed sharing secrets was a necessity for their emotional health. They did not need the social science research to tell them so—they knew that if they didn't have a close friend with whom they could talk intimately, they would go "wacko." Justin, who is half Puerto Rican and half European American, indicated at the age of 15: "My ideal best friend is a close, close friend who I could say anything to ...'cause sometimes you need to spill your heart out to somebody and if there's nobody there, then you gonna keep it inside, then you will have anger. So you need somebody to talk to always." George, a Puerto Rican boy, said when asked about why friendships are important: "So I mean, if you just have your mother and your parents [to talk to], then you're just gonna have all these ideas bottled up and you're just gonna go wacko because you can't express yourself even more. So I think, yeah, it's really important." Manny, a Dominican American boy, said:

> You need friends to talk to sometimes, you know like you have nobody to talk to, you don't have a friend, it's hard. You got to keep things bottled up insides, you might just . . . crying or whatever. Like if a family member is beating on you or something and you can't tell a friend, you might just go out, just you know do drugs, sell drugs whatever.

Another Dominican American boy concurs saying that "without friends you will go crazy or mad or you'll be lonely all of the time, be depressed." Boys recognize that in the absence of trusting friendships in which they can "share everything," there will be serious psychological consequences.

Not only did the boys share "deep secrets" with their male best friends but they also discussed and expressed feelings of vulnerability. As Felix, a Puerto Rican student, reflected on his best friendship with David during his sophomore year, he said, "My best friend thinks physical pain is worse than emotional pain and I don't think that's true, 'cause physical pain could last but for so long, but when it's in the mind, it doesn't go away." Acutely attuned to the nuances of the emotional world, Felix is typical of the Latino boys during their freshman and sophomore years. Continuing the theme into his junior year, Felix said,

> I don't give—I don't give my heart out to too many people, you know, especially when it could get broken or hurt easily. I've been through too many times of that. So it's like I don't have any room – I have to recuperate from my heart broken. There's been death in my family, girlfriends, you know, guy friends. I don't have any more for my heart to get stepped on. So I've picked myself up for awhile. I'm walking. But you know, you never know when you fall down again. So I'm trying to just keep my eye out.

Felix vividly expressed the wariness that comes after a broken heart. And in this scene, his heart was not simply broken over a girl or a family member but also by a "guy friend." Feelings for family members, girl friends, and "guy friends" are blended together in a seamless discussion of having his "heart stepped on."

Justin, the boy who is half Puerto Rican and half European American, said in his freshman year when considering whether he would like to be closer to his male friends:

> I think so. But I don't really know if they're gonna stay here for four years. So I feel like I can't get too attached 'cause then if they leave, I still get

attached to them even though 'cause a friend, he, he could come and go even though I really don't want it to happen. But it could come and go. I could make new friends or whatever. So I, doesn't matter if I get attached to them or not. I don't know . . . I don't want to [become attached] because if they leave I really don't, I never really got emotional for a guy before but I don't know if I would or if I wouldn't.

Justin's struggle is palpable as he expresses both his desire for closeness and a fear that if he allows himself to feel "attached" he will get hurt. He attempts to assert the masculine convention ("doesn't matter if I get attached to them or not") but then recognizes that it is not truly what he feels. By the end of the passage, he poses a question to which he already knows the answer.

The vulnerability in boys' stories was often evident when they were asked what they liked and did not like about their friendships. Describing what he likes about his best friend, David, a Dominican American sophomore, said:

I think our relationship is wonderful. Because we like, I can't explain. The feelings that I have for him if something would happen to him, I probably won't feel right. . . . Like when he was sick and I hadn't seen him for like a week and I went to his um house and I, and I asked his grandmother what was wrong with him and he was in the room like he couldn't move. So I went in there. I sat in his house for the whole day talking to him. And like the next day he got up and he felt better.

David's response suggests a sharp attunement to his own vulnerability (e.g., I probably won't feel right) and to his friend's. He also knows, like so many of his male peers, that "talking" (e.g., I sat in his house for the whole day talking to him) is good for his health ("and like the next day he got up and he felt better").

Being direct and open about his feeling of vulnerability, Javier, a Puerto Rican student, said in his junior year:

Yeah 'cause [my best friend] is like a second person you could speak to. . . It's like see how the kids carry a little teddy bear or whatever and when they cry, they'll hold it and stuff. So when like you get upset or something you just walk over to them and they'll loosen, they'll loosen up whatever. They'll be like yeah it's alright, even though it's not.

Javier recognizes both the safety that a friend (or teddy bear) provides but also the expectation to cover over and tell stories that boys know are not true ("They'll be like yeah, it's alright, even though it's not"). In the context of gender and racial stereotypes, Javier's sensitivity and emotional sophistication is surprising. In the context of our studies, it is not.

While some boys were consistently willing to express vulnerability, others peppered their responses with masculine norms or gender stereotypes only to reveal their more vulnerable sides at other points in their interviews. When an interviewer asked Milo, a Puerto Rican boy, how it felt when he was teased by his best friend, he said, "I know he's playing so it doesn't really, it doesn't feel bad, but if I didn't know he was playing, he probably would be able to hurt somebody. He would get somebody mad enough to do something, you know." His switch from the first person (i.e., "I") to the vague reference of "somebody" right at the moment when his vulnerability is made explicit underscores the danger or sense of risk boys feel when expressing vulnerability. Yet the Latino boys in our studies often expressed such vulnerability anyway.

Expressions of vulnerability, care, and empathy were evident not only when boys discussed the details of their friendships but also when they spoke more abstractly about the importance of friendships. During his freshman year, Carlos, a Dominican American student, said about his best friend: "Like we could express our feelings or whatever. And tell each other how we feel. Like if I feel bad one day, I tell him why." He describes his best friend as a brother and uses language such as "we show each other love" to describe the depths of this friendship. "I know the kid inside of him, inside of him. 'Cause I . . . I grew up with that kid." While the Latino boys in our studies occasionally couched these discussions of friendships in more masculine language, they were more willing than the other boys in our study to reveal another story—a story of vulnerability, love, emotional connection, and desire for emotionally intimate friendships with other boys.

Becoming Distrustful and Alone

A simple question asked on the interview protocol provokes the following types of responses that reveal everything about how friendships change as boys reach late adolescence. The question on the protocol is: "How have your friendships changed since you were a freshman in high school?" The responses by two Latino boys, typical of all the boys in our studies during late adolescence, were:

> I don't know, maybe, not a lot, but I guess that best friends become close friends. So that's basically the only thing that changed. It's like best friends become close friends, close friends become general friends and then general friends become acquaintances. So they just . . . If there's distance whether it's, I don't know, natural or whatever. You can say that but it just happens that way.

> Like my friendship with my best friend is fading, but I'm saying it's still there but . . . So I mean, it's still there 'cause we still do stuff together, but only once in a while. It's sad 'cause he lives only one block away from me and I get to do stuff with him less than I get to do stuff with people who are way further so I'm like, yo. . . . It's like a DJ used his cross fader and started fading it slowly and slowly and now I'm like halfway through the cross fade.

At the age of 16 or 17, as their bodies are almost fully grown and their minds are increasingly attuned to cultural messages about manhood, boys begin to distance themselves from their intimate relationships with other boys and to lose connection with their emotionally sensitive selves. "Best friends become close friends, close friends become general friends, and general friends become acquaintances. . . . It just happens that way," says one boy expressing what the conventions of masculinity expects of him. While the Latino boys were more likely to have emotionally intimate male friendships than the non-Latino boys in our studies (see Way, 2011), they were not more or less likely to grow increasingly distrustful and wary of their male peers and, in many cases, lose their friendships entirely. As boys reach late adolescence and as the suicide rate nationwide rises dramatically during this developmental period and becomes four times the rate of girls (Tyre, 2009), boys from many different cultural backgrounds, including Latino, spoke about losing their closest friendships and growing more wary of their peers.

Homophobia was one of the key reasons boys indicated, both directly and indirectly, regarding why they became more emotionally reserved, wary, and found it difficult to maintain their emotionally intimate male friendships. In an American culture where vulnerable emotions are frequently characterized as "gay" or "girlish" and where "intimacy" is most often associated with sexual relations, this finding is not surprising. By late adolescence, boys turned our questions about close male friendships into questions about their sexual orientation. A common response from the boys when we asked about their close male friendships during late adolescence was: "I'm not gay." Despite their strong desires for intimate male friendships evident throughout adolescence, the boys' desire not to be perceived as "gay" or "girlish" consumed their interviews in late adolescence and prevented them from maintaining the very friendships they valued dearly. "No homo" became a common phrase following intimate statements of how they felt about their current or former close male friends.

When Fernando, a Dominican American boy, is asked in his junior year, what he likes about his best friend, whom he has already stated is not as close to him as before, he said, "everything, the way that we just relate, *no homo*, just the way we talk to each other." According to Urban Dictionary (2010), "no homo" is a "slang phrase used after one inadvertently says something that sounds gay." During late adolescence, Latino boys believed that questions about close friendships, the very relationships they actively desired, sounded "gay."

Addressing the question of good friends during his freshman year interview, Carlos said, "Like we could express our feelings or whatever. And tell each other how we feel. Like if I feel bad one day, I tell them why." He used language such as "we show each other love" to describe the bonds with his friends. Asked how he knew he could trust his best friend, he says, " 'Cause I know the kid inside of him. 'Cause I grew up with that kid, you understand? I know who he really is." By his sophomore year, however, something has shifted. When asked what he likes about his best friend, he said, "It's cool man. We could do anything. We joke around whatever. 'Cause I don't want to have a serious friend. That's boring, yo. Like I want a friend that I could joke around with. If I mess up he won't, you know, just laugh or I don't know." Mirroring ideals of masculinity that encourage boys to be strong and 'make it on their own' ("cause I don't want a serious friend") but then undercutting it with more sensitive views ("If I mess up he won't, you know, just laugh"), Carlos reveals a central conflict for boys during late adolescence. Boys typically want to have an "understanding" friendship but also typically want to be perceived as a heterosexual man.

By his junior year, Carlos' fears are directly stated as he repeated "no homo" every time he said something intimate about his best friend. In response to a question about what he does with his close friends, Carlos tells the interviewer "that question sounded homo, that sounded homo." When the interviewer expressed confusion as to how her question sounded "homo," he laughed and said that "we just do whatever, man, we like, we do whatever we can do. If we don't have money, we stay in his house, watch TV." No longer are Carlos and his friends "expressing feelings" as he indicated in his freshman year; they now do "whatever we can do." When asked about his "best friend" during his senior year interview, a friend whom he rarely sees but whom he still considers his "best friend": "The relationship, I mean it's a good relationship. It's um it's a tight bond whatever. Um, I can trust him. I don't know how to explain it. Somebody you feel chemistry. No homo." His qualification of "no homo" on the heels of expressing closeness (in traditional romantic terms) as well as his response of "it's a tight bond, *whatever*" suggests a discomfort with his feelings but a continued willingness to have a close male friendship.

Other boys, however, were not so lucky. Guillermo, a Bolivian American student, interviewed for the first time in his junior year, said when asked if he has a best friend this year:

> Not really. I think myself. The friend I had, I lost it . . . That was the only person that I could trust and we talked about everything. When I was down, he used to help me feel better. The same I did to him. So I feel pretty lonely and sometimes depressed. Because I don't have no one to go out with, no one to speak on the phone, no one to tell my secrets, no one for me to solve my problems . . . I think that it will never be the same, you know. I think that when you have a real friend and you lost him, I don't think you find another one like him. That's the point of view that I have . . . I tried to look for a person, you know, but it's not that easy.

The yearning specifically for an intimate male friendship is evident in his response as is the sense of loss and the feeling of inevitability associated with that loss. Boys' responses suggested a sensitivity that is similar to their response to betrayal. Once they lost a best friend, they find it difficult, if not impossible, to find a replacement. In addition, as evident in Guillermo's response, references to psychological well-being were evident throughout the boys' descriptions of the loss of their closest male friend. Guillermo's open admission of feeling "lonely" and "depressed" underscores the psychological costs these boys experience as a result of this loss.

While Guillermo's interviews explicitly deal with the sadness he feels surrounding the loss of his best friend, other boys described their frustration and anger with their growing inability to trust their male peers. Fitting with the masculine expectation that was articulated directly by Nick, a Puerto Rican boy, ("I'm not gonna get mad because you dissed me, I'm gonna get mad 'cause I missed you, but I'll probably show it to you like I'm gonna get mad because you dissed me"), anger and frustration was often a way for boys to express their sadness. When Joseph, a Dominican American student who had had a best friend for ten years, is asked whether he has a best friend in his junior year he said, "No I don't trust nobody . . . Can't trust nobody these days." He said that the reason for this break in trust is that his former best friend got him in trouble for "breaking the elevator" in the school.

Although the degree of distrust varied, the boys in our studies were angry at "being dissed" by their friends and they often chose, as a consequence, to retreat from their male peers entirely. Boys expressed anger at their friends for spreading their secrets, "lying" to them, "stealing" their girlfriends, or talking about them "behind their backs" and these experiences led them not to trust their peers. Milo who referred to the "circles of love" among him and his two best friends said by his third year of high school that he has been betrayed by them too many times to trust them any longer. Stories of being teased by his "best friends" for his beliefs (e.g., he goes to church) and of his friends not being "there" for him are the basis of why Milo feels angry and betrayed. Instead of finding replacements for these friends, Milo does not have any "real" best friends any longer.

When Albert, a Puerto Rican student, was asked in his senior year why he still does not have a best friend (he hasn't had a best friend since early adolescence), he said,

> You know, I can't trust—I don't trust 'em too much. I had a friend and he [tried to steal my tapes and my girlfriend] and you know I can't trust nobody else. [I have] a kind of friend, you know but to have another best friend, that would be pretty hard now, can't trust nobody else no more . . . Can't trust people no more.

When asked in his junior year if he wanted a best friend, Mateo, a Puerto Rican boy, said,

> I really, it really doesn't matter to me no more. Cause when now-a-days like you can't really have a best friend. It's like the person who you think would never do something to you, out of nowhere something happens. And I don't . . . I ain't gonna be crying because something happens to me, or I feel like so badly through my inside and I ain't tryin' to you know feel like that.

Mateo, like most of the boys in our studies, is trying to find ways "not to, you know, feel like that."

Justin, the emotionally expressive boy who we have heard from before in this chapter, said during his junior year:

> I don't tell nobody my business so it's not like, it's not a trust thing. It's just something that I don't do. So with money—of course if my friend needs it I give him, he'll give it back or whatever so it's not really a big thing. So with feelings though I don't tell nobody so it's not basically a trust thing it's my personal reason not to tell nobody nothing.

Latino boys who have been portrayed as macho gangsters and rap star wannabees spoke to us about "breaking apart" or suffering if other boys got "inside" of their heads.

Patterns of Desire

> Asked whether he has a best friend, Victor, a boy from Ecuador, said in his junior year:
>
> I wouldn't say . . . I don't say I would 'cause I feel that a friend is going to be there for you and they'll support you and stuff like that. Whether

they're good and bad times, you can share with them, you could share your feelings with them, your true feelings. That's why I don't think I have any real close friends. I mean, things can travel around in a school and things would go around, and the story would change from person to person. Yeah. Basically, I hate it, I hate it, 'cause you know I wouldn't mind talking to somebody my age that I can relate to 'em on a different basis.

Like the route toward manhood, the expressed desire for intimate male friendships, heard so often in boys' interviews during late adolescence, took different forms. For some such as Victor, it was direct ("I hate it, I hate it…") and for others, it was more reserved: "Well, no, I don't really wish I had a best friend, but if I had one, I wouldn't mind."

Francisco, a Dominican American student, said in his fourth year interview that he would like a friend who is "sensitive like me … Like understanding like me … but um that's about it … Like I see movies, in the theater, I start to cry and stuff … No, none of my friends is like that." Boys explicitly desired, even into late adolescence, "sensitive" friends with whom they could "talk about everything" and who were loyal and trusting. They wanted friendship with whom, as Lorenzo told us, "When you need a shoulder to cry on, inside, you need an arm to punch when you are mad and things like that."

The desire for a close male friendship was revealed in boys' responses to different types of questions. Asked to articulate why his friendships are so important, Jorge, a Puerto Rican student, said in his junior year:

'Cause you always need somebody there for you. That's the way I see it. I always need somebody there. Someone that I could count on to talk to whenever I need anything. So I, I think they are really important, friendships. I don't, I mean if you're going to grow up being lonely like always, there's going to be something wrong. Either you're going to be mean to people, lonely, you're going to feel lonely all the time.

Asked what type of friendship he would like to have, Jorge said:

The best of all? Well, I kind of have it now, but even better. But I would like it to get even tighter. I would like it – you know. I like … with the person, I can trust them with anything. But like—deeper, deeper than it is now would be cool.

Boys such as Jorge wanted the "deeper" friendships that were so common during early and middle adolescence. As Sullivan noted about boys from very different socioeconomic and cultural backgrounds, the boys in our studies, including the Latino boys, wanted "chums" with whom to share their secrets and who would "be there" for them in times of need. And they knew the dire consequences for their mental health of not having such friends.

DISCUSSION

The obvious question after listening to the interviews of Latino boys during adolescence is how they are able to be so emotionally expressive and have emotionally intimate male friendships when they live in such a rigidly gendered context where the "cool pose" (Majors & Billson, 1992) dominates, and where ethnic and racial stereotypes about hyper-masculinity are rigidly enforced? How is it possible that Latino boys are able to discuss their intense feelings for their male friends in a culture that often equates such talk with being gay, feminine, or immature? And why were these patterns of emotional expression particularly evident among the Latino boys in our studies? Our qualitative data suggests that the answers to these questions lie in the home, in the school, and in an ethnic context that allows for such emotional expression.

Our qualitative interviews suggested that mothers were a central source of support in the lives of the Latino boys in our studies and were occasionally identified as "best friends." The Latino boys who were most passionate and expressive about their male best friends were often those who had the closest relationships with their mothers. Close friendships did not compensate for poor parent/child relationships but seemed to be enhanced by intimate relationships with mothers. In his junior year, Ricky, a Puerto Rican young man, said, "My best friend? I would like to say that I only have one friend—one best friend and that is my mother." His mother is the person to whom he shares his thoughts and feelings even though he also has numerous friendships with boys from his school. He trusts his mother to "be there" in times of need and to keep his secrets. Although fathers were occasionally mentioned, close relationships with mothers were more often evident among the boys with very close male friendships.

Developmental psychology has long contended that mother/child (as well as father/child) relationships help promote children's friendships. More specifically, John Bowlby and Mary Ainsworth in their theory of Attachment revealed how a close relationship between a primary caretaker, typically the mother, and the child is critical for the health and well-being of the child (Ainsworth, 1964; Ainsworth, Blehar, Waters, & Wall, 1978; Ainsworth & Wittig, 1969; Bowlby, 1969/1982)). A relationship in which the child feels secure with the primary caretaker's attention and love provides the child with an "internal working model" (Bowlby, 1969/1982) that promotes the child's sense of self worth and thus his or her ability to seek out and provide emotional support to others outside of the family.

In a study of six public middle schools,[2] Santos (2010) finds in a sample of 426 African American, Latino, European American, and Asian

American boys that those who reported higher self esteem and more supportive relationships with mothers were more likely to report sharing feelings with and being interdependent with their friends. Furthermore, reports of high levels of mother support in sixth grade predicted an increase in sixth to eighth grade in boys' reports of sharing feelings with and being interdependent with their friends. Mothers appear to play a key role in helping boys of diverse ethnic and racial groups maintain emotionally intimate and supportive friendships during early and middle adolescence.

In addition to mothers as sources of support for boys' intimate friendships, our qualitative observational data suggested that the social dynamics at school also supported boys' ability to have intimate male friendships. The boys, including the Latino boys, who seemed the most willing and able to openly discuss their vulnerabilities and desire for close friendships were those with the most social power with their peers in school. Social power among peers was acquired through numerous routes including the familiar ones for boys such as being athletic, tall, conventionally good looking, and having a good sense of humor (Brown, Lamb & Tappan, 2009). Our participant observations in the schools these boys were in suggest that having these attributes resulted in greater social power which, in turn, appeared to give boys the freedom to have the relationships they wanted without fear of being labeled as girlish or gay (Way, 2011). Felix, for example, was one of the boys in our studies who was extremely popular, funny, and confident in his ability to attract girls as well as in his ability to express vulnerability without being perceived as a "wuss." Psychologist Lyn Mikel Brown and her colleagues (2009) note a similar pattern in their book *Packaging Boyhood*: "The good news for parents is that being successful at sports not only protects a boy from being called gay but also gives him permission to do well academically, show sensitivity, and stick up for kids who are bullied" (p. 222). Boys who succeeded in sports and/or who appeared "manly" did not seem to feel as much pressure as the other boys to prove their masculinity or their heterosexuality.

Our data also indicated that looking the part in and out of school is contingent on race, ethnicity, immigrant status, and, of course, sexual orientation of the boys themselves and the stereotypes associated with these social categories. In American culture with its abundance of stereotypes, being African American makes a boy look more masculine than being Chinese American. Looking American (e.g., baseball cap, untucked shirt, untied athletic shoes) makes a boy seem more masculine than looking like an immigrant (e.g., button up shirts, tucked in shirt, and tied shoes). Similarly, looking "straight" (e.g., baseball cap, untucked shirt, untied athletic shoes), the same look as looking

"American," makes a boy seem more masculine than looking "gay" (e.g., skinny jeans and tight shirts). The look of masculinity, which is based on a set of stereotypes about race, ethnicity, social class, nationality, and sexual orientation, is part of the same embedded set of masculine conventions that equates emotional stoicism, physical toughness, autonomy, and heterosexuality with being a man.

Within the context of our studies, the boys who had the desired "look" of masculinity, according to their peers, were the Puerto Rican boys.[2] These were the boys who the non-Puerto Rican teens—particularly the non-Puerto Rican Latinos in our studies—wanted to be (Way et al., 2008). They wanted to be Puerto Rican because of their "between" skin tone ("between White and Black" according to one student) and hair, which is neither stereotypically Black nor White and their general hip and urban personal style. The Puerto Rican students were also idealized by their immigrant peers because they were American citizens. In schools such as the ones in which we conducted our research where being "an immigrant" is a considered a racial slur, adolescents sought identities that were clearly American (Way et al., 2008).

The Puerto Ricans were also the boys who were the most likely among the Latinos to openly resist conventions of masculinity including emotional stoicism by talking with great passion about their love for their male best friends. Although most Latino boys spoke with warmth and affection about their closest male friends, it was the Puerto Rican boys who were the most poetic in their language and fierce in their determination to maintain emotionally intimate male friendships. Our qualitative data suggest that these patterns of "resistance" were fostered by their high social status in school as such status allows boys to challenge gender stereotypes without the risk of being ostracized by their peers (Brown et al., 2009). The Puerto Rican boys seemed to know that they could get away with it without being teased.

In addition to these family and school level factors, the cultural context of being "Latino" also likely enhanced boys' abilities to have intimate male friendships. From the literature of Gabriel Garcia Marquez or Junot Diaz to the poetry of Pablo Neruda, emotional expression clearly plays a central role in the construction of Latin American identities and culture. Research has repeatedly found that Latino families, as well as Latino males, strongly value the open expression of emotions and interpersonal relationships more generally (Azmitia et al., 2006; Falicov, 1998; Gloria, Castellanos, Scull, & Villegas, 2009; Hurtado & Sinha, 2008; Lopez et al., 2009). Melzi and Fernández (2004), for example, finds in their narratives studies of Peruvian children and parents that, contrary to most studies of Anglo American children, mothers used more emotional language when they talked with their sons than when they talked with their daughters. Such gender socialization at home likely leads Latino boys to be comfortable using such language to express their feelings about their friends than their non-Latino peers.

Yet the variation among Latino boys, with the Puerto Rican boys being more likely than the other Latino boys to be emotionally expressive, suggests that the family, school, and ethnic contexts weave together to create various possibilities for Latino boys. None of these factors in isolation determines boys' experiences of their friendships. The very fact that the boys who reported having poor quality relationships with their mothers and being verbally harassed by their peers were the least likely among the Latinos to have emotionally intimate friendships and to speak in emotional terms about their friendships suggests that the proximal context (i.e., family and school) makes a difference as does the distal context of sociocultural values and beliefs. The variability among the Latino boys reveals the ways in which contexts are multi-layered and shape the nature of developmental processes.

Yet this pattern of emotional expressiveness diminished significantly by late adolescence for all the boys in our studies including the Latino boys. As boys reached late adolescence, they grew increasingly suspicious of their male peers and were less willing to speak in emotional terms about their male friendships. Strikingly, however, these boys continued to speak about their desires for such intimate friendships and they also spoke of increased sadness, depression, and isolation. These patterns of loss, distrust, and sadness among the boys are likely the product of an American culture of masculinity that does not value intimacy among males. As Latino boys become men in American culture, they experience the pressures that all boys in the United States experience—the pressures to be a heterosexual man in all of its stereotypical meanings.

The loss in friendships and trust was not what the Latino boys in our studies wanted and was clearly not good for their mental health. Although mainstream culture has framed such losses as a product of "maturity" as boys grow increasingly interested in girls, the boys themselves do not see these losses as positive and speak of feelings of isolation and depression as a result of such losses. These losses may be at the root, at least in part, of why the nationwide suicide rate of boys jumps to nearly 4 times the rate of girls from the ages of 16–19 years old. The boys in our studies, even those with girlfriends, spoke of going crazy if they did not have a friend to share their thoughts and feelings. The boys' stories indicate, as do the research findings from decades of social science research, that supporting boys' desires for emotionally intimate male friendships will sig-nificantly enhance their emotional, psychological, and academic adjustment over the long term. The research on adults suggests that those without strong social networks, including close friendships, are more at risk for numerous mental and physical health problems (Adams & Allan, 1998). Studies have even found that close friendships are more important than a close spousal relationship for various health related problems (Orth-Gomer et al., 1993). The challenge is to find ways to support the bonds these boys already expe-rience and wish to maintain in the midst of an American culture that says that such relationships are signs of immaturity, or girlish or gay behavior.

While our research studies present contextually rich evidence of the importance of friendships for Latino boys, our findings are specific to Latinos in a particular context and may not generalize to Latinos elsewhere. As this handbook reveals, the Latino population in the United States is not a monolithic entity but rather a group rich in diversity across a range of demo-graphic variables—country of origin, race, social class, and immigration experiences, to name only a few. Our research was carried out with predomi-nantly poor and working class Dominican American and Puerto Rican urban boys. While our findings contribute to a growing body of research emphasiz-ing the mental health benefits of close friendships, it remains to be explored whether the patterns presented are true of Latino boys from different ethnic and social class backgrounds (e.g., middle class Mexican boys) or in different contexts. It is likely, for example, that the high status of Puerto Ricans in our studies, for example, is specific to a New York context. In addition, the themes of loss may have been heightened by the low-income status of the families in our studies who typically experience more residential transitions than more middle and upper class families (Putnam, 2000). However, our studies do reveal that poor, working class Puerto Rican and Dominican American boys from urban contexts are having and wanting close friendships and that these friendships are perceived to be a core component of their mental health throughout adolescence. Supporting such relationships among Latino boys seems to be the critical next step toward improving their mental health.

NOTES

1. Parts of this chapter are drawn from Niobe Way's book *Deep Secrets: Boys' Friendships, and the Crisis of Connection* (Harvard University Press).

2. This study is from the Center for Research on Culture, Development and Educa-tion at New York University. The study is funded by the National Science Foundation.

3. A study done in the Midwest also reported on this phenomenon of "wanna-bee" Puerto Ricans among White youth (Wilkins, 2004).

REFERENCES

Adams, R., & Allan, G. (1998). *Placing friendship in context*. Cambridge: Cambridge University Press.

Ainsworth, M. (1964). Patterns of attachment behavior shown by the infant with his mother. *Merrill-Palmer Quarterly 10*, 51–58.

Ainsworth, M., Blehar, M., Waters, E., & Wall, S. (1978). *Patterns of attachment: A psychological study of the strange situation*. Hillsdale, NJ: Erlbaum.

Ainsworth, M., & Wittig, B. A. (1969). Attachment and the exploratory behaviour of one-year-olds in a strange situation. In B. M. Foss (Ed.), *Determinants of infant behavior* (pp. 113–136). London: Methuen.

Azmitia, M., Kamprath, N., & Linnet, J. (1998). Intimacy and conflict: The dynamics of boys' and girls' friendships during middle childhood and early adolescence. In L. H. Meyer, H. Park, M. Grenot-Scheyerm, I. S. Schwartz, & B. Harry (Eds.), *Making friends: The influences of culture and development* (pp. 171–187). Baltimore, MD: Paul H. Brookes.

Azmitia, M., & Cooper, C. (2001). Good or bad? Peer influences on Latino and European American adolescents' pathways through school. *Journal of Education for Students Placed at Risk 6*(1–2), 45–71.

Azmitia, M., Ittel, A., & Brenk, C. (2006). Latino-heritage adolescents' friendships. In X. Chen, D. French, & B. Schneider (Eds.), *Peer relationships in cultural context* (pp. 426–451). New York, NY: Cambridge University Press.

Berndt, T. (1981). Relations between social cognition, nonsocial cognition, and social behavior: The case of friendship. In J. Flavell & L. Ross (Eds.), *Social cognitive development* (pp. 176–189). New York: Cambridge University Press.

Bigelow, B., & La Gaipa, J. (1980). The development of friendship, values and choice. In H. Foot, A. Chapman, & J. Smith (Eds.), *Friendship and social relations in children* (pp. 15–44). Chichester: Wiley.

Bishop, J., & Inderbitzen, H. (1995). Peer acceptance and friendship: An investigation of their relation to self-esteem. *Adolescence 15*(4), 476–89.

Bowlby, J. (1969/1982). *Attachment and loss: Volume 1, Attachment*. New York: Basic Books.

Bronfenbrenner, U. (1979). *The ecology of human development*. Cambridge MA: Harvard University Press.

Brown, L. M., Lamb, S., & Tappan, M. (2009). *Packaging boyhood: Saving our sons from superheroes, slackers and other media stereotypes*. New York: St. Martin's Press.

Chen, X., French, D., & Schneider, B. (2006). *Peer relationships in cultural context*. New York, NY: Cambridge University Press.

Decker, S. H., & Van Winkle, B. (1996). *Life in the gang: Family, friends, and violence*. New York, NY: Cambridge University Press.

Eccles, J.S., & Roeser, R.W. (1999). School and community influences on human development. In M.H. Bornstein & M.E. Lamb (Eds.), *Developmental psychology: An advanced textbook* (pp. 503–554). Hillsdale, NJ: Erlbaum.

Erdley, C., Nangle, D., Newman, J., & Carpenter, E. (2001). Children's friendship experiences and psychological adjustment: Theory and research. In D. Nangle and C. Erdley (Eds.), *The role of friendship in psychological adjustment* (pp. 5–24). San Francisco: Jossey-Bass.

Falicov, C. (1998). *Latino families in therapy: A guide to multicultural practice.* New York, NY: Guilford Press.

Furman, W., & Bierman, K. (1984). Children's conceptions of friendship: A multimethod study of developmental changes. *Developmental Psychology 20*, 925–933.

Gloria, A.M., Castellanos, J., Scull, N.C., & Villegas, F.J. (2009). Psychological coping and well-being of male Latino undergraduates: Sobreviviendo la Universidad, Hispanic *Journal of Behavioral Sciences 31*, 317–338.

Gordon, R. A., Lahey, B. B., Kawai, E., Loeber, R., Stouthamer-Loeber, M., & Farrington, D. P. (2004). Antisocial behavior and youth gang membership: Selection and socialization. *Criminology 42*, 55–87.

Gutmann, M. C. (1996). *The meanings of macho: Being a man in Mexico City.* Berkeley: University of California Press.

Hill, J., & Lynch, M. (1983). The intensification of gender-related role expectations during early adolescence. In J. Brooks-Gunn & A. Peterson (Eds.), *Girls at puberty: Biological and psychosocial perspectives* (pp. 201–228). New York: Plenum.

Hurtado, A., & Sinha, M. (2008). More than men: Latino feminist masculinities intersectionality. *Sex Roles 59*(5–6), 337–349.

Kimmel, M. (2008). *Guyland: The perilous world where boys become men.* New York, NY: HarperCollins.

Ladd, G. W., & Troop-Gordon, W. (2003). The role of chronic peer difficulties in the development of children's psychological adjustment problems. *Child Development 74*(5), 1344–1367.

Levitt, M., Guacci-Franco, N., & Levitt, J. (1993). Convoys of social support in childhood and early adolescence: Structure and function. *Developmental Psychology 29*(5), 811–818.

López, S., García. J.I.R., Ullman, J.B., Kopelowicz, A., Jenkins, J., Breitborde, N.J.K., & Placencia, P. (2009). Cultural variability in the manifestation of expressed emotion. *Family Process 48*(2), 179–194.

Majors, R. G., & Billson, J. (1992). *Cool pose: The dilemmas of Black manhood in America.* New York: Lexington Books (MacMillan).

Melzi, G., & Fernández, C. (2004). Talking about past emotions: Conversations between Peruvian mothers and their preschool children. *Sex Roles 50*(9–10), 641–657.

Miller, B. (1991). *Adolescents' relationships with their friends* (Unpublished doctoral dissertation). Harvard University, Cambridge, MA.

Nangle, D.W., & Erdley, C.A. (Eds.). (2001). *New directions for child and adolescent development: The role of friendship in psychological adjustment.* San Francisco: Jossey-Bass.

Oldenburg, C., & Kerns, K. (1997). Associations between peer relationships and depressive symptoms: Testing moderator effects of gender and age. *Journal of Early Adolescence 17*, 319–337.

Orth-Gomer, K., Rosengren, A., Wilhelmsen, L. (1993). Lack of social support and incidence of coronary heart disease in middle-aged Swedish men. *Psychosomatic Medicine 55*, 37–43.

Padilla, F. M. (1992). *The gang as an American enterprise.* New Brunswick, NJ: Reuters University Press.

Pelkonen, M., Marttunen, M., & Aro, H. (2003). Risk for depression: A 6-year follow-up of Finnish adolescents. *Journal of Affective Disorders 77*(1), 41–51.

Phinney, J. S., Cantu, C. L., & Kurtz, D. A. (1997). Ethnic and American identity as predictors of self-esteem among African American, Latino, and White adolescents. *Journal of Youth and Adolescents 26*, 165–185.

Putnam, R. D. (2000). *Bowling alone: The collapse and revival of American community.* New York: Simon & Schuster.

Radmacher, K., & Azmitia, M. (2006). Are there gendered pathways to intimacy in early adolescents' and emerging adults' friendships? *Journal of Adolescent Research 21*(4), 415–448.

Rubin, K. H., Bukowski, W. M., & Laursen, B. (Eds.). (2009). *Handbook of peer interactions, relationships, and groups.* New York, NY, US: Guilford Press.

Santos, C. E. (2010). *The missing story: Resistance to ideals of masculinity in the friendships of middle school boys (Unpublished doctoral dissertation).* New York University: New York, NY.

Sax, L. (2007). *Boys adrift: The five factors driving the growing epidemic of unmotivated boys and underachieving young men.* New York: Basic Books.

Spencer, M. B. (2006). Phenomenology and ecological systems theory: Development of diverse groups. In W. Damon & R. Lerner (Eds.), *Handbook of child psychology* (pp. 829–893). New York: Wiley.

Strauss, A., & Corbin, J. (1990). *Basics of qualitative research: Grounded theory procedures and techniques.* Thousand Oaks, CA: Sage.

Sullivan, H.S. (1953). *The interpersonal theory of psychiatry.* New York: Norton.

Townsend, M., McCracken, H., & Wilton, K. (1988). Popularity and intimacy as determinants of psychological well-being in adolescent friendships. *The Journal of Early Adolescence 8*(4), 421–436.

Tyre, P. (2008). *The trouble with boys: A surprising report card on our sons, their problems at school and what parents and educators must do.* New York: Crown Publishing.

Urban Dictionary: No Homo. (n.d.). In *Urban Dictionary.* Retrieved month, day year from http://www.urbandictionary.com/define.php?term=no+homo

Ureño, S. (2003). The constructions of masculinity as expressed through gang involvement in African-American and Puerto Rican inner-city youth. *Dissertation Abstracts International*, AAT 3088959.

Vernberg, E. (1990). Experiences with peers following relocation during early adolescence. *American Journal of Orthopsychiatry 60*, 466–472.

Vitaro, F., Boivin, M., & Bukowski, W. M. (2009). The role of friendship in child and adolescent psychosocial development. In K. H. Rubin, W. M. Bukowski & B. Laursen (Eds.), *Handbook of peer interactions, relationships, and groups* (pp. 568–585). New York, NY, US: Guilford Press.

Way, N. (2011). *Deep secrets: Boys' Friendships, and the Crisis of Connection.* Cambridge, MA: Harvard University Press.

Way, N., & Chen, L. (2000). Close and general friendships among African American, Latino, and Asian American adolescents from low-income families. *Journal of Adolescent Research 15*, 274–301.

Way, N., Cowal, K., Gingold, R., Pahl, K., & Bissessar, N. (2001). Friendship patterns among African American, Asian American, and Latino adolescents from low-income families. *Journal of Social and Personal Relationships 18*, 29–53.

Way, N., Santos, C., Niwa, E., & Kim-Gervey, C. (2008). To be or not to be: An exploration of ethnic identity development in context. In M. Azmitia, M. Syed, & K. Radmacher (Eds.), *The intersections of personal and social identities: New directions for child and adolescent development* (pp. 61–79). San Francisco: Jossey-Bass.

Way, N., & Robinson, M. G. (2003). A longitudinal study of the effects of family, friends, and school experiences on the psychological adjustment of ethnic minority, low-SES adolescents. *Journal of Adolescent Research 18*, 324–346.

Wilkins, A. (2004). Puerto Rican wannabes: Sexual spectacle and the marking of race, class, and gender boundaries. *Gender and Society 18*(1), 103–121.

Chapter 8

UNDERSTANDING THE ROLE OF SOCIAL SUPPORTS IN LATINA/O ADOLESCENTS' SCHOOL ENGAGEMENT AND ACHIEVEMENT

Kathryn R. Wentzel, Shannon Russell, Encarnacion Garza, Jr., and Betty M. Merchant

American schools are failing to prepare many of their students for college and the workplace, especially those who are members of ethnic minority groups. As members of the largest and fastest growing minority group, Hispanic students are of particular concern in light of recent reports suggesting that they are at much greater risk of not meeting academic standards of proficiency and attainment than their non-Hispanic peers (President's Commission on Educational Excellence for Hispanic Americans, 1996). In 2002, only 4 percent of Latino students were proficient or higher in twelfth grade mathematics nationwide; 28 percent of Hispanic students dropped out of high school (U.S. Department of Education, 2002). In Texas, where 44 percent of the total student population is Hispanic (U.S. Census Bureau, 2000), the numbers of Hispanic students who are not meeting educational standards is even higher. In 2009, only 65 percent of Hispanic students in grades six through eight met the minimum standards on the Texas Assessment of Knowledge and Skills (TAKS; Texas Education Agency). In 2008–09, the attrition rate for Hispanic students in Texas was 42 percent compared to 17 percent for Caucasian students; this gap in attrition rates has widened since 2005 (Intercultural Development Research Organization, 2010). Despite the growing concerns about these indicators of academic proficiency and attainment, however, the basic reasons for these less than optimal outcomes are not well understood. Much less is known about those factors that support the high levels of achievement of Hispanic students who stay in school, exceed minimum standards on national tests, and excel academically.

It is clear that a wide range of factors can influence a student's success at school, including individual differences such as temperament and gender, home-based practices such as parenting styles, parental involvement with schools, and the ecologies of extended families, neighborhoods, and culture. However, when focusing on school-based practices, many scholars recognize the nature of classroom experiences as having a strong, consistent, and direct influence on children's adjustment to school (Rutter & Maughan, 2002). Moreover, researchers are beginning to acknowledge that the social and interpersonal climate of classroom settings can have a profound impact on the degree to which students come to value and actively engage in learning activities. Indeed, a growing body of research suggests that experiencing a range of social and academic supports from teachers and peers is related strongly to positive motivational and academic outcomes for many students (Wentzel, 1999). Of potential relevance for understanding the achievement patterns of Hispanic children is that ethnographic accounts often conclude that at least some of these students experience school as a place where positive social supports are lacking and efforts to succeed are undermined by conflicting sets of values and expectations from parents, peers, and teachers (Phelan, Davidson, & Cao, 1991; Romo & Falbo, 1996; Valenzuela, 2000). In general, however, little is known about how Hispanic students perceive their social experiences at school, especially the extent to which they believe that their interactions with teachers and classmates afford them the opportunities and resources necessary for them to succeed academically.

In light of these concerns, the current chapter focuses on the role of Hispanic students' social supports and experiences at school in facilitating positive social and academic outcomes. We include discussion of social behavioral outcomes given that students' social competencies at school often reflect their willingness to contribute to a positive classroom and school climate, and the strong association of positive social behavior at school to students' academic performance (Wentzel, 1999, 2004). Toward this end, we describe a general model of social supports and student adjustment to school and present evidence to support the model. Next, we discuss the relevance of the model for understanding the role of social supports from teachers, peers, and parents in promoting Hispanic students' engagement and academic achievement during the early adolescent years. Finally, we will discuss the implications of this work for policy and practice.

A MODEL OF CLASSROOM SOCIAL SUPPORT

A growing body of empirical evidence supports the notion that socially supportive classroom contexts can promote positive aspects of school adjustment. In this literature, social supports most often take the form of emotionally warm and caring relationships with teachers and peers. For example, adolescents' perceptions that teachers are emotionally supportive and caring are related to positive aspects of academic engagement, including the pursuit of goals to learn and to behave prosocially and responsibly, academic interest, educational aspirations and values, and positive self-concept (e.g., Wentzel, 1994, 1997). Having supportive relationships with teachers also predicts academic performance (Wentzel, 2002b) and in part, whether students at this age drop out of school (Rumberger, 1995). Adolescents also report that their peer groups and crowds provide them with a sense of emotional security and a sense of belonging (Brown, Eicher, & Petrie, 1986). As with teacher support, perceived peer support at school has been associated with academic engagement, including pursuit of academic and prosocial goals and interest in academic subject matter (DuBois, Felner, Brand, Adan, & Evans, 1992; Harter, 1996; Wentzel, 1994, 1997, 1998). Conversely, young adolescents who do not perceive their relationships with peers as positive and supportive tend to be at risk for academic problems and antisocial forms of behavior (e.g., Goodenow, 1993; Midgley, Feldlaufer, & Eccles, 1989; Wentzel, 1994).

Of central concern for understanding the role of social supports in promoting the academic success of young adolescents is that students of this age tend to experience a heightened sensitivity to social aspects of classroom life (Eccles & Midgley, 1989; Harter, 1996). This sensitivity is often compounded with a transition to a new middle school environment that results in adolescents' perceptions that adults no longer care about them, and decreased opportunities to establish meaningful relationships with peers (Eccles & Midgley, 1989). Coupled with findings that Hispanic students at this age tend to be at greater risk for academic problems and school drop out than their non-Hispanic peers (Rumberger, 1995), these developmental challenges support a more careful consideration of the early adolescent years as a critical time for social interactions and relationships to influence the development of Hispanic adolescents' positive orientations toward school.

Adopting a perspective that social supports are important precursors to school success, however, also raises several important conceptual issues. First, work in this area is still in its infancy with respect to understanding the nature of social supports at school and the mechanisms whereby supports have influence on students' adjustment to school. To illustrate, most research on the supportive nature of teachers and peers focuses on fairly global notions of social relatedness; operational definitions typically reflect beliefs that teachers or peers "care about me." This conceptualization, however, masks the multiple forms of support that teachers and peers routinely provide students.

In response to this lack of theoretical specificity, Wentzel (2004) developed a more differentiated model in which social support is defined with respect to specific provisions that can promote academic success at school: emotional nurturance and caring; clear communication of expectations and values related to achievement; instrumental help, advice, and academic instruction; and a safe classroom environment. These dimensions reflect essential components of social support in that: 1) information is provided concerning what is expected and valued in the classroom; 2) attempts to achieve these valued outcomes are met with help and instruction; 3) attempts to achieve outcomes can be made in a safe, non-threatening environment; and 4) individuals are made to feel like a valued member of the group. It is worth noting that models of effective parenting (Grusec & Goodnow, 1994; Laosa & Henderson, 1991) highlight the importance of each of these provisions for the development of intellectual and social competencies in children, and summaries of best practices for educating Hispanic students include these aspects of supportive relationships as essential for effective classroom teaching (Rutherford, 1999; Scribner & Reyes, 1999).

In addition, in-depth understanding of the mechanisms whereby perceived support might influence school-related outcomes is fairly limited. Conceptual models that describe possible mechanisms are not well developed, and empirical work that examines the intervening factors that explain why perceived supports are associated with academic outcomes is rare. In response to this limitation, the model guiding out work describes ways in which social supports and provisions can influence academic outcomes in part, by way of students' engagement in the social and academic life of the classroom. As shown in Figure 8.1, the model predicts that social supports are related to academic outcomes by way of classroom engagement, that is, motivation to achieve social and academic outcomes that are central to the learning process. Engagement can take many forms, including the adoption of socially valued goals such as to behave

Figure 8.1
A Model of Social Supports and Classroom Competence

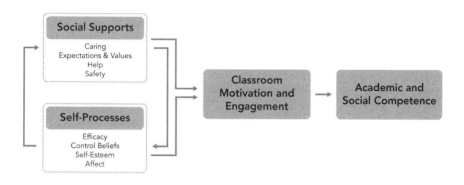

appropriately and to learn, effort and persistence at academic tasks, displays of appropriate classroom behavior, and focused attention on learning and understanding subject matter. In turn, students engaged in positive learning and social activities are more likely to learn more and be able and willing to perform well on academic tests and projects (Wentzel, 1994, 2002).

The model also suggests that the availability of social supports can contribute to social and academic outcomes by way of classroom engagement. To illustrate, evidence suggests that when children enjoy interpersonal relationships with adults and peers that are nurturant and caring, they are more likely to adopt and internalize the expectations and goals that are valued by these individuals than if their relationships are harsh and critical (see Grusec & Goodnow, 1994; Ryan, 1993). When applied to the social worlds of the classroom, it follows that teachers and peers are likely to promote student engagement if they create contexts that make students feel like others care about them and that allow them to be an integral and valued part of the classroom community. Warm and caring relationships with parents are likely to lead students to be more open to developing caring relationships with teachers and peers at school (see Wentzel & Looney, 2007).

Additional supports also are predicted to contribute to classroom engagement. The positive expectations and values for social and academic outcomes that adults and peers communicate to students provide guidance concerning how they should behave and what is important to achieve at school. Teachers and parents are obvious socializers of students' goals and values (see Grusec & Goodnow, 1994). Although not well documented, it also is reasonable to assume that students communicate to each other specific academic values and expectations for performance (e.g., Altermatt, Pomerantz, Ruble, Frey, & Greulich, 2002). Receiving help is a central component of social support in the classroom. Teachers and peers have opportunities on a daily basis to provide children with specific forms of help that promote the development of academic competencies. These resources can take the form of information and advice, modeled behavior, or specific experiences that facilitate learning. Finally, the importance of safety is reflected in outcomes that result when it is absent, such as conflict with and threats from peers, and harsh and critical feedback from teachers. These threatening experiences have been related negatively to middle school students' academic motivation, classroom behavior, and academic accomplishments (e.g., Juvonen, Nishina, & Graham, 2000; Wentzel, 2002; Wentzel, Battle, Russell, & Looney, 2010).

The model shown in Figure 8.1 also suggests that these various aspects of social support can promote classroom engagement indirectly by having an impact on students' beliefs about themselves. Based on the literature on student motivation and self-regulation, several belief systems are likely to be critical in this regard. Self-perceptions of academic efficacy reflect the extent that a student believes she has the ability to achieve specific goals such as doing well in math (Bandura, 1986). Perceived control concerns beliefs that the achievement of one's goals is governed by internal or external reasons, for instance, "I can do well in math if I try hard" versus "I won't do well in math if my teacher doesn't like me" (Skinner, Zimmer-Gembeck, & Connell, 1998). Affect associated with academic pursuits can take the form of negative arousal or anxiety associated with taking tests, or positive attitudes and a sense of well-being when provided with appropriate challenges that promote feelings of competence (Meece, Wigfield, & Eccles, 1990). Each of these self-perceptions are academically relevant constructs central to theories of motivation that are consistent predictors of academic outcomes, including goals, values, interest, and positive forms of classroom behavior (see Wentzel & Wigfield, 2009).

In summary, the model guiding our work allows for a differentiated definition of social support and provides a more complex and complete picture of how perceived supports might influence academic engagement and learning in the classroom. Specifically, the model predicts that social support in the form of emotional nurturance and caring; clear communication of expectations for behavior and achievement; instrumental help, advice, and instruction; and a safe classroom environment can promote positive engagement in the social and academic life of the classroom in part, by influencing the psychological and emotional functioning of students.

Empirical Support for the Model

In general, the positive role of perceived social supports for young Hispanic adolescents has gained some support in the literature. The potential relevance of the multiple dimensions of support in our model for understanding the school adjustment of Hispanic middle school students also can be gleaned from Wentzel's work on Caucasian and African American adolescents (see also Wentzel, 2005, 2009 for reviews). Evidence from Wentzel's program of research and from studies focused specifically on Hispanic students is summarized in the following sections.

Perceived Caring

As noted earlier, most research on school-based supports has focused primarily on emotional aspects of social support. In Wentzel's work on Caucasian and African American adolescents, perceiving teachers and peers to be emotionally supportive and caring has been related to the pursuit of goals to learn and to behave prosocially and responsibly, as well as displays of positive forms of classroom behavior and academic achievement (Wentzel, 1994, 1997, 2003). In addition, perceived support from teachers and peers in a new classroom has been related to changes in aggressive behavior as well as academic outcomes from one year to the next (Wentzel, Williams, & Tomback, 2005, 2006).

Similar findings have been reported in research on Hispanic students. For example, perceived emotional support from teachers and peers is related positively to academic outcomes (e.g., grades) in samples of Hispanic high school and college students (Crosnoe, Johnson, & Elder, 2004; Scribner & Reyes, 1999). During middle school, perceived caring from teachers has been related to student engagement and interest in school (Garcia-Reid, 2007), mastery orientations toward learning (Stevens, Hamman, & Olivarez, 2007), positive classroom behavior (Wooley, Kol, & Bowen, 2009), and positive levels of self-esteem (Carlson, Uppal, & Prosser, 2000). In elementary school, Hispanic students' sense of belonging has been associated with social self-efficacy (Morrison, Cosden, O'Farrell, & Campos, 2003) and with decreasing levels of aggression over time (Meehan, Hughes, & Cavell, 2003).

Perceived Expectations for Achievement and Social Behavior

The extent to which young adolescents perceive their teachers and peers as expecting and wanting them to succeed academically also can have a strong, positive effect on their levels of engagement. Wentzel and colleagues have documented significant, positive relations between Caucasian and African American middle school students' perceptions of teacher expectations for academic performance and positive social behavior to aspects of social and academic motivation, classroom behavior, and academic grades (Wentzel, 2002; Wentzel, Filisetti, & Looney, 2007). Similarly, Caucasian middle-class students often report that their classmates expect them to perform well academically at school (Wentzel et al., 2010). Additional findings indicate that perceived peer expectations for positive academic and social outcomes are significant positive predictors of goals to achieve academically and of classroom grades (Wentzel et al., 2007; Wentzel et al., 2006).

Similarly, research on Hispanic elementary and middle school students also indicates that perceived expectations for academic success from teachers are related to students' own educational aspirations (Cheng & Starks, 2002) and academic engagement (Garcia-Reid, 2007). Hispanic middle school students' perceptions of teacher expectations for academic performance also have been related to academic grades (Kuperminc, Darnell, & Alvarez-Jimenez, 2008). In contrast, little is known concerning the influence of peer expectations and pressures on Hispanic adolescents' achievement.

Perceived Availability of Help

Students in Wentzel's non-Hispanic samples who believe that help is readily available from teachers and peers also tend to report positive levels of social and academic motivation (Wentzel et al., 2010). Research on Hispanic high school students also suggests that perceived help from teachers is related to a range of motivation outcomes including academic effort, beliefs about academic efficacy, academic values, and effort (Alfaro, Umaña-Taylor, & Bámaca, 2006; Plunkett, Henry, Houltberg, Sands, & Abarca-Mortensen, 2008), as well as academic grades (Plunkett et al., 2008). In general, however, research on the role of perceived help from teachers and peers in promoting positive outcomes during Hispanic students' early adolescent years has been infrequent.

Perceived Safety

Finally, the importance of students' perceptions of classroom safety for understanding academic engagement is supported in the literature. Conflict with and threats from peers, and harsh and critical feedback from teachers have been related negatively to middle school students' academic motivation, classroom behavior, and academic accomplishments (e.g., Juvonen et al., 2000; Wentzel, 2002; Wentzel et al., 2010). Most research on peer harassment has focused on White, middle-class samples. Moreover, research on nationally representative samples indicates that Caucasian adolescents are more likely to be involved in bullying activities than are African American or Hispanic adolescents (Nansel et al., 2001). However, peer harassment in the form of discrimination is of unique relevance to ethnic minority students. In this case, discriminatory behaviors communicate to students that they are not a member of the "in group," either because of their minority status (Crocker, Major, & Steel, 1998) or because they are viewed as "acting White" (Fordham & Ogbu, 1986). Such behaviors also can convey that students have characteristics that make them inferior to their peers, especially with respect to intellectual abilities (Steele & Aronson, 1995). The negative consequences of these forms of discrimination are well documented. Of specific interest for understanding Hispanic adolescents' academic engagement are findings that levels of neighborhood safety are associated with commitment to learning (Garcia-Reid, 2007).

Summary

The literature on multiple social supports from teachers and peers suggests that emotional nurturance and caring; clear communication of expectations, and values related to achievement; instrumental help, advice, and academic instruction; and a safe classroom environment can have a significant and positive impact on academic and social motivation, classroom behavior, and academic performance of middle-class Caucasian and African American students. In contrast, research on these various aspects of classroom supports in Hispanic students has not been as frequent, although the extant literature provides some initial support for the model guiding our work especially with regard to the positive role of perceived caring from teachers. In general, however, evidence that results from non-Hispanic samples are generalizable to Hispanic populations has not been forthcoming.

Of additional interest for the current discussion is that Hispanic adolescents are likely to be highly connected to parents and family members, with levels of family interdependence and closeness being related positively and strongly to healthy academic and social functioning (Ceballo, 2004; Martinez, DeGarmo, & Eddy, 2004; Phinney, Kim-Jo, Osoria, & Vilhjalmsdottir, 2005). Therefore, enjoying supportive relationships at home might be a relatively strong, positive predictor of school success for these young ado-lescents even when positive supports are experienced at school. Moreover, having a supportive family system might also negate the potentially nega-tive effects of having weak or no supports from teachers and peers.

Several studies support the centrality of parental influence on Hispanic students' lives at school. For example, when perceived parent supports have been examined in conjunction with perceived teacher or peer sup-ports, parent caring, expectations for academic success, and help has been related to students' motivation, engagement, (Alfaro et al., 2006; Cheng & Starks, 2002; Garcia-Reid, 2007) and classroom grades (Plunkett et al., 2008), over and above supports from teachers and peers. Few researchers, however, have examined young adolescent students' perceptions of multi-ple supports from parents, teachers, and peers in a single study. As a con-sequence, little is known about the unique contributions of these various sources of support to student outcomes.

In response to these gaps in the literature, in the following section we report on findings of a recent study that focused on young adolescent stu-dents' perceived caring, expectations for academic and social outcomes, and help in relation to their classroom engagement, social behavior, and grades. Of particular interest to us were the degree to which findings from Wentzel's studies of non-Hispanic middle-class students were generalizable to a subset of Hispanic students, low-income Mexican American adolescents, and the degree to which parental supports were related to school-based out-comes when supports from teachers and classmates were taken into account.

A Study of Multiple Supports from Parents, Teachers, and Peers

The sample for our study consisted of 464 fifth- and sixth-grade stu-dents from ten schools in a school district in Texas. In the participating schools, 75 percent of the fifth and sixth grade population met Texas Assessment of Knowledge and Skills (TAKS) requirements for math and science and 80 percent met the requirements for reading; 75 percent of the student population was Hispanic (as labeled by the school district), with five of the schools classifying more than 90 percent of their students as Hispanic; and, approximately 88 percent of the students were classified as economically disadvantaged. In the participating classrooms, the aver-age years of teacher experience was 9.4; the student-teacher ratio was 22:1; and 75 percent of the teachers were female. Nineteen percent of the participating students were classified as ESL. Information on individ-ual students' ethnicity, levels of acculturation, family SES, and language spoken at home was not available. Students were administered a set of questionnaires that assessed their perceptions of their parents', teachers', and classmates' emotional nurturance and caring, expectations for academic and social competence at school, and academic help and guidance. The measures were those used in Wentzel's studies of primarily Caucasian middle-class adolescents (e.g., Wentzel et al., 2010).

Of importance for a discussion of generalizability across groups of students is the degree to which students respond to measures in similar ways. With regard to this issue, the measures used in the study showed adequate levels of internal reliability (Cronbach's alphas) in this Mexican American sample. Moreover, internal reliabilities were comparable to those reported in Wentzel's previous work (see Table 8.1). As shown in Table 8.1, mean levels of perceived supports were fairly high. When compared with average scores from Wentzel's non-Hispanic samples, the scores of the

Table 8.1
Descriptive Statistics

Variables	Texas Sample			Comparative Samples		
	Alpha	Mean	Std Dev	Alpha	Mean	Std Dev
Perceptions of Supports						
Caring-Teachers	.72	4.20	.80	.87	3.37	1.04
Caring-Classmates	.83	3.64	.96	.84	3.46	.97
Caring-Parents	.79	2.69	.47	.81	3.97	.77
Help-Classmates	.84	3.55	.85	.72	3.41	.85
Help-Teachers	.84	4.11	.81	.73	3.79	.92
Help-Parents	.62	3.17	.58	.81	3.77	.56
Academic Expectations-Teachers	.81	2.56	.61	.74	3.10	.43
Social Expectations-Teachers	.75	2.50	.64	.67	3.87	.79
Academic Expectations-Parents	.80	3.46	.50	.75	4.51	.46
Social Expectations-Parents	.74	3.53	.60	NA	NA	NA
Academic Expectations-Classmates	.67	2.35	.68	.70	3.41	.68
Social Expectations-Classmates	.80	2.14	.86	.85	3.40	.69
Self-Processes						
Efforts to learn	.65	4.42	.92	.77	3.81	1.17
Efforts to perform well academically	.76	3.91	1.07	.78	4.09	1.13
Efforts to follow rules	.66	4.11	.66	.83	3.87	.87
Academic efficacy	.85	5.00	.91	.86	5.04	.91
Self-esteem	.53	2.03	.92	.74	2.16	1.02

Mexican American students indicate that these students enjoyed a higher level of perceived caring and help from teachers and peers. In contrast, scores for perceived caring from parents, and for social and academic expectations from teachers, peers, and parents were lower for the Mexican American sample when compared to the non-Hispanic sample. With regard to self-processes, Mexican American students reported more frequent efforts to learn and to follow rules, whereas non-Hispanic students reported more frequent efforts to perform well academically.

Of additional interest, is whether these perceived supports and expectations translated into higher levels of motivation and achievement for these low-income Mexican American students. As shown in Table 8.2, perceived supports in all areas were related significantly and positively to student reports of efforts to behave in prosocial and compliant ways and to learn and perform well academically. Moreover, each of the perceived supports was related positively to beliefs about academic efficacy and to levels of self-esteem (with the exception of peer expectations, which were not related significantly to self-esteem). These findings correspond to results reported for Caucasian middle-class samples (see Wentzel, 2004, 2005, 2009 for reviews).

Finally, we found patterns of significant correlations between perceived supports and classroom behavior (i.e., teacher-rated compliance to rules) and grades. As shown in Table 8.2, most supports were related to classroom behavior, including perceived caring from all sources, help from classmates, academic expectations from teachers and parents, and social expectations from parents and classmates. Of interest is that follow-up correlations, in which the effects of multiple sources of support were partialled out, indicated that only caring from peers, academic expectations from teachers, and social expectations from classmates and parents remained significant predictors of classroom behavior. Therefore, provisions of supports from multiple sources appeared to be important for understanding the classroom behavior of these students, with perceived caring and social expectations from classmates being especially strong predictors.

For grades, perceived parent and teacher caring, help from parents, and academic expectations from teachers and parents were significant correlates. In contrast to results for behavior, however, only parental supports remained significant predictors of student grades when supports from teachers and classmates were taken into account. Significant correlations between teacher supports and grades became non-significant when parental supports were partialled out.

In summary, our findings provide initial evidence of the utility of the model guiding our work for understanding classroom engagement of

Table 8.2
Intercorrelations among Variables

	Caring			Help			Academic Expectations			Social Expectations	
	Teacher	*Classmate*	*Parent*	*Teacher*	*Classmate*	*Parent*	*Teacher*	*Classmate*	*Parent*	*Classmate*	*Parent*
Efforts to learn	.37	.28	.14	.37	.30	.17	.35	.31	.19	.36	.29
Efforts to perform well	.33	.32	.11	.36	.32	.22	.29	.27	.23	.29	.27
Efforts to follow rules	.56	.54	.16	.52	.55	.27	.43	.53	.39	.55	.39
Efficacy	.35	.32	.20	.29	.21	.27	.29	.22	.28	.31	.23
Self-esteem	.12	.26	.15	.12	.12	.33	.12	.07	.20	.07	.10
Behavior	.19	.20	.13	.07	.11	.08	.09	.02	.11	.18	.14
Grades	.10	.03	.19	.03	.03	.12	.06	.04	.14	.03	.04

Note: All correlations at or above .10 were significant at $p < .05$. Correlations for behavior and grades shown in shaded boxes remained significant when perceived supports from other sources were partialled out.

young adolescent Mexican American students. Specifically, the multiple supports were related to all aspects of classroom motivation and engagement, and many were related to classroom behavior and grades. Of particular interest is that perceived supports from teachers were relatively weak predictors of student outcomes, whereas parental supports were significant predictors of behavior and grades even when taking supports from teachers and peers into account. Supports from parents and classmates appeared to be the strongest predictors of classroom behavior. In addition, results based on measures used previously with Caucasian middle-class samples proved to be generalizable to our low-income Mexican American sample in that they yielded similar psychometric properties and variables were correlated with each other in similar fashion.

CONCLUSION

In this chapter, we have focused on the role of Hispanic students' social supports and experiences at school in facilitating positive social and academic outcomes. We presented a model that describes multiple dimensions of support as influencing academic adjustment and social behavior in part, by way of psychological processes reflecting beliefs about one's self and affective functioning. In addition, we described the potential role of social supports from teachers, peers, and parents in predicting social and academic competencies at school. In general, our findings support the model, along with the notion that supports from parents and family can have a potentially powerful impact on Mexican American students' ability to thrive academically at school. In addition, supports from peers appeared to play a significant role in supporting positive behavioral outcomes.

As work progresses in this area, several issues deserve further attention. First, in addition to the supports described herein, other aspects of parenting and family functioning are likely to contribute to adolescents' success at school. For example, parents' own educational background and economic status can provide adolescents with experiences and resources that can enhance and supplement learning at school. In middle-class samples, these resources can range from books, tutors, and trips to museums to willingness and time to become involved in school activities. However, in low income, less privileged families such as those in our study, resources provided by parents can take the form of modeling collaborative efforts with fellow migrant workers, negotiating contracts with growers, and teaching skills that promote resiliency and creative problem solving in light of discriminatory practices. Family income also can determine the quality of schools, health care, housing, and neighborhoods, which in turn, can have an enormous impact on children's success at school. Finally, other aspects of parenting such as levels of monitoring of children's activities, spousal support, and access to support from extended family also have the potential to make a difference in adolescents' lives at school. All of these potential impacts on adolescent achievement deserve further study.

Similarly, understanding the contribution of peers to school success can be extended to studies of different types of peer relationships. For instance, it is possible that an adolescent's friends, the larger peer group they interact with, or broader gang allegiances can have a differential impact on Hispanic adolescents' positive engagement in school. The role of peer learning contexts, such as collaborative or cooperative learning activities at school also is a potentially important but understudied aspect of classmates' contribution to each others' academic success (see Wentzel & Watkins, in press). Continued work in this area is especially important for understanding the achievement of Mexican American children. For example, in a study of cooperative vs. competitive behaviors of White, Black, Mexican American, and Mexican elementary school children (Madsen & Shapira, 1970), White and Black students were more competitive than Mexican American and Mexican students. Similarly, Kagan and Madsen (1971) conducted an experiment involving learning activities with Mexican National, Mexican American, and White children. The first controlled activity was based on typical middle class White competition, and the White children outperformed the Mexican American children, who in turn outperformed the Mexican children. They conducted a second learning activity, but based on cooperation rather than competition. In this case, the Mexican children outperformed the Mexican American children and both outperformed the White children.

Finally, the research described in this chapter does not acknowledge the critical impact that instructional practices and resources can have on student learning. Whereas supports from parents, teachers, and peers might play an important role in motivating students to engage in the positive academic and social activities of the classroom, effective teaching is needed to translate motivation and engagement into actual learning and academic gains. In addition, although parent and peer supports appeared to have a stronger impact on student outcomes in our work, the role of teacher supports should not be discounted. For example, it is possible that teachers' supports moderate the impact of parent and peer supports on student outcomes; teachers are likely to respond to students in supportive or unsupportive ways depending on whether they view parental or peer supports as positive or negative. It is clear, therefore, that future studies of social supports and student achievement should also include assessments of classroom instruction and teacher practices.

Other aspects of minority students' experiences at school also deserve further study. Perceived discrimination in the form of differential access to resources as well as stereotyped judgments can pose threats to a student's emotional security and safety; in turn, these threats can result in alienation and disengagement from the social and academic life of the classroom (Crocker, Major, & Steele, 1998; Phelan et al., 1991). Recent work suggests that a strong sense of ethnic identity in conjunction with a positive sense of self-worth tend to act as buffers against the negative effects of prejudice and derogatory behavior on academic achievement (Wong, Eccles, & Sameroff, 2003). Mexican American students who navigate their school experiences successfully overcome psychosocial stress factors (sociocultural variables) associated with their lifestyle and culture. They develop protective resources (personal and environmental) that make them invulnerable. Students "at-risk" who succeed possess a multitude of coping strategies that make them resilient to the stressful factors of acculturations (Garmezy, 1983, 1991; Garza, Reyes, & Trueba, 2004). Therefore, additional work on how ethnic identity might support resilience in the face of school-based forms of discrimination is clearly needed.

In addition, we often assume that students understand how they are supposed to behave and what it is they are supposed to accomplish while at school. However, for some students these expectations are not always immediately obvious. In particular, students who are raised in cultures with dissimilar goals and values to those espoused by American educational institutions might need explicit guidance with respect to the social and academic goals they are expected to achieve at school (Ogbu, 1985). In addition, teachers do not always communicate clearly their own goals for their students, and being academically "successful" can mean different things to teachers and students. Therefore, the more explicit and clearly defined that school administrators and teachers can make the social and academic expectations of their schools, the more likely students will at least understand the goals they are expected to achieve.

In a related vein, a focus on students' beliefs concerning the opportunities and affordances available from teachers and peers highlights the notion that subjective beliefs concerning support from classmates and teachers are likely to reflect to some degree cultural and familial expectations and belief systems (see, e.g., Fordham & Ogbu, 1986; Okagaki & Sternberg, 1993; Phelan et al., 1991). Indeed, beliefs such as what it means to "care," what it means to be a friend, or what an appropriate teacher-student relationship should entail are likely to vary as a function of race, gender, neighborhood, and family background (see e.g., Valenzuela, 1999). In this regard, little is known about how Hispanic students perceive the social climate of their classrooms and the extent to which their perceptions are congruent with those of their teachers and peers. Moreover, perceptions of teacher and parent expectations also might not be congruent. To illustrate, teacher expectations for students' academic accomplishments might be higher than those of parents or, parental expectations could be higher than those of teachers. In the former case, students might learn to devalue education despite the best efforts of teachers; in the latter case, teachers' low expectations for minority students might result in self-fulfilling prophecies despite the best efforts of parents. In any case, if students' beliefs about the nature and quality of supports and relationships at school are not positive, and if familial expectations do not match those of the classroom, students are likely to feel alienated from school and to disengage from learning and academic pursuits.

Finally, research in this area could profit from more complex theoretical models, research methods, and designs. For example, the model described herein was designed specifically to address the role of multiple social supports in explanations of student outcomes. However, this model could focus even more closely on highly differentiated aspects of support (e.g., different types of help, multiple aspects of parental involvement), or more broadly to include the role of supports as they are nested in different types of classroom or family structures, various socioeconomic strata, or levels of acculturation.

In addition, most of the studies reviewed in this chapter are based on correlational designs that do not provide strong bases for drawing causal inferences. Therefore, research could benefit from more in-depth, qualitative designs useful for theory development and more nuanced understanding of classroom contexts and interpersonal supports, as well as more controlled experimental studies that can begin to identify causal mechanisms. More attention to sampling strategies also is necessary. In this regard, researchers need to take into account the likelihood that categorizations of individuals according to ethnicity can undermine our understanding of the impact of potentially powerful contextual factors and individual differences on student achievement.

REFERENCES

Alfaro, E. C., Umaña-Taylor, A. J., & Bámaca, M. Y. (2006). The influence of academic support on Latino adolescents' academic motivation. *Family Relations 55*(3), 279–291.

Altermatt, E. R., Pomerantz, E. M., Ruble, D. N., Frey, K. S., & Greulich, F. K. (2002). Predicting changes in children's self-perceptions of academic competence: A naturalistic examination of evaluative discourse among classmates. *Developmental Psychology 38*, 903–917.

Bandura, A. (1986). *Social foundations of thought and action: A social cognitive theory*. Englewood Cliffs, NJ: Prentice-Hall.

Brown, B. B., Eicher, S. A., & Petrie, S. (1986). The importance of peer group ("crowd') affiliation in adolescence. *Journal of Adolescence 9*, 73–96.

Carlson, C., Uppal, S., & Prosser, E. C. (2000). Ethnic differences in processes contributing to the self-esteem of early adolescent girls. *The Journal of Early Adolescence, 20*(1), 44–67.

Ceballo, R. (2004). From Barrios to Yale: The role of parenting strategies in Latino families. *Hispanic Journal of Behavioral Sciences 26*, 171–186.

Cheng, S., & Starks, B. (2002). Racial differences in the effects of significant others on students' educational expectations. *Sociology of Education 75*(4), 306–327.

Crocker, J., Major, B., & Steele, C. (1998). Social stigma. In D. M Gilbert, S. T. Fiske, & G. Lindzey (Eds.), *The handbook of social psychology* (4th ed., Vol. 2, pp. 504–553). New York: McGraw Hill.

Crosnoe, R., Johnson, M. K., & Elder, G. H. (2004). Intergenerational bonding in school: The behavioral and contextual correlates of student-teacher relationships. *Sociology of Education 77*, 60–81.

DuBois, D. L., Felner, R. D., Brand, S., Adan, A. M., & Evans, E. G. (1992). A prospective study of life stress, social support, and adaptation in early adolescence. *Child Development 63*, 542–557.

Eccles, J. S., & Midgley, C. (1989). Stage-environment fit: Developmentally appropriate classrooms for young adolescents. In C. Ames & R. Ames (Eds.), *Research on motivation in education: Vol. 3* (pp. 139–186). New York: Academic Press.

Fordham, S., & Ogbu, J. U. (1986). Black students' school success; Coping with "the burden of 'acting White.' " *The Urban Review 18*, 176–206.

Garcia-Reid, P. (2007). Examining social capital as a mechanism for improving school engagement among low income Hispanic girls. *Youth & Society 39*(2), 164–181.

Garza, E., Reyes, P., & Trueba E. (2004). *Resiliency and success: Migrant children in the U.S.* Boulder, CO: Paradigm Publishers.

Garmezy, N. (1983). Stressors in childhood. In N. Garmezy & M. Rutter (Eds.), *Stress, coping and development in childhood* (pp. 43–84). New York: MacGraw Hill.

Garmezy, N. (1991). Resiliency and vulnerability to adverse developmental outcomes associated with poverty. *American Behavioral Scientist 34 (4)*, 416–430.

Goodenow, C. (1993). Classroom belonging among early adolescent students: Relationships to motivation and achievement. *Journal of Early Adolescence 13*, 21–43.

Grusec, J. E., & Goodnow, J. J. (1994). Impact of parental discipline methods on the child's internalization of values: A reconceptualization of current points of view. *Developmental Psychology 30*, 4–19.

Harter, S. (1996). Teacher and classmate influences on scholastic motivation, self-esteem, and level of voice in adolescents. In J. Juvonen & K. Wentzel (Eds.), *Social motivation: Understanding children's school adjustment* (pp. 11–42). New York: Cambridge.

Intercultural Development Research Organization (2010). Retrieved February 9, 2010 from *www.IDRA.org*

Johnson, R. L. (2005). *Little improvement in Texas school holding power—Texas Public School Attrition Study, 2004–2005*. IDRA Newsletter. San Antonio, TX: IDRA.

Juvonen, J., Nishina, A., & Graham, S. (2000). Peer harassment, psychological adjustment, and school functioning in early adolescence. *Journal of Educational Psychology 92*, 349–359.

Kagan, S. L., & Madsen, M. C. (1971). Cooperation and competition of Mexican-American and Anglo-American children of two ages under four instructional sets. *Developmental Psychology 5,* 32–39.

Kuperminc, G. P., Darnell, A. J., & Alvarez-Jimenez, A. (2008). Parent involvement in the academic adjustment of Latino middle and high school youth: Teacher expectations and school belonging as mediators. *Journal of Adolescence 31*(4), 469–483.

Laosa, L. M., & Henderson, R. W. (1991). Cognitive socialization and competence: The academic development of Chicanos. In R. R. Valencia (Ed.), *Chicano school failure and success: Research and policy agendas for the 1990s* (pp. 161–199). New York, NY: Falmer Press.

Madsen, W. (1966). *Mexican-Americans of south Texas*. New York, NY: Holt, Rhinehart, & Winston.

Madsen, M. C., & Shapira, A. (1970). Cooperative and competitive behavior of urban Afro-American, Anglo-American, Mexican-American and Mexican village children. *Developmental Psychology 3*(1), 16–20.

Martinez, C. R., DeGarmo, D. S., & Eddy, J. M. (2004). Promoting academic success among Latino youths. *Hispanic Journal of Behavioral Sciences 26*, 128–151.

Meece, J. L., Wigfield, A., & Eccles, J. S. (1990). Predictors of math anxiety and its influence on young adolescents' course enrollment intentions and performance in mathematics. *Journal of Educational Psychology 82*, 60–70.

Meehan, B. T., Hughes, J. N., & Cavell, T. A. (2003). Teacher-student relationships as compensatory resources for aggressive children. *Child Development 74*, 1145–1157.

Midgley, C., Feldlaufer, H., & Eccles, J. (1989). Student/teacher relations and attitudes toward mathematics before and after the transition to junior high school. *Child Development 60*, 981–992.

Morrison, G. M., Cosden, M. A., O'Farrell, S. L., & Campos, E. (2003). Changes in Latino students' perceptions of school belonging over time: Impact of language proficiency, self-perceptions and teacher evaluations. *California School Psychologist 8*, 87–98.

Nansel, T. R., Overpeck, M., Pilla, R. S., Ruan, J., Simons-Morton, B., & Scheidt, P. (2001). Bullying behaviors among US youth: Prevalence and association with psychosocial adjustment. *JAMA, 285*, 2094–2100.

Ogbu, J. U. (1985). Origins of human competence: A cultural-ecological perspective. *Child Development 52*, 413–429.

Okagaki, L., & Sternberg, R. J. (1993). Parental beliefs and children's school performance. *Child Development 64*(1), 36–56.

Phelan, P., Davidson, A. L., & Cao, H. T. (1991). Students' multiple worlds: Negotiating the boundaries of family, peer, and school cultures. *Anthropology and Education Quarterly 22*, 224–250.

Phinney, J. S., Kim-Jo, T., Osorio, S., & Vilhjalmsdottir, P. (2005). Autonomy and relatedness in adolescent-parent disagreements: Ethnic and developmental factors. *Journal of Adolescent Research 20*, 8–39.

Plunkett, S. W., Henry, C. S., Houltberg, B. J., Sands, T., & Abarca-Mortensen, S. (2008). Academic support by significant others and educational resilience in Mexican-origin ninth grade students from intact families. *The Journal of Early Adolescence 28*(3), 333–355.

President's Commission on Educational Excellence for Hispanic Americans (September, 1996). *Our Nation on the Fault Line: Hispanic American Education*. Washington, DC: White House Initiative on Educational Excellence for Hispanic Americans.

Romo, H. D., & Falbo, T. (1996). *Latino high school graduation: Defying the odds*. Austin, TX: University of Texas Press.

Rumberger, R.W. (1995). Dropping out of middle school: A multilevel analysis of students and schools. *American Educational Research Journal 32*, 583–625.

Rutherford, W. (1999). Creating student-centered classroom environments: The case of reading. In P. Reyes, J. D. Scribner, & A. P. Scribner (Eds.), *Lessons from high-performing Hispanic schools: Creating learning communities* (pp. 131–168). New York, NY: Teachers College Press.

Rutter, M., & Maughan, B. (2002). School effectiveness findings 1979–2002. *Journal of School Psychology 40*(6), 451–475.

Ryan, R. M. (1993). Agency and organization: Intrinsic motivation, autonomy, and the self in psychological development. In J. Jacobs (Ed.), *Nebraska symposium on motivation, Vol 40* (pp. 1–56). Lincoln, NB: University of Nebraska Press.

Scribner, J. D., & Reyes, P. (1999). Creating learning communities for high performing Hispanic students: A conceptual framework. In P. Reyes, J. D. Scribner, & A. P. Scribner (Eds.), *Lessons from high-performing Hispanic schools: Creating learning communities* (pp. 188–210). New York, NY: Teachers College Press.

Skinner, E. A., Zimmer-Gembeck, M. J., & Connell, J. P. (1998). Individual differences and the development of perceived control. *Monographs of the Society for Research in Child Development 63*, Nos. 2–3.

Steele, C., & Aronson, J. (1995). Stereotype threat and the intellectual performance of African Americans. *Journal of Personality and Social Psychology* *69*, 797–811.

Stevens, T., Hamman, D., & Olivárez, A., Jr. (2007). Hispanic students' perception of White teachers' mastery goal orientation influences sense of school belonging. *Journal of Latinos and Education 6*(1), 55–70.

Texas Education Agency (2010). Retrieved February 9, 2010 from *www.tea.state.tx.us*

U.S. Department of Education, National Center for Education Statistics (2002) *The condition of education 2002 in brief*, NCES 2002–011, Washington, DC.

U.S. Census Bureau (2000). Retrieved November, 30, 2009 from *www.census.gov /main/www/cen2000.html*

Valenzuela, A. (1999). *Subtractive schooling: U.S.-Mexican youths and the politics of caring*. Albany, NY: SUNY Press.

Valenzuela, A., (2000). The significance of the TAAS test for Mexican immigrant and Mexican American adolescents: A case study. *Hispanic Journal of Behavioral Sciences 22*, 524–539.

Wentzel, K. R. (1999). Social-motivational processes and interpersonal relationships: Implications for understanding students' academic success. *Journal of Educational Psychology 91*, 76–97.

Wentzel, K. R. (1994). Relations of social goal pursuit to social acceptance, classroom behavior, and perceived social support. *Journal of Educational Psychology 86*, 173–182.

Wentzel, K. R. (1997). Student motivation in middle school: The role of perceived pedagogical caring. *Journal of Educational Psychology 89*, 411–419.

Wentzel, K. R. (1998). Social support and adjustment in middle school: The role of parents, teachers, and peers. *Journal of Educational Psychology 90*, 202–209.

Wentzel, K. R. (2002). Are effective teachers like good parents? Interpersonal predictors of school adjustment in early adolescence. *Child Development 73*, 287–301.

Wentzel, K. R. (2003). School adjustment. In W. Reynolds & G. Miller (Eds.), *Handbook of psychology, Vol. 7: Educational psychology* (pp. 235–258). New York: Wiley.

Wentzel, K. R. (2004). Understanding classroom competence: The role of social-motivational and self-processes. In R. Kail (Ed.), *Advances in child development and behavior, Vol. 32* (pp. 213–241). New York, NY: Elsevier.

Wentzel, K. R. (2005). Peer relationships, motivation, and academic performance at school. In A. Elliot & C. Dweck (Eds.), *Handbook of competence and motivation* (pp. 279–296). New York, NY: Guilford.

Wentzel, K. R. (2006). Social motivational perspective on classroom management. In C. Evertson and C. Weinstein (Eds.), *Handbook of classroom management—research, practice, and contemporary issues* (pp. 619–644). Mahwah, NJ: Erlbaum.

Wentzel, K. R. (2009). Students' relationships with teachers as motivational contexts. In K. Wentzel and A. Wigfield (Eds.), *Handbook of motivation at school* (pp. 301–322). Mahwah, NJ: LEA.

Wentzel, K. R., Battle, A., Russell, S., & Looney, L. (2010). Teacher and peer contributions to classroom climate in middle school. *Contemporary Educational Psychology 35*, 193–202.

Wentzel, K. R., Filisetti, L., & Looney, L. (2007). Adolescent prosocial behavior: The role of self-processes and contextual cues. *Child Development 78*, 895–910.

Wentzel, K. R., & Looney, L. (2007). Socialization in school settings. In J. Grusec & P. Hastings (Eds.), *Handbook of social development* (pp. 382–403). New York, NY: Guilford.

Wentzel, K. R., & Watkins, D. E. (2011). Peer relationships and learning: Implications for instruction. In R. Mayer and P. Alexander (Eds.), *Handbook of research on learning and instruction* (pp. 322–343). New York: Routledge.

Wentzel, K. R., & Wigfield, A. (2009). *Handbook of motivation at school*. New York, NY: Taylor Francis.

Wentzel, K. R., Williams, A. Y., & Tomback, R. M. (2005, April). *Relations of teacher and peer support to classroom behavior in middle school*, paper presented at the annual meeting of the American Educational Research Association, Montreal, QC.

Wentzel, K. R., Williams, A. Y., & Tomback, R. M. (2006, April). *Relations of teacher and peer support to academic achievement in middle school*, paper presented at the annual meeting of the American Educational Research Association, San Francisco, CA.

Wong, C. A., Eccles, J. S., & Sameroff, A. (2003). The influence of ethnic discrimination and ethnic identification on African American adolescents' school and socioemotional adjustment. *Journal of Personality 71*, 1197–1232.

Woolley, M. E., Kol, K. L., & Bowen, G. L. (2009). The social context of school success for Latino middle school students: Direct and indirect influences of teachers, family, and friends. *The Journal of Early Adolescence 29*(1), 43–70.

Chapter 9

FAMILIES, PEERS, AND MEXICAN-HERITAGE ADOLESCENTS' NEGOTIATION OF SCHOOL TRANSITIONS

Margarita Azmitia

> For Latino/as, as for many other groups of Color in the United States, educational achievement cannot be conceptualized as an individual process. Context, community, and family form a seamless network leading to educational progress.
>
> —Hurtado, Cervantez, & Eccleston, 2010, p. 284

Considerable research has highlighted the educational challenges of Latino children and adolescents. Latinos have the lowest high school graduation rates of any major ethnic group in the United States; 53 percent of Latinos graduate from high school compared to 71 percent of Native Americans, 72 percent of African Americans, 82 percent of Asian Americans, and 84 percent of Whites (U.S. Census, 2004). Latinos also have the lowest percentage of college graduates; in 2005, only 11 percent of Latinos 25–29 years of age had a BA or higher, compared to 34 percent of Whites and 18 percent of African Americans (Gándara, 2008).

If one considers the demographic projections that show that relative to other ethnic groups in the United States, Latinos are a young population—the median age is 25 and 40 percent are under 20—and that by the year 2050, 25 percent of the United States will be Latino (U.S. Census, 2000), their low levels of educational attainment are not merely personally devastating for these adolescents and their families, but also devastating for the United States. In particular, Latino's low high school and college graduation rates forecast an under-prepared workforce that will be unable to keep pace with the requirements of the fastest growing jobs and careers, which increasingly require a college degree (Gills et al., 2006; Gándara & Contreras, 2009; Hurtado et al., 2010). Latino adolescents' vulnerabilities are not confined to education; of all major ethic groups, Latino adolescents have the highest rates of early pregnancy, are increasingly using and abusing drugs, have a significant gang presence, and, with African-heritage adolescents, are the largest racial groups in the criminal justice system (Gonzalez et al., 2009; Grau, Azmitia, & Quattelbaum, 2009; Haney & Zimbardo, 1998; U.S. Census, 2000; Vigil, 2002).

Although the focus on Latino adolescents' academic difficulties has overshadowed their success stories, there is a growing literature on academically successful Latinos (e.g., Cooper, Cooper, Azmitia, Chavira, & Gullat, 2002; Ethier & Deaux, 2004; Gándara, 1995; Grau, Azmitia, & Quattelbaum, 2009; Rivas & Mooney-Drake, 2008). This chapter highlights both assets and vulnerabilities in Latino adolescents' educational pathways. I discuss the role of family and friends in supporting or challenging Latino adolescents' engagement and persistence in school and educational aspirations. I focus on the transitions to middle school and college because these are key turning points in Latino students' school performance and lives. The chapter is organized as follows: I first describe the educational pathways of Mexican-heritage adolescents. I then review research that has shown that understanding how adolescents manage school transitions, and in particular, the transition to middle school and college, can provide a unique window into the challenges and resources adolescents face as they pursue their educational goals. Following this section, I briefly review the theoretical perspectives that have guided research on Latinos academic achievement and aspirations. I then review research that has used these perspectives to investigate Mexican-heritage adolescents' management of the transitions to middle school and college and how family and friends help or challenge adolescents' adjustment to these new school contexts. I conclude with suggestions for future research and social policies that can help these adolescents succeed in school and consequently increase their social mobility and contribute positively to the nation's future.

MEXICAN-HERITAGE ADOLESCENTS: CHARACTERISTICS, STRENGTHS, AND VULNERABILITIES

The term *Latino* or *Hispanic* obscures important historical, geographical, racial, educational, and socioeconomic variations in the diverse Latino populations in the United States. Addressing this diversity is beyond the scope of this chapter. This chapter primarily focuses on Mexican-heritage adolescents because they are the youngest and fastest growing ethnic minority group in the Southwest; their population is also increasing in many Midwestern and Southern states. Historically, their history of colonization has placed Mexican-heritage families in a unique position relative to other ethnic minority groups. Although Native Americans share the history of colonization, Native American families' relegation to reservations and their relatively small numbers have prevented them from exerting the political pressure that has increased the representation of Latinos in government and school administrations in some Southwestern states. It is still the case, however, that the majority of Latinos attend schools without adequate facilities and teachers, thus making it difficult for them to compete with their ethnic majority peers (Gándara & Contreras, 2009). The increase in criminal activities and gang violence in many heavily-Latino urban neighborhoods has prompted businesses to relocate to safer suburban neighborhoods, thus further reducing the tax base of low-income neighborhoods' already under-funded, poor-quality schools.

The shared border between Mexico and the United States also is a continued source of political tension and has resulted in increases in the racism and discrimination that Mexican-heritage adolescents experience at school and in their home communities. The shared border has also led to family fragmentation as some family members make their way into the United States and others stay behind in Mexico. Suárez-Orozco, Suárez-Orozco, and Todorova (2008) have noted that family loss and separation can play an important role in Latino students' school performance and increase their vulnerability to depression.

Among Latinos, Mexican-heritage children and adolescents have the highest rates of academic difficulties and school dropout, and in the case of immigrants, also tend to have parents with lower levels of education than other immigrant groups. By the year 2050, they will constitute one in three K-12 students in the Southwest, and they already constitute almost half of the student population in California and Texas (Gándara, 2008). Mexican-heritage families have high rates of poverty; 34 percent of first generation families and 25 percent of second and third generation families qualify for health and social services, although contrary to the prevailing stereotype, they are less likely than non-Latino families to use these services (Fry & Passel, 2009).

Like other immigrant families, many Mexican-descent parents brave enormous hardships during and following their immigration to the United States so that their children will receive a good education and not suffer the same hardships and poverty their parents and relatives endured in their home countries or in the low-paying, demanding, unsafe jobs adults usually obtain after arriving in the United States. Unfortunately, soon after their arrival, many families realize that the United States is not the bastion of democracy and equal opportunity that politicians underscore in their impassioned speeches and that sustain these families' dreams for the future. These realizations can prompt the adolescents and their families to revisit and revise their American dreams.

Despite the prevailing belief that second and their generation Latinos often develop oppositional and resistant attitudes towards school (Ogbu, 2008), many second-and third-generation Mexican-heritage adolescents are excelling in school and entering the middle class and high status professions (Mooney & Rivas-Drake, 2008; Portes & Fernández-Kelly, 2008). Many of these upwardly mobile Latinos attribute their success to their families' encouragement, determination, and *consejos* and stories about positive and negative developmental pathways (Ceballo, 2004; Delgado-Gaitán, 1984; Gándara, 1995; Lopez, 2001). Still, family emotional support is not enough to ensure upward mobility (Coleman, 1988). Researchers are only beginning to investigate the characteristics of Mexican and Central American adolescents that succeed in school and move up the socioeconomic ladder. As I will elaborate in more detail in a subsequent section, research has shown that adolescents' intrinsic motivation, optimism, agency, and skill at finding a mentor are associated with their academic success (Gándara & Contreras, 2009; Suárez-Orozco et al., 2008). Adolescents who succeed in middle school and college also form friendships with peers who value schooling and have a strong sense of obligation to their families and the community (Cooper et al., 2002). Finally, sustained participation in community organizations and academic outreach programs appears to play an important role in helping these students succeed in school and attain their career goals (Azmitia & Cooper, 2001; Cooper et al., 2002; Gándara & Contreras, 2009; Suárez-Orozco et al., 2008).

SCHOOL TRANSITIONS AND THE EDUCATIONAL PIPELINE

School transitions provide rich opportunities for observing adolescents' strengths, resources, and vulnerabilities. School transitions can be stressful because they are typically accompanied by changes in adolescents, families, and schools. In particular, these transitions bring with them new expectations for academic and social responsibilities and shifts in peer, parent-adolescent, and teacher-adolescent relationships. Research has consistently shown that the transition to middle school plays a key role in adolescents' educational trajectories; while many adolescents continue on positive educational and life pathways, others disengage from school, gravitate towards peer groups that endorse risky behaviors and antisocial activities, and in general, slide into the 'bad path of life' (Azmitia & Brown, 2002). The transition to college also brings with it stresses and turning points. For many adolescents, college presents a more impersonal school structure in which they must make sense of a wide range of academic and social opportunities without their parents' guidance. Many college students also encounter a more diverse peer group and must learn to balance social activities and academic work. Because 20 percent of first year students do not return for their sophomore year, increasingly researchers and policy makers have turned their attention to factors that increase adjustment to and persistence in college (Gerdes & Mallinckrodt, 1994, Terenzini & Reason, 2005; Tinto, 1993)

Ironically, at the same time that adolescents need their families and friends' emotional support and guidance to adjust to the new middle school or college contexts, these relationships are also changing and can become key sources of stress (Shaver, Furman, & Buhrmester, 1985). For example, while many early adolescents want to be more independent from their parents and to spend more time with their friends, many parents of early adolescents increase their monitoring and supervision of their children because they fear that they will succumb to peer pressure to engage in risky behavior (Azmitia & Brown, 1992; Azmitia, Ittel, & Brenk, 2006). Ethnic minority adolescents who want to leave home to attend college can also experience resistance from parents who fear that going away to college will distance their children from the family. Parents of daughters can be more likely than parents of sons to prevent their children from attending college away from home because parents fear for their daughters' safety and worry that their daughters will change their values and engage in activities of which the parents disapprove. Thus, it is not uncommon for ethnic minority adolescents, and in particular Latinos, who are admitted to prestigious universities to chose to attend less prestigious schools in their home communities (Pérez & McDonough, 2008).

Adolescents' friends can be important sources of support as adolescents' renegotiate their relationships with their families. They can also support adolescents through school transitions and provide important information about school, relationships, and other important aspects of adolescents' lives. In their conversations with friends, adolescents can explore their educational goals, their gender, ethnic and sexual identities, and for poor and working class adolescents, how class will contour and constrain their upward mobility. Friends are important contexts for identity exploration because they provide intimate spaces for self-disclosure. Because their friends are also exploring their identities, reciprocal discussions of possibilities, resources, and concerns can help adolescents become aware of their choices and commit to possible identities.

As they move through middle school, adolescents also become identified with groups who share the same interests, skills, level of social acceptance, and reputation. These crowds provide further opportunities for adolescents to assess the positioning of their various identities within the school and society at large. However, for poor and working class adolescents who are upwardly mobile, these peer crowds can exert pressure to conform to working class values and behavioral practices and lead them to feel ambivalent about their upwardly mobile goals (Eckert, 1989; Willis, 1997). Ogbu (2008) has also noted similar pressures on ethnic minority adolescents who excel in school and are accused by their peers of "acting White."

In addition to pressuring them to conform, friends can also challenge adolescents' loyalties. The transitions to middle school and college are characterized by an influx of new peers, which can strain relationships as adolescents try to incorporate new friendships into their extant circle of friends. It is not unusual for adolescents, and especially girls, to feel excluded, which can lead to loneliness and other stresses (Azmitia, Kamprath, & Linnet, 1998). Adolescents' romantic relationships can also be sources of support and challenge as partners negotiate intimacy and find ways to spend time with their romantic partners and their friends. Adolescents who do not attend college in close proximity to their romantic partner can experience the additional strain of maintaining a long-distance relationship while meeting the academic and social demands of college. At times, adolescents feel conflicted between staying in college and returning home to be closer to their romantic partner (Azmitia, Syed, Radmacher, & Gills, in preparation). I now explore the transitions to middle school and college in more depth.

The Transition to Middle School

The transition to middle school marks the beginning of adolescents' pursuit of college-going or vocational pathways. Math achievement, in particular, seems to play a key role in early adolescents' college readiness; research suggests that adolescents who have not completed Algebra 1 by the end of ninth grade are less likely to attend college than those who complete this benchmark in middle school or at least, by ninth grade (Azmitia et al., 2009). In their work with European- and African-heritage students, Eccles and Midgley (1989) proposed that the transition to middle school poses a developmental mismatch for most adolescents. Puberty and changes in friendships and peer relationships prompt early adolescents to seek more independence from parents, which can lead to conflicts and declines in adolescents' perceptions of their parents' emotional support (Grotevant & Cooper, 1988). In contrast to parents, middle school teachers expect early adolescents to be more independent in managing their classwork and homework, but often fail to provide sufficient guidance about how to manage these increased demands for personal responsibility (Ecces, Midgley et al., 1993). Moreover, middle school teachers can provide conflicting messages to their students because on the one hand, they expect more self-governance, but on the other hand, they often focus more attention than elementary school teachers on behavioral control, which can make early adolescents perceive them as distant and punitive (Eccles & Midgley, 1989). Taken together, these shifts in parents' and teachers' expectations and guidance have been associated with declines in self-esteem, academic engagement and performance, and negative perceptions of teachers' support and the school climate (Eccles & Midgley, 1989). The declines seem to be greater for boys than girls, in part because teachers and administrators seem to be especially vigilant of boys' negative behavior, which can lead boys to perceive the school as unfair and unsupportive (Eccles & Midgley, 1989; see also Kuperminc, Wilkins, Roche, & Alvarez-Jimenez, 2009).

Seidman, Allen, Aber, Mitchell, and Feinman (1994) replicated and extended Eccles's and Midgley's (1989) findings in their study of Latino and African American early adolescents transitioning to middle school in New York City. Their results replicated the declines in early adolescents' self-esteem, grades, and engagement in extracurricular activities. These declines in school engagement and performance were associated with an increased orientation to peers with antisocial attitudes and low-school motivation and the adolescents' negative perceptions of the school climate, thus extending previous work on the middle school transition to include peers (see also Kuperminc et al., 2009). Contrary to expectations, no gender differences in the decline in grades and increased affiliation with low-achieving peers obtained. However, numerous studies since then have shown that boys are more likely to than girls to exhibit these patterns, thus increasing the gender gap in achievement (Azmitia & Cooper, 2001; Burciaga, Huber, & Solorzano 2010; Gándara & Contreras, 2009).

The Transition to College

College students are expected to take the initiative for contacting and developing relationships with staff and professors, an expectation that can be stressful and make students feel inadequate, confused, and, in the case of students who are the first in their families to attend college, result in them feeling like they do not belong in college (Orbe, 2004; Ostrove, 2003). This sense of belonging, of fitting in, plays an important role in college students' persistence and retention (Hoffman, Richmond, Morrow, & Salomone, 2002–2003; Tinto, 1993). Students who feel like they do not fit in with their peers or who find the multiplicity of academic choices and responsibilities too overwhelming can experience declines in self-efficacy and self-esteem and increases in depression. These mental health difficulties are correlated with students' decision to drop out of college (Gerdes & Mallinckrodt, 1994; Tinto, 1993).

In their longitudinal study of the transition to college, Azmitia, Syed, Radmacher, and Gills (2005) found that peer groups played an especially important role in diverse college students' adjustment to college. Participation in supportive peer groups increased students' sense of belonging and, for ethnic minority students, provided safe spaces from discrimination (see also Cooper et al., 2002). Interestingly, few of these college students indicated that a mentor had helped them adjust to college. Indeed, many indicated that the lack of mentors and advisors as one of their greatest challenges. This finding is important given that research has consistently shown the importance of mentors in successful Latino students' educational pathways (Gándara & Contreras, 2009; Suárez-Orozco et al., 2008). Students who adjusted successfully to college also reported close, positive relationships with their families. For all ethnic groups, emotional support from parents had a stronger association with students' mental health than their informational or financial support, further highlighting the role of positive family relationships in successful adjustment to college.

Mexican-Heritage Students' Transition to Middle School

Much of the research on Latino students' adjustment to middle school has not differentiated between the adjustment profiles of the various Latino groups. Thus, most the findings that I will describe pertain to Latinos as a whole. Like most adolescents, many Latino students find the transition to middle school challenging, as evident from decreases in grades and increases in truancy and other forms of misbehavior (Azmitia & Cooper, 2001). Researchers have identified vulnerabilities that are specific to Latino students. As a group, Latinos perform more poorly in elementary school than other ethnic groups, and consequently, in middle school many of these students are tracked into vocational tracks or remedial courses that are not intellectually engaging (Gándara & Contreras, 2009). Many middle schools also have limited support for immigrant students who are not proficient in English, and thus, early adolescents placed in mainstream classes fall increasingly behind or are, from the start, placed in remedial or special education classes from which it is hard to transition into grade-level courses (Gándara & Contreras, 2009; Suárez-Orozco et al., 2008). Because students who have behavioral difficulties and negative attitudes towards school often populate remedial classes, low-achieving Latino early adolescents can befriend peers who are disengaged from school and consequently, become disengaged academically.

However, limited English proficiency is not, by itself, an explanation of Latino students' academic difficulties. As Kao and Tienda (1998) and Suárez-Orozco and Suárez-Orozco (2001) have shown, many first generation students often outperform second generation students in school, a finding that suggests that language barriers are not the principal cause of the educational difficulties of Latino students (see also Hurtado et al., 2010). This *immigrant optimism* appears to stem, at least in part, from students' sense of obligation to their families (Fuligni & Pereira, 2009), and their families' support, monitoring,[1] and encouragement (Azmitia, Cooper, & Brown, 2009, Grau et al., 2009). Ogbu (2008) suggested that immigrant families often believe that the racism and discrimination that they experience are only temporary, and that with hard work and time, their situation will improve. This positive framing of racism and discrimination can serve as a protective factor for adolescents who must endure the negative stereotypes of Latinos that are prevalent in local and national portrayals of Latinos in the United States. Immigrant Latinos' optimism may play a role in the finding that as a group, first generation Latinos have better physical and mental health than second and third generation Latinos (Gonzales, Fabrett, & Knight, 2009).

Importantly, as they move into middle school, some Latino early adolescents, and especially children of Mexican immigrants, begin to exceed their parents' level of schooling, and thus, their parents are less able to help with homework and monitor their academic work. Although parents can recruit older siblings to help, the quality of this sibling guidance depends on their siblings' own academic skills and engagement in school. Parents can also encourage their children to seek help from teachers, thus helping their children build a network of academic support and guidance. Although it appears that despite their low levels of schooling, many Mexican-heritage parents help their adolescent children access familial and school academic networks (Azmitia, Cooper, & Brown, 2009), it is the case that as a group, Mexican-heritage parents are less directly involved in their children's educational pathways, which can lead to poor parental monitoring of their children's progress and to increase teachers' perceptions that the parents do not value school (Azmitia, Cooper, García, & Dunbar, 1996).

Parents cannot protect their early adolescent children against racism and discrimination. In their study of the negative experiences and hassles of a diverse group of Latino middle school students, Kuperminc, Henrich, Meyers, House, and Sayfi (2007) found that at least 25 percent of their participants reported being treated unfairly and a larger percentage reported seeing friends being treated unfairly because of their race. These negative experiences also extend to the community, where Latino early adolescents report being followed by security officers in stores, having racial slurs being directed to them or other Latinos, and being denied employment (Cooper, Jackson, Azmitia, & Lopez, 1998). Early adolescents' negative perception of their school and community climates can lower their self-esteem, increase their risk for depression, and reduce their engagement in school (Gándara & Contreras, 2009; Kuperminc, Leadbetter, Emmons, & Blatt, 1997). Currently, depression and suicide ideation in Latino adolescents are special concerns amongst researchers, educators, and community leaders because the incidence of these and other psychological disorders in Latino adolescents has increased significantly in the last two decades. Due to cultural prescriptions against discussing problems outside the family and seeking therapy and lack of access to mental health practitioners, Latino adolescents are less likely than their White peers to seek treatment (Gándara & Contreras, 2009; Kuperminc et al., 2009), which puts them at risk for long-term psychological problems and school dropout.

Taken together, Latino early adolescents' experiences during the transition to middle school can play an important role in their identity development. In supportive family, school, and peer contexts, early adolescents can craft identities and access emotional and informational support networks that keep them on the good path of life. However, Latino early adolescents who perceive high levels of hassles at school, find the material academically uninteresting, and, in general, perceive the school and their teachers negatively can craft identities in which succeeding in school is akin to participating in an institution that discriminates against them and thus, lose their motivation to succeed (Ogbu, 2008).

Latino Students' Transition to College

Research has yielded substantial within-group differences in the role of family and friends in Latino college students' educational trajectories. However, it is the case that Mexican-descent students have the lowest rates of college completion. One reason for their low college completion is that Mexican-heritage adolescents are less likely than other groups to enroll in college immediately after high school graduation and more likely than other Latino groups to enter higher education through the community college system and to attend college part-time. Often, these students are unaware that their course work will not transfer to a four-year university or take courses that are not furthering their degree completion (Fry, 2002). Many Latino students are also unaware of the advantages of attending two- vs. four-year colleges and the differences in the prestige and resources of public and private universities. Pérez and McDonough (2008) found that even high-achieving Latinos did not engage in extensive college choice, but rather, tended to use a selection process characterized by chain migration wherein they attended institutions recommended by parents, their parents' friends, or their own friends without attention to the quality of the institution or whether it was a good fit for their career aspirations.

College students, and especially those who are the first in their families to go to college, can also struggle to construct academic identities that are compatible with their home cultures and family values. As they move through college, these students can feel that they are distancing themselves from their families and friends from home and yet, are not fully accepted by their college peers, faculty, and staff (Orbe, 2004). These perceptions can increase their feelings of marginalization and alienation, thus affecting their academic engagement and self-efficacy. It appears that Latino college students' cultural beliefs and family interdependence can serve a protective function by keeping them grounded in their cultural goals and practices and prompting them to join Latino-oriented organizations that emphasize the positive features of Latino culture, provide safe spaces from discrimination and oppression, and encourage them to work for social change (Cooper et al., 2001; Ethier & Deaux, 1990; Quintana & Scull, 2009; Sidanius, Van Laar, Levin, & St. Clair, 2004).

Friendship and peer relationships play a key role in Latino students' adjustment to college. Several studies have shown that Latino students' friendships with co-ethnic peers can increase their sense of belonging and persistence in college. Through their friendships peers who are more familiar with the social interaction practices and expectations of college, Latino students can gain valuable information for negotiating college and thus, increase their chances of success. Indeed, universities have begun to recognize the important role of peer mentors in students' success and created informal or formal opportunities for more advanced students to socialize and mentor less advanced students (Azmitia, Syed, Radmacher, & Gills, in preparation; Cooper et al., 2002).

Developing creative institutional ways for helping Latino students become aware of and access support programs is important for helping Latino students adjust to and succeed in college. As universities become attuned to the reality that due to family or work commitments most Latino adolescents do not participate in organizations, they have created support structures and curricular demands that increase Latino students knowledge of campus resources and familiarize them with the culture of the university. For example, San Jose State University has incorporated into its course requirements for lower division courses projects that require them to gather information about a variety of university support programs and activities (Robert G. Cooper, personal communication, February 1, 2010). At many universities, Latino students can also take courses on the ins and outs of the university's culture. These courses are facilitated by staff who provide opportunities for students to check-in about their experiences as well as provide advice, help them solve problems that range from difficulties with their roommates to brokering enrollment in courses requirements for their majors and thus, like the Puente program counselors, make Latino students feel at home and encourage them to persist in their studies.

Taken together, the research suggests that family, friends, and mentors can support Mexican-heritage adolescents through the transitions to middle school and college. However, adolescents' initiative to establish academic networks with peers and teachers, their intrinsic motivation, and their reliance on cultural values to counteract the negative impact of racism of discrimination appear to differentiate academically resilient adolescents from those who perform poorly at school or drop out. I now turn to three theoretical approaches that have been useful for understanding Latino students' educational trajectories. While the Sociocultural and Ecocultural approaches have paid more attention to the elementary school years, the Social Capital and Acculturation perspectives have included children and adolescents.

THEORETICAL APPROACHES TO THE ROLE OF FAMILY AND FRIENDS IN LATINO ADOLESCENTS' EDUCATIONAL TRAJECTORIES

Researchers examining the role of family and friends in Latino adolescents' transitions to middle school and college have drawn primarily on three theoretical perspectives, the *Ecological or Sociocultural Perspective*, the *Social Capital Perspective*, and the *Acculturation Perspective*. None of these approaches was specifically developed to study Latinos. However, their emphasis on family values, goals, and social interaction practices help researchers conceptualize Latino families' assets and deficiencies for helping their children succeed in U.S. schools, the role of friends as sources of support and information, and the stresses, opportunities, and choices that Latino adolescents make as they pursue their educational goals renders them useful theoretical lenses to examine Latino adolescents' school transitions and educational trajectories.

Proponents of the *Ecological or Sociocultural Perspective* emphasize the role of values, goals, and social interaction practices in children and adolescents' schooling (Greenfield, Quiroz, & Raef, 2002; Parke & Buriel, 1998; Tharp & Gallimore, 1988; Rogoff, 2003). Researchers that draw on this theoretical perspective have mostly studied the role of families in Latino adolescents' academic performance and goals. These researchers propose that Latino families' emphasis on interdependence and obligations to family is often at odds with mainstream schools' emphasis on independence and self-actualization. In a series of studies, Tharp and Gallimore (1988) and Greenfield et al. (2002) showed that these differences between home and school led teachers to misinterpret Latino students' behavior in the classroom. For example, Latino families' practice of encouraging sibling caretaking and collaboration led Latino children to help their peers in the classroom, a behavior that was interpreted by teachers as cheating. Latino parents' emphasis on sibling caretaking can also result in students, and especially girls, taking on responsibility for classroom chores and devoting less time to academic tasks (Azmitia, Cooper, García, & Dunbar, 1996).

In a study teachers' perception of Latino parents' attitudes towards school, Reese, Balzano, Gallimore, and Goldenberg (1995) noted that teachers often interpreted parents' concerns about their children's behavior in the classroom—which is a key component of the Latino value on being *bien educado* as a lack of interest in their children's academic performance, a major emphasis of the school. In turn, parents interpreted teacher's emphasis on academics and parent involvement in the classroom and meetings as insensitive to their home and job responsibilities and as a failure to understand their priorities and goals for their children's development (Valdés, 1986).

Greenfield et al. (2002) and Tharp and Gallimore (1988) proposed that the mismatch between parents' and teachers values and expectations can lead to conflicts and misunderstandings between teachers and parents and have the unfortunate consequence of creating the impression that Latino parents do not value school. They recommend that schools provide opportunities for parents and teachers to discuss their practices, values, expectations, and goals with the goal of creating mutual understanding and respect for the home and school cultures and to find ways to develop a partnership that benefits their children's academic performance and allows them to attain their educational and career goals.

Another important research direction within this theoretical perspective has been to examine the specific school learning practices of the home and the school. This research has primarily focused on early literacy and numeracy because preschools and elementary schools are more likely to have a parent-involvement component than middle schools and high schools. As reviewed by García and Scribner (2009), the educational practices that Latino parents, and especially immigrants, use to help their children succeed in school often reflect the practices learned in their home country or in low-quality U.S. schools and thus, tend to emphasize drill and memorization more than the open ended, conceptual approaches favored by middle class teachers and peers (see also Gallimore & Goldenberg, 1993; Laosa, 1982). García and Scribner (2009) also underscore the role of parents' limited English language proficiency and the dismantling of bilingual education in the academic difficulties that Latino children experience in the early elementary school grades. They provide convincing evidence showing that Latino children who receive support in school for developing their first and second languages at school fare better academically than those who enter school with limited first language development and are then immersed in English-only instruction. Because academic skills build on each other, Latino students' academic deficiencies in the primary grades play an important role in the achievement gap between Latinos and other ethnic groups (see also Burciaga et al., 2009; Gándara & Contreras, 2000; Hurtado et al., 2010).

Considerably less information about the educational practices and goals of the Latino families of middle school and college students is available. One promising research direction has involved examining parents and their adolescent children's discussions about school and the future. In their longitudinal study of low-income Mexican- and Central-American heritage adolescents transitioning to middle school in two small cities in California, Azmitia et al. (2009) found that parents often discussed their educational futures with their children, but that these discussions were unrelated to their math grades. Catsambis (2001) reported a similar result using the NELS longitudinal database, which involved a larger, more representative sample of Latino adolescents. Importantly, Catsambis (2001) identified social-class variations in the association between parent-adolescent discussions about the future and Latino adolescents' grades. In particular, although the association between these discussions and low-income Latinos academic performance was not statistically significant, this association was significant for middle-class adolescents. Catsambis suggested that this finding might reflect middle class parents' greater familiarity with U.S. schools and proposed that interventions focus on helping working class and immigrant parents acquire specific knowledge about the practices and expectations of U.S. schools, the specific focus of *Social Capital Approaches* to Latino adolescents' educational trajectories.

On a more positive note, analyses of Latino adolescents' endorsement of cultural values, practices, and goals—their ethnic identity—have shown that ethnic identity can serve a protective function for Latino adolescents by keeping them grounded in their cultural goals and practices and prompting them to befriend co-ethnic peers and join Latino-oriented organizations that emphasize the positive features of Latino culture, provide safe spaces from discrimination and oppression, and encourage them to work for social change (Cooper et al., 2001; Ethier & Deaux, 1990; Quintana & Scull, 2009; Sidanius, Van Laar, Levin, & St. Clair, 2004). Thus, on a broader level, Latino cultural values, goals, and practices can be protective assets in adolescents' academic performance and development. Before exploring ethnic identity in more depth, I review the Social Capital Perspective, which has focused on mapping Latino families' assets vis-à-vis schooling.

School and college knowledge are at the heart of the *Social Capital Approach* to Latino adolescents' educational pathways. Social Capital approaches to schooling are based on assessing resources or assets—financial, information, cultural, social networks—that students have for education (Coleman, 1988). Unlike the Sociocultural and Ecocultural perspectives, this approach incorporates social class as an important context for mapping students' academic performance and goals. In her landmark studies of working class White parents in the Midwest, for example, Lareau (1989) documented the differences in working class and middle class parents' school-related practices and how working class parents' home practices and their lack of participation in the traditional parent involvement activities of volunteering in the classroom, attending school meetings, and initiating contact with teachers when their children were performing poorly, led teachers to infer that working class parents did not value school and to lower their expectations for their children's academic performance. Lareau's research suggests that many of the factors that place Latino adolescents at risk for educational failure are not unique to Latino culture per se, but rather, reflect the role of socioeconomic status, and in particular, poverty, in adolescents' schooling and life pathways.

As applied to Latino families, proponents of the Social Capital perspective have differentiated between parents' emotional support and encouragement and their knowledge of the U.S. school system and the requirements for college eligibility. In his seminal work, Coleman (1988) argued that emotional support and encouragement are not enough to help students succeed in school. Parents need specific information about school practices and goals and access to social networks that can help students with schoolwork and homework if they lack the educational background to provide this help (see also Gándara & Contreras, 2009). In support of Coleman's proposal, Valenzuela and Dornbusch (1994) found that by itself, family emotional support did not predict Latino adolescents' academic performance in high school. Rather, it was the parents' educational attainment, and in particular, whether they had graduate from high school, coupled with their emotional support, that was positively correlated with high school students' grades (but see Azmitia et al., 2009). Consistent with Valenzuela and Dornbush's (1994), Rumbaut's (1995) analysis of the academic success of immigrant groups in California showed that with the exception of Cambodian, Laotian, and Vietnamese refuges, Asian immigrant parents typically have more schooling and in many cases, hold university degrees, a factor that contributes to the greater academic success of their children relative to their less-schooled Mexican and Central American counterparts. Indeed, Latino immigrants from South America, and especially Colombia, Chile, and Argentina, tend to be middle-class professionals, which accounts for their more successful academic profile than that of Puerto Rican, Dominican, and Mexican, and Central Americans (Hurtado et al., 2010).

By focusing on a lack of information and not on deficient educational values, the social capital approach creates opportunities for intervention. For example, this approach is consistent with school and community efforts to empower parents to get involved in their children's schooling and a greater attention to the role of academic tracking in constraining students' college eligibility and consequently, their opportunities to attain the American Dream (McDonough, 1997; Oakes, 1986). This asset-mapping and building approach is also consistent with efforts to identify family and community resources that can help Latino adolescents' succeed, such as siblings (Tierney & Auerbach, 2004), community organizations (Cooper, in preparation), and peers (Stanton-Salazar, 2001).

Stanton-Salazar (2001) has underscored the importance of developing peer networks that support Latino adolescents' schooling. He argues that given parents' limited schooling and challenging work schedules, it may be unrealistic to expect them to be the primary agents of their children's academic socialization and future ideation. He suggests that peers might be in a better position to serve this function and proposed interventions that create peer networks that support Latino adolescents' academic performance and career ideation. Taken together, interventions based on the Social Capital perspective emphasize the importance of creating connections or networks for Latino families that can help support their educational and occupational goals and increase the chances that their children will graduate from high school and attend college. Social Capital perspectives underlie successful intervention programs such as *Head Start*, *Gear Up*, *Puente*, *Upward Bound*, and *MESA*. These interventions vary in the degree of required parent participation, with *Head Start* and *MESA* having the highest and *Upward Bound* the lowest levels of family involvement. Gándara and Contreras (2009) suggest that these differences in parent involvement play a role in the finding that Latino students who participate in programs with formal family involvement components are more likely to finish high school and enroll in college than students that do not involve families. They suggest that these differences in family involvement also forecast the counselor's engagement with program participants. For example, while Puente counselors see their jobs as mentors and fictive kin to their students, Upward Bound counselors typically have less involvement more distant relationships with their participants. These differences are associated with the programs' success in increasing high school graduation and college enrollment amongst their participants; Latinos who participate in Puente are more likely to finish high school and enroll in college than Latinos who participate in Upward Bound (Gándara & Contreras, 2009).

Thus far, I have discussed models that focus on the current ecological conditions of Latino students' schooling or the assets that Latino families bring (or do not bring) to their children's education. The *Acculturation Perspective* emphasizes Latino families and adolescents' negotiation of Latino and U.S. cultures and the stresses that can accompany this negotiation. For example, by virtue of attending school, an institution that emphasizes mainstream values, and coming into contact with U.S.-born peers, Latino adolescents have more contact with U.S. values and practices than their parents, who tend to be employed in jobs with other immigrants or to inhabit ethnic enclaves that preserve their cultural values, goals, and practices. This difference in opportunities for coming into contact with mainstream U.S. values and practices results in children and adolescents acculturating faster to their new country than their parents, thus increasing parent-adolescent conflicts as adolescents try to pressure their parents give them the independence and time with peers that their more acculturated Latino peers or their non-Latino peers enjoy (Phinney, Ong, & Madden, 2000; Umaña-Taylor & Alfaro, 2009).

The Acculturation Perspective also emphasizes adolescents' negotiation of their ethnic identities. For example, in her study of immigrant and non-immigrant Mexican-descent adolescents, Matute-Bianchi (1991) showed that immigrant students' greater identification with the Mexican culture played a protective function against prejudice and discrimination and was associated positively with academic performance and school engagement. Subsequent studies have focused on how Latinos integrate their home (Latino) and host (U.S.) cultures. Some of this work has replicated Matute-Bianchi's finding that Latinos who value their cultural background and have high levels of ethnic identity have higher self-esteem than Latinos who assimilate into U.S. culture (Phinney & Chavira, 1992). Although the evidence is mixed, some studies have shown that Latino students with high ethnic identities or Latinos who form bicultural identities that integrate their Latino and American cultures perform better in school than Latinos who assimilate to the U.S. cultural practices and values (Cooper et al., 2002; Rumbaut, 1995, but see Quintana & Scull, 2009).

Fuligni and Pereira (2009) propose that although the value that immigrant families place on family interdependence and family obligations can help them persist in school, it can also create stress for first- and second-born adolescents who bear the burden of blazing the academic trail for their younger siblings. In support of this proposal, Fuligni, Yip, and Tseng (2002) found that Chinese adolescents that perceived high levels of family academic pressure had poorer mental health than Chinese adolescents who experienced moderate or low levels of family academic pressure. Although to our knowledge, comparable large-scale quantitative studies are not available for Latinos, smaller scale studies and analyses of qualitative interviews provide support for Fuligni and Pereira's finding. These studies show, however, that some Latino first- and second-born adolescents perceive their families' educational pressures as a good burden that helps them weather their negative school experiences and thus, do not show the mental health challenges that afflict Latino adolescents who find their parents' high expectations burdensome (Azmitia, Syed, & Radmacher, 2008; Cooper et al., 2002). Cooper et al. (2002) suggest that this positive spin on family pressures and obligations contributes to Latino adolescents' goal of using their educational accomplishments in the service not only of their families, but to also help their communities.

As evident from the work on the role of family obligations and immigrant optimism on first generation Latinos' academic performance and trajectories, relative to other theoretical perspectives on Latino adolescents' schooling, acculturation models have paid more attention to generational variations in Latino adolescents' academic performance and goals. Despite widespread belief that immigrants' optimism results in first generation adolescents outperforming second and third generation Latino adolescents, as a group second and third generation adolescents are performing better in school and are more likely to go to college and enter the middle class (Gándara & Contreras, 2009) than first generation Latinos. This misperception of second- and third-generation Latino adolescents' disengagement and opposition to school stems, at least in part, from the problem-focused approach to Latino adolescents' schooling that emphasizes resistance, disengagement, and rejection of mainstream educational values that adolescents perceive as racist and oppressive (Ogbu, 2008).

Contrary to Ogbu's (2008) and Rumbaut's (1995) findings of a dimming of Latino adolescents academic performance and aspirations from the first to the second and third generations, large-scale studies of Latino adolescents' educational and career goals have revealed that the majority of second and third Latino generation students share their parents' goals that they graduate from high school and attend college. It is the case, however, that as they progress through middle school and high school and are tracked into non-college preparatory classes, some Latino adolescents and their parents downgrade their educational aspirations and abandon their dream of going to college (Gándara & Contreras, 2009; Villalpando, 2010). As Mooney and Rivas-Drake (2008) suggest, more research on middle and upper class Latino adolescents is needed to present a clearer picture of the factors that promote upward mobility in Latinos.

CONCLUSIONS AND FUTURE DIRECTIONS

This chapter provided a brief overview of the role of family and friends in Mexican-heritage adolescents' educational pathways. I focused on the transitions to middle school and college because these are key junctions in students' prospects for upward mobility. Although some of the factors that contribute to Mexican-heritage adolescents may be unique to this group, such as their history of colonization, the parents' low levels of education, and their choice of colleges based on their families' needs, many of the positive and negative influences on Latino adolescents' schooling are likely shared with other groups who value interdependence and experience high rates of poverty.

Investigating the family practices and educational trajectories of middle class Latinos is an important direction for future research in policy. To date, the focus on recent immigrants and especially, immigrants living in poverty and attending low-quality schools has deflected attention away from the growing Latino middle class, many who have been in the United States for several generations. Much is to be learned about their pathways to success.

Because most of the work on family involvement in their children's schooling has focused on early childhood and elementary school, we also lack information how families of middle school, high school, and college students participate in their children's schooling. Certainly considerable research has shown that these Latino parents have high academic aspirations for their children. However, beyond knowing that their children report that they help with homework, monitor their behavior, and discuss their problems and their future, little is known about the content of their help, monitoring, and conversations. Observations of family interactions and in-depth interviews of Latino parents and adolescents will begin to fill this gap in the literature. More information is also needed about teachers' perceptions of Latino parents and successful strategies for involving them in their children's education. How do teachers and schools form successful partnerships with parents with limited English proficiency and academic skills and whose jobs and other responsibilities make it difficult for them to attend school functions or meetings? The current economic crisis has resulted in many successful programs being cut or downsized, yet, never has providing academic support for Latino families and students been so critical. Research that examines successful family and friend involvement programs in middle school and provides more information about the role of families and friends in Latino college students' adjustment and persistence will be invaluable for creating the infrastructure that the fastest growing ethnic minority group in the United States needs to succeed.

NOTE

1. First generation Latino children and adolescents are more likely than second and third generation Latino children and adolescents to grow up in two-parent families with access to other relatives or fictive kin, such as compadres and comadres (Fry & Passel, 2009; Grau et al., 2009).

REFERENCES

Azmitia, M., & Brown, J. (2002). Latino immigrant parents' beliefs about the "path of life" of their adolescent children. In J. M. Contreras, K. A. Kerns, &

A. M. Neal-Barnett (Eds.). *Latino children and families in the United States: Current research and future directions* (pp. 77–105), Westport, CT: Praeger.

Azmitia, M. Cooper, C. R, & Brown, J. R. (2009). Support and guidance from families, friends, and teachers in Latino early adolescents' math pathways. *Journal of Early Adolescence 29*, 142–169

Azmitia, M., Cooper, C. R., García, E. E., & Dunbar, N.D. (1996). The ecology of family guidance in low-income Mexican-American and European-American families. *Social Development 5*, 1–23.

Azmitia, M., Ittel, A., & Brenk, C. (2006) Latino heritage adolescents' friendships. In X. Chen, D. C. French, & B. H. Schneider (Eds.), *Peer relationships in cultural context* (pp. 426–451). NY: Cambridge.

Burciaga, R. Huber, L. P., & Solorzano, D. (2010). Going back to the headwaters: Examining Latina/o educational attainment and achievement through a framework of hope. In E. G. Murillo, Jr., S. A. Villenas, R. T. Galván, J. S. Muñoz, C. Martínez, & M. Machado-Casas (Eds.), *Handbook of Latinos and education. Theory, research, and practice* (pp. 422–437). NY: Routledge.

Catsambis, S. (2001). Expanding knowledge of parental involvement in children's secondary education: connections with high school seniors' academic success. *Social Psychology of Education 5*, 149–177.

Coleman, J. S. (1988). Social capital in the creation of human capital. American *Journal of Sociology Supplement 95*, 95–120.

Cooper, C. R., Cooper, R. G., Azmitia, M., Chavira, G., & Gullat, Y. (2002). Bridging multiple worlds: How African American and Latino youth in academic outreach programs navigate math pathways to college. *Applied Developmental Science 6*, 73–87.

Cooper, C. R., Jackson, J. F., Azmitia, M., & Lopez, E. M. (1998) Multiple selves, multiple worlds: three useful strategies for research with ethnic minority youth on identity, relationships, and opportunity structures. In V. C. McLoyd & L. Steinberg (Eds.), Studying minority adolescents: Conceptual, methodological, and theoretical issues (pp. 111–125). Mahwah, NJ: Erlbaum.

Delgado-Gaitán, C. (1994). Consejos: The power of cultural narratives. *Anthropology and Education Quarterly 25*, 298–316.

Eccles, J. S., & Midgley, C. (1989). Stage/environment fit: Developmentally appropriate classrooms for early adolescents. In R. E. Ames & C. Ames (Eds.), *Research on motivation in education, Vol. 2*, NY: Academic Press.

Eckert, P. (1989). *Jocks and burnouts. Social categories and identity in high school*. NY: Teachers College Press.

Ethier, K., & Deaux, K. (1990). Hispanics in ivy: Assessing identity and perceived threat. *Sex Roles 22*, 427–440.

Fry, R. (2002). *Latinos in higher education: Many enroll, too few graduate*. Washington, D. C.: Pew Hispanic Center.

Fuligni, A. J., & Perreira, K. M. (2009). Immigration and adaptation. In F. A. Villarruel, G. Carlo, J. M. Grau, M. Azmitia, N. J. Cabrera, T. J. Chahin (Eds.), *Handbook of U.S. Latino psychology* (pp. 99–114). Thousand Oaks, CA: Sage.

Fuligni, A., Yip, T., & Tseng, V. (2002). The impact of family obligation on the daily activities and psychological well-being of Chinese American adolescents. *Child Development 73*, 302–314.

Gallimore, R., & Goldenberg, C. (1993). Activity settings of early literacy: Home and school factors in children's emerging. In E Forman, N. Minick, & C. A. Stone (Eds.), *Contexts for learning: Sociocultural dynamics in children's development* (pp. 315–335). Oxford, UK: Oxford University Press.

Gándara, P. (2008). The crisis in the education of Latino students. *National Education Association, Issues in Education*, Retrieved October 21, 2009 from www. Nea.org/achievement/gandara/08.

Gándara, P. (1995). *Over the ivy walls: The educational mobility of low-income Chicanos*. Albany: State University of New York Press.

Gándara, P., & Contreras, F. (2009). *The Latino education crisis. The consequences of failed policies*. Cambridge, MA: Harvard.

García, E.E., & Scribner, K. (2009). Latino pre-K–3 education: A critical foundation. In F. A. Villarruel, G. Carlo, J. M. Grau, M. Azmitia, N. J. Cabrera, T. J. Chahin (Eds.), *Handbook of U.S. Latino psychology* (pp. 267–290). Thousand Oaks, CA: Sage.

Gerdes, H., & Mallinckrodt, B. (1994). Emotional, social, and academic adjustment of college students: A longitudinal study of retention. *Journal of Counseling & Development 72*(3), 281–288.

Gills, J., Schmukler, K., Azmitia, M., & Crosby, F. (2006). Affirmative action and ethnic minority students: Enlarging pipelines to support success. In C. Wainryb, J. Smetana, & E. Turiel, (Eds.), *Social development, social inequalities, and social justice.* (pp. 81–108). Mahwah, NY: Lawrence Erlbaum Associates.

Gonzales, N. A., Fabrett, F. C., & Knight, G. P. (2009). Acculturation, enculturation, and the psychosocial adaptation of Latino youth. In F. A. Villarruel, G. Carlo, J. M. Grau, M. Azmitia, N. J. Cabrera, T. J. Chahin (Eds.), *Handbook of U.S. Latino psychology* (pp. 115–134). Thousand Oaks, CA: Sage.

Grau, J. M., Azmitia, M., & Quattelbaum, J. (2009). Latino families: parenting, relational, and developmental processes. In F. A. Villarruel, G. Carlo, J. M. Grau, M. Azmitia, N. J. Cabrera, T. J. Chahin (Eds.), *Handbook of U.S. Latino psychology* (pp. 153–179). Thousand Oaks, CA: Sage.

Greenfield, P. M., Quiroz, B., & Raeff, C. (2000). Cross-cultural conflict and harmony in the social construction of the child. In S. Harness, C. Raeff, & C. M. Super (Eds.), *Variability in the social construction of the child. New directions for child and adolescent development*, (pp. 93–108). San Francisco, CA: Jossey-Bass.

Grotevant, H. D., & Cooper, C. R. (1988). Individuality and connectedness in adolescent development: Review and prospects for research on identity, relationships, and context. In E. Aspaas Skoe & A. L. von der Lippe (Eds). *Personality development in adolescence: A cross national and life span perspective* (pp. 3–37). London: Routledge.

Haney, C., & Zimbardo, P. (1998). The past and future of U.S. prison policy. Twenty-five years after the Stanford Prison experiment. *American Psychologist 53*, 709–727.

Hoffman, M., Richmond, J., Morrow, J., Salomone, K. (2002–2003). Investigating sense of belonging in first year college students. *Journal of College Student Retention, Theory, and Practice 4*, 227–256.

Hurtado, A., Cervantez, K., & Eccleston, M. (2010). Infinite possibilities, many obstacles: Language, culture, identity, and Latino/a educational achievement. In E. G. Murillo, Jr., S. A. Villenas, R. T. Galván, J. S. Muñoz, C. Martínez, & M. Machado-Casas (Eds.), *Handbook of Latinos and education. Theory, research, and practice* (pp. 284–300). NY: Routledge.

Kao, G., & Tienda, M. (1995). Optimism and achievement: The educational performance of immigrant youth. *Social Science Quarterly 76*, 1–19.

Kuperminc, G. P., Henrich, C., Meyers, J. House, D., & Sayfi, S. (2007, June). The role of perceived discrimination in the academic adjustment of Latino youth from immigrant families. In N. Wilkins (Chair). *Academic attainment among Latino youth: A social justice issue.* Symposium presented at the biennial meeting of the Society for Community Research and Action, Pasadena, CA.

Kuperminc, G. P., Leadbeater, B. J., Emmons, C., & Blatt, S. J. (1997). Perceived school climate and difficulties in the social adjustment of middle school students. *Applied Developmental Science 1*(2), 76–88.

Kuperminc, G. P., Wilkins, N. J., Roche, C., & Alvarez-Jimenez, A. (2009). Risk, resilience, and positive development among Latino youth. In F. A. Villarruel, G. Carlo, J. M. Grau, M. Azmitia, N. J. Cabrera, T. J. Chahin (Eds.), *Handbook of U.S. Latino psychology* (pp. 213–234). Thousand Oaks, CA: Sage.

Laosa, L. (1982). School, occupation, culture, and family: The impact of parental schooling on the parent-child relationship. *Journal of Educational Psychology 74*, 791–827.

Lareau, A. (2000). *Home advantage: Social class and parental intervention in elementary education.* Latham, MD: Rowland and Littlefield Publishers.

Lopez, G. R. (2001). The value of hard work: Lessons on parent involvement from an (im)migrant household. *Harvard Educational Review 7*, 416–437.

McDonough, P. (1997). *Choosing colleges: How social class and schools structure opportunity.* Albany: NY: State University of New York Press.

Mooney, M., & Rivas-Drake, D. (2008, March 28). Colleges need to recognized and serve the 3 kinds of Latino students. *Chronicle of Higher Education,* p. A37

Oakes, J. (1996). *Keeping track: How schools structure inequality.* New Haven: Yale University Press.

Ogbu, J. (2008). *Minority status, oppositional culture, and schooling.* NY: Routledge.

Orbe, M. P. (2004). Negotiating multiple identities within multiple frames: An analysis of first-generation college students. *Communication Education 53*, 131–149

Ostrove, J. M. (2003). Belonging and wanting: Meanings of social class background for women's constructions of their college experiences. *Journal of Social Issues 59*, 771–784.

Parke, R. D., & Buriel, R. (1998). Socialization in the family: Ethnic and ecological perspectives. In N. Eisenberg (Ed). *Handbook of child psychology (Vol. 3): Social, emotional, and personality development*. (pp. 463–552). NY: Wiley.

Pérez, P. A., & McDonough, P. M. (2008). Understanding Latina and Latino college choice: A social capital and chain migration analysis. *Journal of Hispanic Higher Education 7*, 249–265.

Phinney J., S., & Chavira, V. (1992). Ethnic identity and self-esteem: An exploratory longitudinal study. *Journal of Adolescence 15*, 271–281

Phinney, J. S., Ong, A., & Madden, T., (2000). Cultural values and intergenerational value discrepancies in immigrant and non-immigrant families. *Child Development 71*, 528–539.

Quintana, S. M., & Scull, N. C. (2009). Latino ethnic identity. In F. A. Villarruel, G. Carlo, J. M. Grau, M. Azmitia, N. J. Cabrera, T. J. Chahin (Eds.), *Handbook of U.S. Latino psychology* (pp. 81–98). Thousand Oaks, CA: Sage.

Reese, L., Balzano R., Gallimore, R, & Goldenberg, C. (1995). The concept of educación: Latino family values and American schooling. *International Journal of Educational Research 23*, 57–81.

Rogoff, B. (2003). *The cultural nature of human development*. New York: Oxford University Press.

Rumbaut, R. (1995). The new Californians: Comparative research findings on the educational progress of immigrant children. In R. Rumbaut and W. Cornelius (Eds.), *California's immigrant children: Theory, research, and implications for educational policy*. La Jolla: Center for U.S.-Mexican Studies, University of California, San Diego.

Seidman, E., Allen, L., Aber, J. L., Mitchell, C., Feinman, J.(1994). The impact of school transitions in early adolescence on the self system and the perceived context of poor urban youth. *Child Development 65*, 507–522.

Sidanus, J., Van Laar, C., Levin, S., & Sinclair, S. (2004). Ethnic enclaves and the dynamics of social identity on the college campus: The good, the bad, and the ugly. *Journal of Personality and Social Psychology 87*, 96–110.

Shaver, P., Furman W., & Burhmester, D. (1985). Transition to college: Network changes, social skills, and loneliness. In S. Duck and D. Perlman (Eds.), *Understanding personal relationships: An interdisciplinary approach*. (pp. 193–219). Thousand Oaks, CA: Sage Publications.

Stanton-Salazar, R. D. *Manufacturing hope and despair: The kin and school support networks of U.S.-Mexican youth*. NY: Teachers College Press.

Suárez-Orozco, C., Suárez-Orozco, M. (2001). *Children in immigration*. Cambridge, MA: Harvard.

Suárez-Orozco, C., Suárez-Orozco, M., & Todorova, I. (2008). *Learning a new land*. Cambridge, MA: Harvard.

Terenzini, P T., & Reason, R. D. (2005, November). *Parsing the first year of college: A conceptual framework for studying college impacts.* Paper presented at the Association of Higher Education, Philadelphia, PA.

Tharp, R. G., & Galliomore, R. (1988). *Rousing minds to life. Teaching, learning, and schooling in social context.* NY: Cambridge.

Tierney, W., & Auerback, S. (2006) Toward developing an untapped resource: The role of families in college preparation. In W. Tierney, Z. B. Corwin, & J.E. Colyar (Eds.), *Preparing for college: Nine elements of effective outreach* (pp. 29–48). Albany, NY: State University of New York Press.

Tinto, V. (1993). *Leaving college: Rethinking the causes and cures of student attrition* (2nd ed.). Chicago: University of Chicago Press.

Umaña-Taylor, A., & Alfaro, E. (2009). Acculturation stress and adaptation. In F. A. Villarruel, G. Carlo, J. M. Grau, M. Azmitia, N. J. Cabrera, T. J. Chahin (Eds.), *Handbook of U.S. Latino psychology* (pp. 135–152). Thousand Oaks, CA: Sage.

U.S. Census Bureau, Population Division Branch. (2000). *Population projections.* Data set available on-line: http://www.census.gov.

Valdés, G. (1996). *Con respeto: Bridging the distances between culturally diverse families and schools: An ethnographic portrait.* New York: Teachers College Press.

Valenzuela, A., & Dornbusch, S. M. (1994). Familism and social capital in the academic achievement of Mexican origin and Anglo adolescents. *Social Science Quarterly 75*, 18–36.

Vigil, J. D. (2002). *Rainbow of gangs. Street culture in the mega city.* University of Texas Press.

Villapando, O. (2010). Latinas/os in higher education: Eligibility, enrollment, and educational attainment. In E. G. Murillo, Jr., S. A. Villenas, R. T. Galván, J. S. Muñoz, C. Martínez, & M. Machado-Casas (Eds.), *Handbook of Latinos and education. Theory, research, and practice* (pp. 232–249). NY: Routledge.

Willis, P. (1992). *Learning to labour.* NY: Columbia University Press.

Chapter 10

SOCIAL-EMOTIONAL CHALLENGES FOR NEWCOMER LATINO YOUTH IN EDUCATIONAL SETTINGS

Francisco X. Gaytán and Carola Suárez-Orozco

Latino students now constitute the fastest growing group of students in our elementary and secondary schools. Nationally, they represent more than one-fifth of all public school students enrolled in kindergarten through twelfth grade (Planty, Hussar, Snyder, Provasnik, Kena, Dinkes, Ramani, & Kemp, 2008). In some states, such as California, Latinos constitute nearly half the student population (Pérez-Huber, Huidor, Malagón, Sánchez, & Solórzano, 2006). Findings from a number of recent studies suggest that although some Latinos are successfully navigating the American educational system, a majority are struggling academically and leaving schools without acquiring the skills necessary to compete in the knowledge-intensive U.S. economy (Gándara & Contreras 2009). Latinos have the highest high school dropout rates and the lowest college attendance rates among all racial and ethnic groups (Pérez-Huber et al., 2006), foreshadowing less-than-optimal outcomes in today's economy. Many face lives at or below the poverty line laboring at the lowest levels of the service-sector economy.

In considering Latinos, we must acknowledge their extraordinary diversity, and resist the inclination to categorize their complex experiences using simplified generalizations. Some Latinos can trace their ancestors to individuals who were settled on what is now U.S. territory, long before the current borders were set, through conquest and land purchases. More recently, large numbers of Latinos have been immigrating from dozens of countries that fuel this burgeoning population. Today, an estimated two-thirds of Latinos are either immigrants or the children of immigrants (Suárez-Orozco & Gaytán 2009).

The sending countries, the areas of settlement, the historical timing of the migration, and the economic circumstances vary considerably for Latinos from different backgrounds. Although educational attainment and achievement varies among these Latino populations, the limited data available often lead researchers to treat Latinos as if they were a homogeneous group and report general findings for an aggregated Latino population. However, even when Latino immigrants and native-born Latinos are considered separately, findings indicate that both groups are struggling in the educational system.

This chapter considers the social-emotional challenges that exist in the lives of Latino immigrant youth in relation to their experience in school. In some cases these challenges may contribute to their poor educational performance, and in others they are the result of academic pressures and the quality of support that the educational system provides; this is indicative of the complex nature of the lives of immigrant and Latino youth and the diversity within these groups as well as the multifaceted nature of educational institutions. In some cases, the relationship between social-emotional well-being and academics is unidirectional, but more often it represents a dynamic association among many factors that must be considered carefully depending upon the particular context of the individual or group in question. In the initial section, we report on the overall trends of the U.S. Latino population as a whole, including both the U.S.- and foreign-born. We then turn to exploring the dynamics that shape opportunity including family-of-origin resources, socioeconomic status, neighborhood characteristics such as poverty and school segregation, and the schools attended by the majority of Latino students. Because human experience is not solely the product of structural forces, we also consider how individual student academic engagement, language skills, and networks of relations mediate academic outcomes. In addition, we explore the social-emotional challenges that may result from experiences in schools. Given the large proportion of *immigrant-origin* Latinos currently in the United States, we will particularly consider the challenges of the immigrant experience in this paper. Throughout the chapter, we intersperse our discussion with findings from the Longitudinal Immigrant Student Adaptation (LISA) study, a mixed-methods, five-year longitudinal study using data collected from student, parent, and teacher perspectives to document the factors associated with the cultural and academic adaptation of immigrant youth (Suárez-Orozco et al., 2008). A sample of 309 newcomer immigrant adolescents arriving within five years of the start of the study (from Central American, Chinese, Dominican, Haitian, and Mexican backgrounds and roughly evenly split between males and females) was followed over the course of the study.[1] We conclude with a discussion of research and policy implications for this significant and growing population.

STRUCTURING SOCIAL-EMOTIONAL AND ACADEMIC SUPPORT

Whether or not Latino students will be successful in school is determined by a convergence of supports (or absence thereof) that also affect their social-emotional well-being. We use a social and cultural capital framework to describe the resources that Latino immigrant families possess upon their arrival in a new land (Perreira, Harris, & Lee, 2006). Social capital has been described as the resources that one is connected to through social connections to individuals and institutions (Coleman, 1988; Putnam, 2000). We compliment this perspective with notions of cultural capital and human capital (termed "family capital" and "student resources" here). Cultural capital considers cultural knowledge and the degree to which an individual or group has access to the culturally bound opportunity structure (Bourdieu & Passeron, 1977) and human capital refers to demographic and socio-economic resources. The specific types of capital we consider include: *family capital* (including poverty, parental education, and whether they are authorized migrants); the kinds of *schools* that Latino immigrant students encounter (school segregation, the language instruction they are provided, how well prepared their teachers are to provide services to the them); *student resources* (their social-emotional challenges, their facility in acquiring a second language, and academic engagement); and their *networks of relational supports*. This complex constellation of variables underscores the dynamic relationship between social-emotional well-being and academic integration and adaptation.

Below, we review key factors that are shared by many Latino origin youth and distinguish those factors that are particular salient for the social-emotional well-being of immigrant origin.

Family-of-Origin Capital

Poverty

Poverty has long been recognized as a significant risk factor for social-emotional problems and poor educational outcomes among all youth (Luthar, 1999; Weissbourd, 1996). Children raised in socioeconomic deprivation are vulnerable to an array of distresses including difficulties concentrating and sleeping, anxiety and depression, and a heightened propensity for delinquency and violence. Those living in poverty often experience the stress of major life events as well as the stress of daily hassles that significantly impede academic performance. Poverty frequently coexists with other factors that augment risks, such as single parenthood, residence in neighborhoods plagued with violence, gang activity, and drug trade, as well as school environments that are segregated, overcrowded, and poorly funded. High poverty is also associated with high rates of housing mobility and concurrent school transitions, which are highly disruptive to educational performance (Gándara & Contreras, 2009).

Although some Latino students come from privileged backgrounds, large numbers suffer today from the challenges associated with poverty. In 1999, 22.8 percent of Latinos were living in poverty, compared with 7.7 percent of Whites (Ramirez & Therrien, 2000). In 2006, the poverty rate for Latino students (28 %) was double of that of White children (16%) (Fry & Gonzales, 2008). For immigrant Latino families, poverty reaches much higher rates; 35 percent of foreign-born Latino students live in poverty, compared with 27 percent of their native-born counterparts. Immigrant children are more than four times as likely as native-born children to live in crowded housing conditions, and 37 percent of Latino immigrant families report difficulties affording food (Capps, 2001). A large proportion of these children are raised in families where parents are working, but many are employed in very low paying professions with erratic working conditions. Further, while the majority of the children are citizens themselves, approximately a quarter have parents who are unauthorized[2] migrants who thus do not access social services that could serve to mitigate the harshest conditions of their poverty. The large proportion of Latino and immigrant youth that are living in poverty thus puts this group at a greater risk for the social-emotional stresses summarized above for a general child and youth population (Luthar, 1999; Weissbourd, 1996). While this deduction makes intuitive sense, there is little empirical work that directly examines the interplay between poverty, education, and social-emotional well-being poverty of youth in Latino families in particular. Studies that examine the process of how these three variables relate to each other among Latino youth as they develop over time would fill an important gap in the literature.

Unauthorized Status

An estimated 11.1 million immigrants live in the United States without authorization; of that population, 78 percent are from Mexico and Latin

America (Bean & Lowell, 2007). Among the undocumented population in the United States, 1.8 million are children or adolescents (Passel, 2006). These undocumented youth often arrive after multiple family separations and traumatic border crossings (Suárez-Orozco, Todorova, & Louie, 2002). In addition, an estimated 3.1 million U.S.-citizen children live in households headed by at least one undocumented immigrant (Passel, 2006).

Unauthorized children and youth in households with unauthorized members often experience fear and anxiety around being separated from family members if they or someone they love are apprehended or deported (Capps, Castañeda, Chaudry, & Santos, 2007); such psychological and emotional duress can take a heavy toll on the academic experiences of children growing up these homes on top of the social-emotional stresses discussed throughout this paper that exist for U.S.-born Latino youth and Latino immigrant youth with legal status. Further, while unauthorized youth have equal access to K–12 education under federal policies, they do not have equal access to health, social services, or jobs (Gándara & Contreras, 2009). In addition, undocumented students with dreams of graduating from high school and going on to college will find that their legal status stands in the way of their access to postsecondary educational opportunities (Gándara & Contreras, 2009; Suárez-Orozco, Suárez-Orozco, & Todorova, 2008). Thus, immigrant Latinos who are unauthorized or who come from unauthorized families suffer from a particular burden of unequal access.

Family Educational Background

The educational background of parents matters. Highly literate parents are better equipped to guide their children in studying, accessing, and making meaning of educational information. Children with more educated parents are exposed to more academically oriented vocabulary and interactions at home, and they tend to be read to more often from books that are valued at school (Goldenberg, Rueda, & August, 2006). More educated parents understand the value of and have the resources to provide additional books, a home computer, and Internet access. They are also more likely to seek information about how to navigate the educational system in the new land.

Unfortunately, however, many Latino parents have limited schooling. The number of Latino students who have no parent with a high school diploma will grow from 37 percent to 59 percent by 2015 (National Task Force on Minority High Achievement, 1999). For those Latino parents who do have higher levels of education, concern for their children may be unwarranted in this regard, but the overrepresentation of Latino parents among those with lower levels of education is a reason for concern. Such disadvantaged backgrounds have implications for the smoothness of the educational transition into a new context while simultaneously affecting social-emotional adjustment. Not surprisingly, youth arriving from families with lower levels of education tend to struggle academically, while those who come from more literate families and with strong skills often flourish (Kasinitz, Mollenkopf, Waters, & Holdaway, 2008). Moreover, low parental education is compounded by parents' limited English language skills, which may index the support children receive for learning English at home (Portes & Hao, 1998).

Apart from level of education, a limited understanding of the implicit cultural rules and expectations that guide parental and student engagement and behavior may add another layer of social-emotional stress that affects the academic performance of Latino youth. Immigrant Latino parents often do not possess the kind of cultural capital that serves middle-class mainstream students well (Perreira et al., 2006); not knowing the dominant cultural values of the new society limits immigrant Latino parents' ability to provide an upward academic path for their children. Parental involvement may not be a cultural practice in their countries of origin nor a luxury that their financial situation in this country typically allows. Many Latino immigrants come from cultural traditions where parents are expected to respect teachers' recommendations rather than to advocate for their children (Delgado-Gaitan, 2004). Not speaking English and having limited education may make them feel inadequate. Lack of documentation may make them worry about exposure to immigration raids (Capps et al., 2007). Low-wage, low-skill jobs with off-hour shifts typically do not provide much flexibility to attend parent-teacher conferences and childcare. The impediments to coming to school are multiple and are frequently interpreted by teachers and principals as "not valuing" their children's education. Ironically, however, Latino immigrant parents often frame the family narrative of migration around providing better educational opportunities to their children (Suárez-Orozco et al., 2008). While they may care deeply about their children's education and may often urge their students to work hard in school so they do not have to do hard physical labor as their parents do, Latino immigrant parents frequently do not have first-hand experience in the American school system or in their own native system (Lopez, 2001). Because Latino immigrants are typically a self-selecting group, their barriers to educational success likely have a social-economic component that would challenge them in either the United States or their home country; however, these class issues are most likely compounded by social-emotional stress associated with not having the requisite cultural resources to successfully manage within U.S. schools. They also may have restricted access to social networks that could provide the educational resources to help them navigate the complicated college pathway system in the United States (Auerbach, 2004). Thus, they may have limited capacities to help their children successfully "play the educational game" in their new land. Capturing gaps in understanding of subtle cultural nuances is a real challenge for researchers, but it clearly makes sense that there is a considerable amount of social and emotional stress associated with engaging an unfamiliar cultural context and that this could likely have an impact on educational outcomes for Latinos. Finding ways to show this process of cultural negotiation and its relationship to social-emotional health in school contexts would therefore be an important area for future investigation.

School Resources

School Contexts

Segregation in neighborhoods and schools has negative consequences on academic success for minority students (Massey & Denton, 1993; Orfield & Lee, 2006; Orfield & Yun, 1999). In all but a few "exceptional cases under extraordinary circumstances, schools that are separate are still unquestionably unequal" (Orfield & Lee, 2006, p. 4). Nationally, Latinos tend to settle in highly segregated and deeply impoverished urban settings and attend the most segregated schools of any group in the United States today. In 1996, only 25 percent of Latino students attended majority-White schools. The degree of segregation results in a series of consequences; in general, Latinos who settle in predominantly minority neighborhoods have virtually no direct, systematic, or intimate contact with middle-class White Americans. This in turn affects the quality of schools they attend and the networks that are useful to access desirable colleges and jobs (Orfield, 1995; Portes, 1996).

Segregation for Latino-origin immigrant students often involves isolation at the levels of race and ethnicity, poverty, and language—aptly named "triple segregation" (Orfield & Lee, 2006). These three dimensions of segregation have been associated with reduced school resources with various negative educational outcomes, including low expectations, difficulties learning English, lower achievement, greater school violence, and higher dropout rates (Gándara & Contreras, 2009). Such school contexts typically undermine students' capacity to concentrate, their sense of security, and hence their ability to learn.

In terms of triple segregation, the Latino groups in the study (Central American, Dominican, and Mexican) were the most likely to attend highly segregated schools. Numerous negative qualities were associated with this level of segregation. For example, when asked to relate their perceptions of school in the new country, many students spoke of crime, violence, gang activity, weapons, drug dealing, and racial conflicts. Students who attended highly segregated schools with high levels of perceived school violence were more likely to demonstrate patterns of academic disengagement and grade decline over time. Indicators of school inequality, including percentages of inexperienced teachers as well as out-of-subject certification rate; greater-than-average school size; dropout rate; daily attendance; higher-than-average suspension and expulsion rates; percentage of students performing below proficiency on the state-administered English language arts and math standardized tests; and a significant achievement gap on the standardized exam between one or more ethnic groups that attend the school were linked to these highly segregated schools and, consequently, lower student performance.

Indicators of school segregation and violence were consistent with poor performance school wide on standardized tests across the Latino groups. The LISA study found that only 20 percent of Dominican and Central American students, and 16 percent of Mexican students, in low-quality schools reached proficiency level or higher on the federally mandated, statewide English language arts exam. There was also a significant relationship between segregated schools and individual achievement outcomes including both grades and students' standardized achievement test scores (Suárez-Orozco et al., 2008).

Segregation places students at a significant disadvantage as they strive to learn a new language, master the necessary skills to pass high-stakes tests, accrue graduation credits, get into college, and attain the skills needed to compete in workplaces increasingly shaped by the demands of the new global economy. Unfortunately, all too many schools that serve the children of immigrants, like schools that serve other disadvantaged students, are those that seem designated to teach "other people's children" (Delpit, 1995). Such segregated, suboptimal schools offer the very least to those who need the very most, structuring and reinforcing inequality (Oakes, 1985).

Individual Child Resources and Challenges

The Migration Process

For many Latino students, their educational journey begins with their migration to the United States. Migration is a transformative process with profound implications for the family as well as the potential for lasting impact on social-emotional development (García-Coll & Magnuson, 1997; Suárez-Orozco & Suárez-Orozco, 2001). By any measure, immigration is one of the most stressful events a family can undergo (Falicov, 1998; Suárez-Orozco & Suárez-Orozco, 2001); it removes family members from predictable contexts—community ties, jobs, and customs— and strips them of significant social ties—extended family members, best friends, and neighbors. New arrivals who experienced trauma (either before migrating or as secondary to the "crossing") may remain preoccupied with the violence and may also feel guilty about having escaped when loved ones remained behind (Lustig, Kia-Keating, Knight, Geltman, Ellis, Kinzie, Keane, & Saxe, 2004). Undocumented new arrivals face the growing realities of workplace raids that can lead to traumatic and sudden separations (Capps et al., 2007).

In the LISA study, one of the most surprising findings regarding the migration process was the frequency of students being separated from parents. Eighty-nine percent of the Domincans (N = 75), 95 percent of the Central Americans (N = 77), and 85 percent of the Mexicans (N = 84) in the sample reported being separated from one or both parents for periods from 6 months to over 10 years. These separations had a significant effect on mental health; children who underwent separations reported significantly more depressive symptoms than those that did not. Araceli[3], a fourteen-year-old Dominican female LISA study participant, describes this sadness:

> The day I left my mother I felt like my heart was staying behind. Because she was the only person I trusted – she was my life. I felt as if a light had extinguished. I still have not been able to get used to living without her.

Youth who were left with a loving caretaker for an extended period of time, often became attached to that caretaker. Although children would be happy about the prospect of "regaining" parents when called on to rejoin them, they would also "lose" contact with the caretakers to whom they had become attached. An eleven-year-old Central American participant of the LISA study, Ricardo, captured the feelings caused by simultaneous gains and losses:

> Once I was in the plane they told me to be calm, not to be nervous, not to cry. I was crying because I was leaving my grandfather. I had conflicting feelings. On the one side I wanted to see my mother, but on the other I did not want to leave my grandfather.

During reunification in the new country, family relationships needed to be renegotiated. The reunited child had to become reacquainted with family members. Often, the children encountered new family constellations that included stepparents, stepsiblings, and siblings they had never met. The father of another study participant, Enrique, a 13-year-old Mexican boy, explained:

> My son and my daughter are not warm towards me. They are still mad that I left them and was separated from them for years. Even when I explain to them that I came here for them, they don't hear, they don't understand. My daughter acted strangely when she first got here, she got jealous when I hugged my wife. She just wanted my attention for herself. Now, that's changed and things are getting back to normal.

Youth in the LISA study responded in a variety of ways to these family separations. If family prepared the children and youth through conversations that prepared them emotionally and psychologically for the for the separation and if the separation is framed as temporary, necessary, and undertaken for the good of the family, the separation was more manageable than if the child felt abandoned. If parents and caretakers managed the separation cooperatively and if the accompanying losses were minimized, the youth, though changed, were not necessarily be damaged by the experience. The mother of Rosario, a 13-year-old Mexican girl, described how her family managed their separation:

> In spite of everything, we have a good relationship because my mother always spoke well of me. She always told her where I was and that some day I would come for her. So there's a certain respect.

New Roles: Adjusting to Life in the United States

For some Latino immigrants, the dissonance in cultural expectations, the cumulative stressors, and the loss of social supports lead to affective and somatic symptoms (Alegría, William Siboney, Woo, Torres, & Peter Guarnaccia, 2007; Mendoza, Joyce, & Burgos, 2007). Some Latino parents are relatively unavailable psychologically owing to their own struggles in adapting to a new country, thus posing a developmental challenge to their children (Suárez-Orozco & Suárez-Orozco, 2001). The immigrant parents of Latino youth, whether their children are of the first or second generation, often turn to them in navigating the new society. Children of immigrants are asked to take on "parentified" roles, including translation and advocacy (Faulstich-Orellana, 2001). Such tasks often fall more to on the shoulders of daughters, leading to both positive and negative consequences for their development (Suárez-Orozco et al., 2005). These changing roles can in turn lead to familial conflict.

Familial Problems

Based on the LISA study, immigrant youth who reported fewer family problems felt better and did better in school. Research has demonstrated that family conflict plays a central role in undesirable psychosocial and educational outcomes (Buehler & Gerard, 2002; Conger, Ge, Elder, Lorenz, & Simons, 1994). To establish whether newcomer adolescents found family conflict to be a significant factor in their lives, we asked students about issues that were a problem in their family after youth had been in the US for almost seven years, on average; these included conflicts about parents working long hours, grades, friends, household responsibilities, changing family constellations due to migration, and conflicting plans for the future. While some of these conflicts are part of adolescent development regardless of immigration status, understanding their impact on immigrant youth in particular is important.

Most students responded to the bulk of these potential family tensions with "not a problem." This corresponded to previous research suggesting that newcomer immigrant youth generally view family as an important resource in their lives that builds resilience despite the stresses of migration (Suárez-Orozco & Suárez-Orozco, 1995). However, those students who reported family problems were more likely to report lower levels of well-being and lower academic performance.

While outright conflicts and problems were not especially an issue for most of these students, the qualitative data revealed a general drift over time in intimacy and ease of communication within the family. As the children matured and as they spent more time in the new country, parents worried about a growing distance between their children and themselves. For some families, this was a result of the natural changes that take place during adolescence. For many, as the children's native language skills atrophied, communication about anything more than basic exchanges declined. For others, cultural changes (often fashion and dating practices) the youth brought into the home appalled immigrant parents. For still others, as the gap between the parents and their children's educational and cultural competence increased, they found less and less in common.

Some of these conflicts may be particularly pronounced among the second generation (Latinos born in the United States to immigrant parents), which makes the need to distinguish them from their Latino immigrant peers important; they often have limited facility in their parents' native language (Portes & Hao, 1998), which presents other challenges in maintaining communication at home with parents (Suárez-Orozco et al., 2008). While American-born Latinos and their first-generation parents may share a lack of access to those who can guide them through the institutions of the unfamiliar dominant society, they are spared the challenges of pre-migratory trauma, status-related stress, and family separations. On the other hand, second generation children often face the stressors of poverty, typically in urban contexts (Noguera, 2006) without the protection of immigrant optimism (Kao & Tienda, 1995) and a dual frame of reference (Suárez-Orozco & Suárez-Orozco, 1995); the burden of forging a trans-cultural identity where they can navigate both their parents' culture and the dominant culture also falls more to them (Suárez-Orozco, 2004).

Challenges of English Language Acquisition

Many Latino children experience difficulties with English in school, which as was already mentioned, may be at the root of many stressors in their lives. In 2000, about three-quarters (71%) of all children who spoke English less than "very well" were Latinos in pre-kindergarten to fifth grade (Capps, Fix, Murray, Ost, Passel, & Herwantoro, 2005). A more recent survey in 2006 revealed that 18.4 percent of all Latino school-age children (5–17) spoke English with difficulty (Planty et al., 2008). The struggle to speak English among Latino students is not just a challenge for immigrant children. Among pre-kindergarten–to-5th-grade Latino children in the United States, 62 percent of foreign-born children spoke English less than "very well," as well as 43 percent of U.S.-born children of immigrants and 12 percent of children of U.S.-born Latinos (Capps et al., 2005).

Learning a second language often takes a long time and being a competent language user at an academic level takes even more. It has been well established that the complexity of oral and written academic English skills generally requires between four and seven years of optimal academic instruction to develop academic second language skills compared to native English speakers (Collier, 1987; 1995; Cummins, 1991; 2000). Struggles with language are well presented in the LISA data; only 7 percent of the sample had developed academic English skills comparable to those of their native-born English-speaking peers after an average of seven years in the United States (Carhill, Suárez-Orozco, & Páez, 2008). As noted earlier, Latino English language learners (ELL) do not typically encounter strong second-language-acquisition educational programs, and often face individual disadvantages and structural linguistic isolation that may explain the poor academic English development seen in our study.

Many Latino immigrant students from poverty-stricken countries enter U.S. schools with little or no schooling, and they often may not read or write well in Spanish. Moreover, growing numbers of Latino immigrants are indigenous speakers who do not speak Spanish as their first language. For these children, English is their third language, doubling the effort to master academic proficiency in English. Research in second-language acquisition suggests that when students are well grounded in their native language and have developed reading and writing skills in that language, they appear to be able to efficiently apply that knowledge to the new language when provided appropriate instructional supports (August & Shanahan, 2006; Butler & Hakata, 2005). Unfortunately, however, many Latino students do not enter schools with this advantage. In addition, many Latino ELL students cannot receive support for learning English from their parents at home. Latino parents often have limited education (National Task Force on Minority High Achievement, 1999) and limited English skills and may thus be unable to provide rich English learning contexts for their children. Indeed, nearly a quarter of Latino students are linguistically isolated (Capps et al., 2005), living in households where all members over age 14 are limited English proficient.

This state of linguistic isolation is a reality in the social contexts of many Latino students who live in segregated neighborhoods. Many Latinos live in predominantly minority neighborhoods that do not promise much direct contact with well-educated native English speakers. At school, ELL students in general and Latino students in particular are also often segregated from their native-English-speaking peers by being relegated to the basement or a wing of the school (Olsen, 1997). In many cases, children have almost no meaningful contact with English-speaking peers (Carhill et al., 2008). Indeed, more than a third of immigrant students in the LISA study reported that they had little opportunity to interact with peers who were not from their country of origin, which no doubt contributed to their linguistically isolated state (Suárez-Orozco et al., 2008). This isolation is clearly detrimental to Latino ELL students by minimizing exposure to the English language that they need to learn. Without such contact, an important source of language modeling is missed. More relevant to the purposes of this piece are the consequent barriers to receiving social support from English speakers, thus ameliorating social-emotional stress. This type of support can and does come from family and friends who are not English speakers, but considering that a considerable amount of stress in the life of a Latino immigrant adolescent can come from challenges related to managing cultural differences, the support from English speakers can be beneficial.

Networks of Relationships

From the time of arrival in a new country, social supports and networks of relations provide families with tangible aid, guidance, and advice as well as emotional sustenance. These supports are critical for newcomers who can find their new environment disorienting. Positive relationships maintain and enhance self-esteem, while providing acceptance, approval, and a sense of belonging. During migration, extended family members—godparents, aunts, uncles, older cousins, and the like—are often important sources of tangible support. Family cohesion and the maintenance of a well-functioning system of supervision, authority, and mutuality can shape the well-being and social outcomes of children.

No family is an island, so wellness is enhanced when it is part of a larger community offering what Felton Earls termed "community agency" (Earls, 1997). For immigrant youth, community agency can inoculate against the toxic elements in their new settings (DeVos, 1992). In immigrant communities, these organizations are often associated with churches or religious organizations. Community-based organizations serving Latino youth in the United States often focus on problem behaviors such as gang interventions or pregnancy prevention. In contrast, however, community-based organizations serving Asian youth tend to emphasize proactive activities such as SAT preparation, math, and English tutoring (Zhou & Li, 2004).

Peers can serve as both positive and negative social capital (Portes, 1998). Peers can encourage maladaptive behavior, promote drug use, and discourage competent academic engagement. In this case, peers serve to distract their classmates from performing optimally in school (Gibson, Gándara, & Koyama, 2004). Peers may contribute to unsafe school and community environments, which can undermine students' ability to concentrate, their sense of security, and their ability to experience trusting relationships in school. On the positive side, peer relationships can prove powerful role models as they provide a sense of belonging and tangible help (Gibson et al., 2004; Stanton-Salazar, 2004). For new Latino immigrant students, the companionship of co-nationals is important as a source of information on school culture (Suárez-Orozco, Pimentel, & Martin 2009). Peers can act as "vital conduits" (Stanton-Salazar, 2004) of information to disoriented newcomers. Peers not only buffer the loneliness new arrivals often experience but also can enhance self-confidence and self-efficacy, providing the sustenance that nourishes the development of new psychosocial competencies (Suárez-Orozco et al., 2008).

Mentoring relationships are often important in the lives of immigrant youth (Crul, 2007; Rhodes, 2002). In stressed families with limited social resources, mentors support healthier relationships by alleviating pressure on the family (Roffman, Suárez-Orozco, & Rhodes, 2003). Bicultural mentors can serve to bridge the old and new cultures (Crul, 2007). Bicultural mentors act as sources of information about the new cultural rules of engagement. Mentors can heal ruptures in relationships that result from long immigrant separations and complicated reunifications. Because Latino immigrant parents are often not available given their work schedules, the guidance and affection from a mentor serves to fill the void in the life of a youngster. Mentoring relationships have been shown to reduce substance abuse, aggressive behavior, and delinquency (Rhodes, 2002). Research suggests that college educated co-ethnic mentors particularly can help their protégés perform better in school by helping them with homework, by providing informed advice about educational access, and through positive role modeling (Crul, 2007; Suárez-Orozco et al., 2008).

Well-Being

Data examining the well-being of immigrant origin populations in general and Latinos in particular across generations and ages reveal mixed results according to country of origin, developmental group, cohort, and age of arrival as well as developmental outcome (Rumbaut, 2004; Takeuchi, Hong, Gile, & Alegría, 2007). While there is a fairly consistent "immigrant paradox" showing a decline across generations with greater length of residency for *physical health* outcomes and engagement in *risk behaviors*, the results are inconsistent regarding the risk to *psychological health*. Further, the body of evidence on the immigrant health has focused on adults and families rather than on adolescents (Lansford, Deater-Deckard, & Bornstein, 2007; Taningco, 2007). Immigrant youth of refugee origin appear to be at greatest risk for affective disorders (Lustig et al., 2004). Latino and immigrant adolescents show patterns of progressive risk-taking behaviors the longer they are exposed to U.S. culture (Vega, Alderete, Kolody, & Aguilar-Gaxiola 1998). Given the limited and mixed evidence on the developmental trajectories of this growing population of urban residing Latino adolescents, more research on indicators of their well-being is needed using both qualitative and quantitative lenses. Important questions that as of yet have not been directly addressed include express comparisons between native-born and immigrant Latino adolescents, considering factors such as legal status, parental background, and language; only by considering the complexity of this heterogeneous group can we gain a better understanding of their social-emotional situation.

RESEARCH AND POLICY IMPLICATIONS

Taking in the panorama of the current social-emotional challenges facing immigrant and Latino youth is a daunting enterprise. As we have considered, a plethora of structural, familial, school, and student-level factors interacts to affect educational opportunity and social-emotional well-being. Given economic and demographic realities that disproportionately affect Latinos, the future does not appear promising if we stand by and do nothing. To develop meaningful interventions and tackle these large-scale issues we need to strengthen our research and evidence. In tandem, we need to implement promising models that address the many needs of Latino students. There is reason for hope; we already have ample evidence that can make a difference in the educational and well-being of Latino immigrant origin youth. Also, we would like to reiterate that Latinos represent a very diverse group. Not all Latinos face the challenges of poverty, low education, unauthorized status, and low levels of English language proficiency; variation in academic success and emotional well-being among immigrant youth can be explained by family support and individual perseverance and motivation among youth and parents (Fuligni, 1997). This does not discount the structural issues that limit the impact of such influences. Figuring out ways to understand and remove these barriers is imperative to the academic and social-emotional well-being of Latino immigrant youth. With this in mind, we make recommendations for research, practice, and policy below.

Research Recommendations

Specifying and Defining Populations

As noted earlier, the term Latino (or Hispanic) encompasses a wide range of individuals from different generational statuses, linguistic and racial backgrounds, and countries of origin. Defining the population under consideration is therefore essential. Researchers need to be specific whenever they include first, second, or third generations in their sample. They should specify country of origin whenever that is available or known (e.g., Mexican for the first generation or Mexican American for the second generation and beyond). Further, it is important to distinguish between children of immigrants and limited English proficient children (defined by the U.S. Census as speaking a language other than English at home and speaking English less than "very well"). Other terms that are sometimes used and that should be carefully defined include English language learners, newcomers, and Latin American immigrants. Further, whenever possible it is important to include comparison groups (Suárez-Orozco & Suárez-Orozco, 1995). These comparison groups can include both a range of immigrant origin populations as well as others from nonimmigrant populations who encounter similar contexts. These comparison groups provide valuable contextualization of findings.

Resiliencies and Strengths

Despite the myriad of challenges facing Latino students and families, it is imperative to not lose sight of the strengths that these families have. Investigating resilience and "funds of knowledge" of the Latino community rather than focusing solely on deficits can serve to improve the educational outlooks of its children and youth. Research consistently shows that Latino parents and children care deeply about education (Gándara, 1995; Suárez-Orozco & Suárez-Orozco, 1995) and that they have numerous familial and cultural resources to draw from in support of both well-being and academics (Falicov, 1998). Taking this starting point along with drawing on the close caring nature of many Latino families can aid in the development of interventions that are truly "additive," incorporating the strengths of both American and Latino culture to achieve their educational success (Valenzuela, 1999).

Policy and Practice Implications

There are no easy solutions to the complex problems facing Latino immigrant students. To ameliorate this pressing issue, we must face head on a challenge that has been created by a combination of structural barriers, cultural and linguistic challenges, and school-wide problems.

After-School Programs and Services in Schools

Many Latino students from low-income families do not have the kind of supports at home that middle-class students have readily at hand— educated parents who can help them organize essays and proofread them, a computer with Internet access, a tutor who can help them master trigonometry or chemistry problems, or a quiet place to work. Not recognizing such educational impediments contributes to augmenting the already-considerable achievement gap. To better serve Latino students, we recommend principals and community leaders collaborate to organize and systematize after-school programs or community education centers where immigrant students can receive benefit from supervision and mentoring (Perkins & Borden, 2003). It is particularly important that these after-school programs provide tangible academic supports, homework help, and meaningful, high-standards future-focused academic information and project a "yes you can!" narrative about academic potential and pathways (Zhou & Li, 2003). After-school programs with a focus on positive Latino cultural identity as well as sports, dance, and other extracurricular activities can also serve a role in positive youth development, but they are not enough to make an academic difference.

In addition, attention needs to be paid to the whole child and the numerous influences on development. Given that Latinos face the challenges of poverty, access to institutions such as health care, and stressors apart from those related to education, comprehensive services during the after-school hours and even during school are needed to truly help their education and well-being. These services should include healthcare, mental health services, and information about finances and nutrition. Only when these basic needs are met can we expect the situation for Latino youth to improve. Full-service schools (Dryfoos, 1994) that integrate such services into the school building both during the school day and after school represent a promising model for utilizing the school space as a "one-stop-shopping" community center that supports Latino communities.

Mentorship

Mentoring relationships often evolve organically in after-school and community organizations and make a tremendous difference in adolescents' lives (Rhodes, 2002; Suárez-Orozco et al., 2008). For youth in stressed families with limited social resources, mentors can support healthier family and peer relationships by alleviating pressure on the family (Roffman, Suárez-Orozco, & Rhodes, 2003). Mentoring relationships could particularly be useful in serving newly arrived immigrant youth, as a bicultural mentor can bridge the old and new cultures; an acculturated mentor can act as font of information about the new cultural rules of engagement. Mentoring relationships can also serve to heal ruptures in relationships that have resulted from long separations and complicated reunifications (Suárez-Orozco et al., 2002). Because immigrant adolescents' parents may not be available given their work schedules, the guidance and affection from a mentor can serve to fill the void. Further, mentoring relationships have been shown to reduce substance abuse, aggressive behavior, and incidences of delinquency (Rhodes, 2002), a path that boys are a greater risk to engage in (Vigil, 2002). In addition, college-educated mentors can help their protégés perform better in school by helping them not only with homework but also by providing them with informed advice about their own path to college.

Building on the Strengths of Latino Families

While immigrant-origin Latino families clearly face a number of academic challenges, they also embody a number of admirable cultural traits and resources that have been associated with positive academic outcomes (Perreira et al., 2006), including school attachment (Johnson, Crosnoe, & Elder, 2001), parental closeness (Fuligni, 2001; White & Glick, 2000); parental monitoring (Anguiano 2004), immigrant optimism (Kao & Tienda, 1995), and the recognition of the value of hard work (Suárez-Orozco & Suárez-Orozco, 1995). Together, these "family-mediated outlooks and values" (Perreira et al., 2006) explain why first generation immigrant students who enter school with the intention pursuing an education (rather than entering the workforce) do relatively well compared with later-born generations who begin to succumb to the frustrations, discouragement, and anomie that plague disenfranchised minority youth (Perreira et al., 2006; Rumbaut, 1997).

The maintenance of these native linguistic and cultural resources is important to positive identity development, higher self-esteem, and, ultimately, academic achievement of Latino and immigrant youth (Tse, 2001; Valenzuela, 1999). A bicultural balance allowing flexible movement between the language and values of each two cultural groups while maintaining positive attitudes toward both can help an individual in the cultural minority develop a healthy sense of self (LaFromboise, Coleman, & Gerton, 1993. There is evidence to support that for Latinos, maintaining a bicultural balance between the native culture and the new culture may protect against negative educational outcomes. For example, research shows that Mexican youth who speak both Spanish and English fluently and whose household members do the same are the least likely to drop out of school (Feliciano, 2001). The maintenance of native language as beneficial as it allows a child to access social support from both family and the larger community, particularly when the family and community are non-English speaking (Rodriguez, Diaz, Duran, & Espinosa, 1995).

Further, a Latino child who experiences his or her home language and culture in an institution such as school will likely feel more valued in that setting and in larger society, making the possibility of his or her academic success seem more likely. Moll, Amanti, Neff, and Gonzalez (1992) present an example of how teachers, researchers, and parents can collaborate to create such a curriculum that respects the home culture of students and their families while preparing them for success in larger society and the dominant culture. Moll and his colleagues had the explicit goal of developing a curriculum for the largely Mexican-descent community that they were working in. Researchers and teachers collaborated in collecting qualitative data to "develop innovations in teaching that draw upon the knowledge and skills found in local households" (1992, p. 132), which they termed the "Funds of Knowledge." The researchers adhered to the Latino value of *confianza*—literally translated, *trust*; the researchers and teachers extended this concept to include the notion of mutual respect for the knowledge that both the researchers/teachers and the families brought to the table. In so doing, teachers were able to bridge the gap between the students' home world and their classroom experience, culminating in a learning module created in collaboration between students, families, researchers, and teachers (Moll et al., 1992).

School-wide efforts should be made to reach out to parents by using Spanish-speaking community liaisons. Flyers in Spanish are not enough; a personal invitation is often much more effective. Calling under positive circumstances instead of simply waiting for a crisis is another important strategy. Providing English-as-a-second-language courses on campus for parents also can bring them to the school. Accommodating schedules as much as is possible will allow greater participation as well. Such promising practices can serve to welcome, engage, and incorporate Latino families into the fabric of the schools.

CONCLUSION

Latinos are now the nation's largest minority group in American schools. The majority are immigrants or the children of immigrants. Latinos, especially those of immigrant origin, share optimism and hope in the future that must be cultivated and treasured; they see schooling as the key to a better tomorrow. Tragically, over time, Latino youth, especially those enrolled in highly impoverished and deeply segregated schools, face negative odds and uncertain prospects. Too many Latino youngsters are leaving schools without developing and mastering the kinds of higher-order skills needed in today's global economy and society. The future of our country will in no small measure be tied to the fortunes of all young Americans. As Latinos, immigrant and U.S.-born, are an increasing part of the American future, harnessing their energy, optimism, and faith in the future is in everyone's interest. Doing so is arguably one of the most important challenges to our country's democratic promise.

NOTES

1. For complete details of the study, see Suárez-Orozco, Súarez-Orozco, and Todorova, 2008.

2. Throughout this piece, we use the terms "unauthorized," and "undocu-mented" interchangeably to identify individuals who were born abroad residing in the United States, who are not U.S. citizens, permanent residents, or authorized visitors. For a detailed discussion of these terms along with the term "illegal immigrant" see Bean and Lowell, 2007.

3. All names are pseudonyms and identifying information has been changed to protect the confidentiality of study participants.

REFERENCES

Alegría, M., Siboney, W., Woo, M., Torres, M., & Guarnaccia, P. (2007). Looking beyond nativity: The relation of age of immigration, length of residence, and birth cohorts to the risk of onset of psychiatric disorders for Latinos. *Research in Human Development 4*, 19–47.

Anguiano, R. P. V. (2004). Families and schools: The effects of parental involvement on high school completion. *Journal of Family Issues 25*, 61–85.

Auerbach, S. (2004). Engaging Latino parents in supporting college pathways: Lessons from a college access program. *Journal of Hispanic Higher Education 3*(2): 125–45.

August, D., & Hakuta, K. (1997). *Improving schooling for language-minority children: A research Agenda*. Washington, DC: National Academy Press.

Bean, F. D., & Lowell, B.L. (2007). Unauthorized migration. In M. Waters and R. Ueda (Eds.), *The New Americans: A Guide to Immigration Since 1965*. (pp. 70–82). Cambridge and London: Harvard University Press.

Bourdieu, P., & Passeron, C. (1977). *Reproduction in education, society and culture*. Los Angeles: Sage.

Buehler, C., & Gerard, J. (2002). Marital conflict, ineffective parenting, and children's and adolescent's maladjustment. *Journal of Marriage and the Family, 64*, 78–92.

Butler, Y. G., & Hakuta, K. (2005). Bilingualism and second language acquisition. In by T. K. Bhatia and W. C. Ritchie (Eds.), *The handbook of bilingualism* (pp. 114–44). London: Blackwell.

Capps, R. (2001). Hardship among children of immigrants: Findings from the 1999 National Survey of America's Families. *Assessing the New Federalism,* Policy Brief B-29. Washington, DC: The Urban Institute.

Capps, R., Castañeda, R. M., Chaudry, A., & Santos, R. (2007). *Paying the price: The impact of immigration raids on America's children.* Washington, DC: The Urban Institute.

Capps, R., Fix, M., Murray, J., Ost, J., Passel, J.S., & Herwantoro, S. (2005). *The new demography of America's schools: Immigration and the No Child Left Behind Act.* Washington, DC: The Urban Institute.

Carhill, A., Suárez-Orozco, C., & Páez, M. (2008). Explaining English language proficiency among adolescent immigrant students. *American Educational Research Journal 45,* 1155–79.

Coleman, J. (1988). Social capital in the creation of human capital. *American Journal of Sociology 94,* S95–S120.

Collier, V. P. (1987). Age and rate of acquisition of second language for academic purposes. *TESOL Quarterly 21,* 617–41.

Conger, R. D., Ge, X., Elder, G. H., Jr., Lorenz, R. O., & Simons, R. L. (1994). Economic stress, coercive family process, and developmental problems of adolescents. *Child Development, 65* 541–561.

Crul, M. (2007). The integration of immigrant youth. In M. M. Suárez-Orozco (ed.), *Learning in the Global Era: International Perspectives on Globalization and Education.* Berkeley: University of California Press.

Cummins, J. (1991). Language development and academic learning. In L.M. Malavé and G. Duquette (Eds.), *Language, Culture, & Cognition,* (pp. 161–175). Clevedon, England: Multilingual Matters.

Delgado-Gaitan, C. (2004). *Involving Latino families in schools: Raising student achievement through home-school partnerships.* Thousand Oaks, CA: Corwin Press.

Delpit, L. (1995). *Other people's children: Cultural conflict in the classroom.* New York: The New Press.

DeVos, G. (1992). *Social cohesion and alienation: Minorities in the United States and Japan.* Boulder, CO: Westview Press.

Dryfoos, J. G. (1994). *Full-service schools: A revolution in health and social services for children, youth, and families.* San Francisco: Jossey-Bass.

Earls, F. (1997). Tighter, safer, neighborhoods. *Harvard Magazine* (November–December): 14–15.

Falicov, C. J. (1998). *Latino families in therapy: A guide to multicultural practice.* New York: Guilford Press.

Faulstich-Orellana, M. (2001). The work kids do: Mexican and Central American immigrant children's contribution to households and schools in California. *Harvard Educational Review 71,* 366–89.

Feliciano, C. (2001). The benefits of biculturalism: Exposure to immigrant culture and dropping out of school among Asian and Latino youths. *Social Science Quarterly 82,* 865–80.

Fry, R., & Gonzales, F. (2008). *One-in-five and growing fast: A profile of Hispanic public school students.* Washington, DC: Pew Hispanic Center.

Fuligini, A. (1997). The academic achievement of adolescents from immigrant families: the roles of family background, attitudes, and behavior. *Child Development 69*, 351–363.

Fuligni, A. J. (2001). Family obligation and the achievement motivation of adolescents from Asian, Latin American, and European backgrounds. In A. J. Fuligni (ed.), *Family Obligation and assistance during adolescence: Contextual variations and developmental implications (New directions in child and adolescent development)*, (pp. 61–76). San Francisco, CA: Jossey-Bass.

Gándara, P. (1995). *Over the ivy walls: The educational mobility of low income Chicanos.* Albany: SUNY Press.

Gándara, P., & Contreras, F. (2009). *The Latino education crisis: The consequences of failed school policies.* Cambridge, MA: Harvard University Press.

García-Coll, C.T., & Magnuson, K.A. (1997). The psychological experience of immigration: A developmental perspective. In A. Booth, A.C. Crouter and N. Landale (Eds.), *Immigration and the Family* (pp. 91–131). Mahwah, NJ: Lawrence Erlbaum Associates.

Gibson, M., Gandara, P., & Koyama, J.P. (2004). *School connections: U.S. Mexican youth, peers, and school adjustment.* New York: Teachers College Press.

Jia, G., & Aaronson, D. (2003). A longitudinal study of Chinese children and adolescents learning English in the United States. *Applied Psycholinguistics 24*, 131–61.

Johnson, M.K., Crosnoe, R., & Elder Jr., G.H. (2001). Students' attachment and academic engagement: The role of race and ethnicity. *Sociology of Education 74*, 318–40.

Kao, G., & Tienda, M. (1995). Optimism and achievement: The educational performance of immigrant youth. *Social Science Quarterly 76*, 1–19.

Kasinitz, P., Mollenkopf, J.H, Waters, M.C., & Holdaway, J. (2008). *Inheriting the city: The children on immigrants come of age.* Cambridge, MA, and New York: Harvard University Press and Russell Sage Foundation.

LaFromboise, T., Hardin. Coleman, L. K., & Gerton, J. (1993). Psychological impact of biculturalism: Evidence and theory. *Psychological Bulletin 114*, 395–412.

Lansford, J. E., Deater-Deckard, K., & Bornstein, M.H. (2007). *Immigrant families in contemporary society.* New York: The Guilford Press.

Lopez, G. R. (2001). The value of hard work: Lessons on parent involvement from an (im)migrant household. *Harvard Educational Review 71*, 416–437.

Lustig, S.L., Kia-Keating, M., Knight, W.G., Geltman, P., Ellis, H., Kinzie, D.J., Keane, T., & Saxe, G. (2004). Review of child and adolescent refugee mental health. *Journal of American Academy of Child and Adolescent Psychiatry 43*, 24–36.

Luthar, S.S. (1999). *Poverty and children's adjustment.* Thousand Oaks, CA: SAGE Publications.

Massey, D., & Denton, N. (1993). *American apartheid*. Cambridge, MA: Harvard University Press.

Mendoza, F.S., Javier, J.R., & Burgos, A.E. (2007). Health of children in immigrant families. In J.E. Lansford, K. Deater-Deckard and M.H. Bornstein (Eds.), *Immigrant Families in Contemporary Society* (pp. 30–50). New York: The Guilford Press.

Moll, Luis C., Cathy Amanti, Deborah Neff, and Norma González. 1992. Funds of knowledge for teaching: Using a qualitative approach to connect homes and classrooms. *Theory into Practice 31*(2): 132–41.

National Task Force on Minority High Achievement. (1999). *Reaching the top*. New York: The College Board.

Noguera, P.A. (2006). Latino youth: Immigration, education, and the future. *Latino Studies 4*, 313–20.

Oakes, J. (1985). *Keeping track: How schools restructure inequality*. New Haven, CT: Yale University Press.

Olsen, L. (1997). *Made in America: Immigrant students in our public schools*. New York: The New Press.

Orfield, G. (1995). *Latinos in education: Recent trends*. Cambridge, MA: Harvard Graduate School of Education.

Orfield, G., & Lee, C. (2006). *Racial transformation and the changing nature of segregation*. Cambridge, MA: The Civil Rights Project, Harvard University.

Orfield, G., & Yun, J.T. (1999). *Resegregation in American schools*. Cambridge, MA: The Civil Rights Project, Harvard University.

Passel, J.S. (2006). *The size and characteristics of the unauthorized migrant population in the U.S.* Washington, DC: Pew Hispanic Center.

Pérez-Huber, L., Huidor, O., Malagón, M.C., Sánchez, G., & Solórzano, D.G. (2006). *Falling through the cracks: Critical transitions in the Latina/o educational pipeline: 2006 Education Summit report*. Los Angeles: UCLA Chicano Studies Research Center.

Perkins, D. F., & Borden, L.M. (2003). Key elements of community youth development programs. In F.A. Villarruel, D.F. Perkins, L.M. Borden, and J.G. Keith (Eds.), *Community youth development: Programs, policy, and practices* (pp. 327–340). Thousand Oaks, CA: SAGE Publications.

Perreira, K.M., Harris, K.M., & Lee, D. (2006). Making it in America: High school completion by immigrant and native youth. *Demography, 43*, 1–26.

Planty, M., Hussar, W., Snyder, T., Provasnik, S., Kena, G., Dinkes, R., Ramani, A.K., & Kemp, J. (2008). *The condition of education 2008*. NCES 2008-031. Washington, DC: U.S. Department of Education, Institute of Education Sciences, National Center for Education Statistics.

Portes, A. (1996). Children of immigrants: Segmented assimilation and its determinants. In A. Portes (ed.), *The Economic Sociology of Immigration: Essays on Networks, Ethnicity, and Entrepreneurship* (pp. 248–280). New York: Russell Sage Foundation.

Portes, A. (1998). Social capital: Its origins and applications in modern sociology. *Annual Review of Sociology 22*: 1–24.

Portes, A., & Hao, L. (1998). E pluribus unum: Bilingualism and loss of language in the second generation. *Sociology of Education 71*, 269–94.

Putnam, R. (2000). Bowling alone: The collapse and revival of American community. New York: Simon & Shuster.

Ramirez, R., & Therrien, M. (2000). *The Hispanic population in the United States: March 2000*. Current Population Report P20-535. Washington, DC: U.S. Census Bureau.

Rhodes, J.E. (2002). *Stand by me: The risks and rewards of youth mentoring relationships*. Cambridge, MA: Harvard University Press.

Rodriguez, J.L., Diaz, R.M., Duran, D., Espinosa, L. (1995). The impact of bilingual preschool education on the language development of Spanish-speaking children. *Early Childhood Research Quarterly 10*, 475–490.

Roffman, J.G., Suárez-Orozco, C, & Rhodes, J.E. (2002). Facilitating positive development in immigrant youth: The role of mentors and community organizations. In F.A. Villarruel, D.F. Perkins, L.M. Borden, and J.G. Keith (Eds.), *Community youth development: Practice policy and research* (pp. 90–117). Thousand Oaks, CA: Sage Press.

Rumbaut, R.G. (2004). Ages, life stages, and generational cohorts: Decomposing the immigrant first and second generations in the United States. *International Migration Review 38*, 1160–1206.

Rumbaut, R.G. (1997). *Passages to adulthood: The adaptation of children of immigrants in Southern California*. New York: Russell Sage Foundation.

Stanton-Salazar, R.D. (2004). Social capital among working-class minority students. In M.A. Gibson, P. Gándara and J.P. Koyma (Eds.), *School connections: U.S. Mexican youth, peer, & school achievement* (pp. 18–38). New York: Teachers College Press.

Suárez-Orozco, C. (2004). Formulating identity in a globalized world. In M.M. Suárez-Orozco and D.B. Qin-Hilliard (Eds.), *Globalization: Culture and education in the new millennium* (pp. 173–202). Berkeley: University of California Press.

Suárez-Orozco, M., & Gaytán, F.X. (2009). Preface to the 2009 edition. In M.M Suárez-Orozco and Páez, M., *Latinos: Remaking America (Second Edition)* (pp. xi–xxi). Berkeley: University of California Press.

Suárez-Orozco, C., & Suárez-Orozco, M.M. (1995). *Transformations: Immigration, family life, and achievement motivation among Latino adolescents*. Palo Alto, CA: Stanford University Press.

Suárez-Orozco, C., & Suárez-Orozco, M.M. (2001). *Children of immigration*. Cambridge, MA: Harvard University Press.

Suárez-Orozco, C., Pimentel, A., & Martin, M. (2009). The significance of relationships: Academic engagement and achievement among newcomer immigrant youth. *Teachers College Record 111*, 712–749.

Suárez-Orozco, C., Suárez-Orozco, M.N., & Todorova. I. (2005). Wandering souls: The interpersonal concerns of adolescent immigrants. In George De

Vos and Eric S. De Vos. Boulder (Eds.) *Narrative themes in comparative context*, vol. 2 of *cross-cultural dimensions in conscious thought* (pp. 463–495). CO: Rowman & Littlefield.

Suárez-Orozco, C. Suárez-Orozco, M., & Todorova, I. (2008). *Learning a new land: Educational pathways of immigrant youth*. Cambridge, MA: Harvard University Press.

Suárez-Orozco, C., Todorova, I., & Louie, J. (2002). 'Making up for lost time': The experience of separation and reunification among immigrant families. *Family Process 41*, 625–43.

Takeuchi, D.T., Hong, S., Gile, K., & Alegría, M. (2007). Developmental contexts and mental disorders among Asian Americans. *Research in Human Development 4*, 49–69.

Taningco, M.T. (2007). *Revisiting the Latino health paradox. Policy brief*. Boston, MA: Tomás Rivera Policy Institute.

Tse, L. (2001). Resisting and reversing language shift: Heritage-language resilience among U.S. native biliterates. *Harvard Educational Review, 71*, 676–708.

Valenzuela, A. (1999). *Subtractive schooling: U.S.-Mexican youth and the politics of caring*. Albany: SUNY Press.

Vega, W.A., Alderete, E., Kolody, B., & Aguilar-Gaxiola, S. (1998). Illicit drug use among Mexicans and Mexican Americans in California: The effects of gender and acculturation. *Addiction 93*, 1839–50.

Vigil, D. (2002). *A rainbow of gangs: Street cultures in the mega-city*. Austin: University of Texas.

Weissbourd, R. (1996). *The vulnerable child*. Reading, MA: Perseus Books.

White, M.J., & Glick, J. (2000). Generation status, social capital, and the routes out of high school. *Sociological Forum 15*, 671–91.

Zhou, M., & Li, X. (2003). Ethnic language schools and the development of supplementary education in the immigrant Chinese community in the United States. In C. Suarez-Orozco and I. L. G. Todorova (Eds.), *New directions for youth development: Understanding the social worlds of immigrant youth* (pp. 57–73). San Francisco: Jossey-Bass.

INDEX

ABOUT THE EDITORS AND CONTRIBUTORS

EDITORS

NATASHA J. CABRERA is Associate Professor at the University of Maryland. Her areas of research include the role of father involvement in children's development, ethnic and cultural differences in fathering and mothering, and the mechanisms that link early experience to children's later development. She is the author of many peer-reviewed articles and the co-editor of the *Handbook of Father Involvement: Multidisciplinary Perspectives* (2002).

HIRAM E. FITZGERALD, PhD, is associate provost for university outreach and engagement and university distinguished professor of psychology at Michigan State University. He is President of the National Outreach Scholarship Conference and is a member of the Native Children's Research Exchange. Fitzgerald's research includes the study of infant and family development, the impact of fathers on early child development, the implementation of systemic models of community process and change, the etiology of alcoholism and coactive psychopathology, the digital divide and youth-computer interface, and broad issues related to university-community engaged scholarship. He has received numerous awards, including the ZERO TO THREE Dolley Madison Award for Outstanding Lifetime Contributions to the Development and Well Being of Very Young Children, and the World Association for Infant Mental Health's designation as Honorary President.

FRANCISCO A. VILLARRUEL received his PhD in human development in 1990 from the University of Wisconsin. He is a University Outreach and Engagement Senior Fellow and a professor of human development and family studies. His research focuses on Latino youth and youth that are in conflict with the law. He sits on the National Board for the Campaign for Youth Justice, the Michigan Council on Crime and Delinquency, and is a consultant to the Office of Juvenile Justice and Delinquency Prevention.

CONTRIBUTORS

DANIELA ALDONEY is a graduate student in the Department of Human Development at the University of Maryland, College Park. She earned her undergraduate degree in psychology from the Universidad de Chile, in Santiago, Chile. Aldoney's research interest includes the study of parent-child relationship in disadvantages population and the ways in which culture and ethnicity may influence parenting practices.

MARGARITA AZMITIA received her PhD in developmental psychology in 1986 from the University of Minnesota. She is a fellow of the American Psychology Association and the American Educational Research Association. Currently, she is a professor of psychology at the University of California at Santa Cruz. Her research focuses on the role of family, peers, and schools in ethnically and socioeconomically diverse adolescents' educational pathways and identity development.

RAYMOND BURIEL is Professor of Psychology and Chicana/o Latina/o Studies at Pomona College. He is a native of Riverside, California, and received his PhD from the University of California at Riverside. He did post doctoral work at the Spanish Speaking Mental Health Research Center at UCLA on a Ford Foundation Fellowship, and was a Scholar of the Tomas Rivera Policy Institute at Claremont, California. His research has focused on the acculturation and adjustment of Mexican immigrant families with a special emphasis on the characteristics of immigrants that are conducive to success in the United States. His work in this area has examined the development of biculturalism as an adaptive strategy, and the deleterious effects of deculturation across successive generations. His current research focuses on children who serve as interpreters for their immigrant parents. He refers to these children as "language and cultural brokers" because they not only interpret and translate, but also explain American culture to their parents.

DINA C. CASTRO is a Senior Scientist at FPG Child Development Institute, University of North Carolina at Chapel Hill. She serves as director of the *Center for Early Care and Education Research: Dual Language Learners*, funded by the U.S. Department of Health and Human Services, Administration for Children and Families. Her research includes a national study of early childhood programs' policies and practices to address the needs of Latino children and their families, and randomized controlled intervention studies to promote school readiness among Latino dual language learners. She also has conducted studies of language and literacy development in young children, factors affecting the well-being of Latino immigrant families, choices of care among Latino families, and family involvement in Head Start.

ALEXANDRA CORDERO is a student in the PhD program in Counseling Psychology at New York University. She received her MA in Counseling and Guidance (Bilingual) from NYU and her AB in Psychology from Harvard University and has also done graduate work at NYU in cultural anthropology. Her research and clinical interests include issues of concern to Latino populations in psychology and education.

JILL DENNER received her PhD in Developmental Psychology from Teachers College, Columbia University. She is the Associate Director of Research at Education, Training, Research (ETR) Associates where she does applied research, with a focus on increasing the number of women and underrepresented minorities in computing. Dr. Denner has been PI on several NSF grants, written numerous peer-reviewed articles, and co-edited two books: *Beyond Barbie and Mortal Kombat: New Perspectives on Gender and Gaming*, published by MIT Press in 2008, and *Latina Girls: Voices of Adolescent Strength in the United States*, published by NYU Press in 2006.

XIMENA FRANCO received her PhD in developmental psychology in 2007 from Florida International University. Currently, she is an Investigator at the Frank Porter Graham Child Development Institute, at the University of North Carolina-Chapel Hill. Her current work focuses on the development of class-wide and small-group interventions in the areas of math and social-emotional development specifically designed to improve the quality of practices for supporting preschool-aged dual language learners. An adjunctive area of work is to develop a professional development plan for teachers to effectively implement these interventions in their classrooms. These interventions are part of the Nuestros Niños School Readiness Intervention Program funded by the National Institute of Child Health and Development.

ENCARNACION GARZA, JR. is an Associate Professor at the University of Texas at San Antonio. The focus of his research is on Latino student success and the preparation of school leaders for social justice.

FRANCISCO X. GAYTÁN is an assistant professor of social work at Northeastern Illinois University in Chicago. He received his PhD in applied psychology from New York University. He also has Masters degrees in education from Harvard's Graduate School of Education and social work from the University of California at Berkeley. His research focuses on the social-emotional and academic development of first and second-generation Latino immigrant youth in the United States.

ELIZABETH C. HAIR received her PhD in Developmental Psychology in 1999 from Texas A&M University. Currently, she is a Senior Research Scientist in the Public Health Area of NORC at the University of Chicago. Her current research focuses on the social, emotional, and physical health of children, adolescents, and families. Previously, Dr. Hair worked at Child Trends for 10 years and was the Program Director of the Health Area.

TAMARA G. HALLE is Co-Director of Early Childhood Research at Child Trends and oversees all Early Childhood projects in Child Trends' DC office. Dr. Halle conducts research on children's early cognitive and social development, early care and education, family and community supports for school readiness, and school characteristics associated with ongoing achievement and positive development. Her recent work focuses especially on early literacy development among English language learning children, and evaluations of early childhood curricula, programs, and professional development aimed at supporting children's school readiness. She is currently Co-Principal Investigator on a project for the Office of the Assistant Secretary for Planning and Evaluation focusing on how best to conceptualize and measure children's school readiness, and is contributing to several projects of the Center for Early Care and Education Research: Dual Language Learners (CECER-DLL). She received her PhD in developmental psychology from the University of Michigan.

TRACY W. KENNEDY received her undergraduate degree in Criminology from the University of Maryland. She is currently a graduate student in Human Development at the University of Maryland, College Park. The focus of her work will be on the developmental outcomes and services to children and families of incarcerated parents. She is also a full-time staff member in the Multicultural Involvement and Community Advocacy Office in the Division of Student Affairs at the University of Maryland.

BRIANNE KONDELIS received her M.Ed. in Human Development from the University of Maryland, College Park in 2010. Prior to completing graduate studies, Brianne was a classroom teacher in Montgomery County, Maryland. Brianne's interests include early childhood education and parent education and intervention programs.

JULIA A. LOVE received her PhD in developmental psychology from Claremont Graduate University. Currently, she is a Research and Evaluation Specialist at Los Angeles Universal Preschool. Her past research has focused on the social-emotional and academic success of children who serve as Language Brokers for their families. Currently, her research is focused on the social-emotional, motor, and cognitive development of children attending LAUP preschools in Los Angeles County.

RUBÉN O. MARTINEZ is the director of the Julian Samora Research Institute at Michigan State University. He is a sociologist with research interests in minority youth education, diversity leadership in higher education, and environmental justice issues in Latino communities. He is currently doing research on the demographic shift and its implications for the nation's economy, particularly with regard to demands for highly skilled labor.

MEAGAN MCSWIGGAN received her B.A. in Psychology and Spanish in 2008 from Wake Forest University. She is currently enrolled in a PhD program in clinical child psychology at the University of Central Florida. Her research has focused on early social-emotional development and factors affecting school readiness. Previously, she was employed at Child Trends as a Senior Research Assistant in the Early Childhood Development area.

BETTY M. MERCHANT received her PhD in Administration and Policy Analysis in 1991 from Stanford University. She is Dean of the College of Education and Human Development at the University of Texas at San Antonio and professor in the Department of Educational Leadership and Policy Studies. She has taught at all grade levels, K–12 in a broad range of cultural contexts, including tribally controlled Native American schools. Her research focuses on the differential effects of educational policies and practices, particularly for students traditionally marginalized by mainstream educational settings, school leadership, and educational decision-making within increasingly diverse contexts.

GWENDELYN RIVERA is a doctoral candidate in Psychological Studies in Education at the University of California, Los Angeles. Her research interests include factors that contribute to the academic and personal resilience of immigrant youth, access to higher education, and the role of after-school programs on youths' developmental outcomes. She is currently a research assistant at the National Center for Evaluation, Standards, and Student Testing.

PHILIP C. RODKIN received his PhD in social psychology at Harvard University in 1994. He is an associate professor of child development in the Departments of Educational Psychology and Psychology at the University of Illinois at Urbana-Champaign. His interests include children's personality and social development, with a focus on peer relationships in childhood and adolescence. One goal of his work is to understand the socialization and development of aggressive behavior, and eventually to devise interventions that use children's existing social networks to reduce problem behavior in schools.

SHANNON RUSSELL is a doctoral candidate in the department of Human Development at the University of Maryland, College Park specializing in Educational Psychology. Her research focuses on teacher student relationships during secondary school.

CARLOS E. SANTOS received his PhD in developmental psychology in 2010 from New York University. He is an Assistant Research Professor at Arizona State University's School of Social and Family Dynamics. His research has focused on gender development, particularly in the context of peer relationships during adolescence, gender-based interventions aimed at improving the socio-emotional development of children and adults, and racial/ethnic identity development during adolescence.

CAROLA SUÁREZ-OROZCO is a Professor of Applied Psychology at NYU and is Co-Director of Immigration Studies at NYU. She publishes widely on the experiences of immigrant families and youth including factors influencing a variety of trajectories of performance, the role of the "social mirror" in identity formation, immigrant family separations, the role of mentors in facilitating youth development, as well as gendered experiences of immigrant youth. Her books include: *Learning a New Land: Immigrant Children in American Society*; *Children of Immigration; Transformations: Migration, Family Life, and Achievement Motivation Among Latino Adolescents*; and *The New Immigration: An Interdisciplinary Reader*. She received an American Psychological Association Presidential Citation in 2006 for her lifetime work on the psychology of immigration, was inducted into the New York Academy of Sciences in 2007, and became a member of the Institute for Advanced Study in Princeton in 2009.

CHRISTINA M. VILLANUEVA is finishing her PhD in social psychology at Claremont Graduate University. Her dissertation investigates language brokering, parental behaviors, and observed familial interactions of Mexican descent families. She is also the Assistant Director of Operations for the Research Infrastructure in Minority Institutions (RIMI) Project at California State University San Bernardino.

LAURA D. WANDNER received her BA from Connecticut College. She is currently enrolled in a PhD program in clinical health psychology at the University of Florida. Her current research focuses on behavioral health. Previously, she was employed at Child Trends as a Senior Research Assistant where her research focused on early childhood development and health.

KAREN M. WATKINS-LEWIS received her PhD in developmental psychology in 2007 from Howard University in Washington, D.C. She was a Fellow with the National Center for Research on Early Childhood Education at the University of Virginia in 2009. Currently, she is a research affiliate and lecturer at the University of Maryland College Park. Her research has focused on socio-cultural and parenting factors associated with cognitive and emotional development among children of color.

NIOBE WAY is Professor of Applied Psychology in the Department of Applied Psychology at New York University. She is also the Director of the Developmental Psychology program and the co-Director of the Center for Research on Culture, Development, and Education at NYU. In addition, she is the President for the Society for Research on Adolescence. She received her doctorate from the School of Education at Harvard University in Human Development and Psychology and was an NIMH postdoctoral fellow in the psychology department at Yale University. Way's research focuses on the intersections of culture, context, and human development, with a particular focus on the social and emotional development of adolescents from low-income families. She is primarily interested in how schools and families as well as larger political and economic contexts influence the developmental trajectories of children and adolescents. Her work also focuses on adolescents' experiences of social identities, including both their gender and ethnic identities.

KATHRYN R. WENTZEL is a professor in the department of Human Development at the University of Maryland, College Park. She received her PhD in education at Stanford University. Her research interests focus on parents, peers, and teachers as motivators of adolescents' classroom behavior and academic accomplishments. She has published over 100 articles and book chapters based on this work and has co-edited books on achievement motivation. She is currently Co-Editor of the *Journal of Applied Developmental Psychology.* Dr. Wentzel is past Vice-President of Division E (Counseling and Human Development, AERA) and a Fellow of the American Psychological Association, Division 15, and of the American Educational Research Association.

TRAVIS WILSON is a doctoral candidate in the department of Educational Psychology at the University of Illinois at Urbana-Champaign. His research focuses on children's social development in the context of schooling: children's social networks, cross-ethnic relationships, and social behavior, and how these factors impinge on academic achievement.